LET'S LUNCH IN LONDON

Corrine Streich
(with Lori Streich)

M

To Frank and Nina

Acknowledgements

While writing this book I talked to hundreds of people about restaurants, and it is impossible to thank them individually, so I wish to offer one grand thank you to them all. In particular, I want to thank Michael Friedman, Laurence Orbach and Sidney and Esther Kramer.

First published 1982 by
PAPERMAC
a division of Macmillan Publishers Limited
4 Little Essex Street, London WC2R 3LF
and Basingstoke

Associated companies in Auckland, Dallas,
Delhi, Dublin, Hong Kong, Johannesburg,
Lagos, Manzini, Melbourne, Nairobi,
New York, Singapore, Tokyo, Washington
and Zaria

ISBN 0 333 33392 6

Designed by Robert Updegraff
Maps by Hilary Evans

Composition in Rockwell by
Filmtype Services Limited,
Scarborough, North Yorkshire

Printed in Great Britain by
Redwood Burn Limited, Trowbridge
and bound by Pegasus Bookbinding, Melksham

Contents

Introduction

If restaurants closed at lunchtime, life in London would become very dull indeed. Eating is only one part of the lunchtime activity. Business deals are opened and closed then, and love affairs begin and end. Lunchtime is when we can see people we feel obliged to see but with whom we would rather not dine, and it is a time to get to know someone a little better, before deciding whether or not to spend an evening together. We lunch to make new friends and contacts, to pass the time of day, to impress clients, or to talk out our hearts.

There are thousands of restaurants in London, yet most people frequent the same few nearby haunts every day. Inevitably though, there are occasions when the restaurant we know and are known in is not the right place, and we don't know where else to go.

Let's Lunch matches the character of the restaurant with the occasion. I have selected over 300 restaurants – posh places, plain places and many in between – and listed them under twelve categories, which cover most reasons for going out to lunch. Where, for instance, should you take conservative Uncle George from St Mawes to ask him for a loan on one of his rare visits to town? Consider the listings under 'Traditional' and 'Formal Elegant'; but if he disdains expensiveness and style, the 'Informal' section will serve you better.

Suppose that you are a job candidate. Your potential employer has invited you to lunch at the place of your choice, but the restaurants where you are known are not quite appropriate. If an expensive, full-service restaurant, one with a *maître d'hôtel*, captains and *sommeliers*, is appropriate, then consider those under 'Traditional' and 'Formal Elegant'. These categories include places that are opulent and showy, those with character as well as excitement, and others that are quiet and dignified.

On the other hand, you are taking your young niece to lunch before putting her on the train at St Pancras station, and she happens to be a confirmed vegetarian. Look through the index, under the food listings, for 'vegetarian'.

Within each category of *Let's Lunch* there is a diversity of styles, types of food, prices and locations. The quality of the food, the service and amenities in all the restaurants range from acceptable to excellent. However, no reader will like them all, nor is meant to.

The descriptions of the restaurants in *Let's Lunch* are designed to guide you to the places that you will enjoy and deter you from going to those that you won't.

INFORMATION The vital statistics about the restaurants listed were current at the time of publication. The London restaurant scene, however, is volatile. In the interim, a place may have changed its chef, decor, management, menu, phone number, location, or it may have closed down. So it is best to phone before a first visit.

BOOKINGS Each restaurant entry indicates when reservations are needed, or where they are or are not accepted. This too is subject to change. A very popular restaurant may lose its following, or a quiet place may suddenly become 'in'. The notation 'suggested' indicates that booking is advisable; the notation 'required' means that reservations should be made a few days in advance.

DRESS Dress restrictions generally apply to men only. Women may wear trousers to every London restaurant. In some restaurants, though, jeans – even pressed, unfaded ones – are not permitted. Jackets or jacket-and-tie requirements are more strictly observed in winter than in warm weather, and often it is left to the discretion of the *maître d'*. If you are going somewhere elegant, double-check about the dress requirements when you make your reservation.

PRICE RANGE The price categories, from 'Very expensive' to 'Inexpensive', indicate the price of lunch for two with wine, based on the *average* bill at each restaurant, in late 1981.

Inexpensive = £12 or less   Expensive   = £20 to £40
Moderate   = £12 to £20   Very expensive = £40 and over

TIPPING The law is quite clear on service being subject to VAT, just as everything from the cover charge to the coffee is subject to 15 per cent Value Added Tax. Money not accounted for on the bill as service but left on the table as a 'tip' is not subject to VAT. It is however subject to the waiter's income tax assessment, which can mean more book keeping for the restaurant. For this reason many restaurants automatically calculate a service charge (from 10 to 15 per cent) and add it to the bill. However, tipping is meant to be an expression of one's pleasure for services rendered. It is not compulsory, even when it is added to the bill.

Formal Elegant

These restaurants are at the top of the totem pole. Some are embued with such quiet good taste they make every guest feel attuned to the subtlest nuances. Others have the seductive grandeur and opulent settings of those old picture palaces, designed to make the customer feel rich for the price of admission. And you should expect what you pay for in these places: a headwaiter who not only writes down your order but listens to it and makes helpful suggestions, no matter how long you take to decide; waiters who remember who has ordered what, without asking, and who give the impression of only bringing beautiful offerings, while the empty plates effortlessly disappear.

These are venues for serious eating and serious talking by low-keyed, high-salaried gastronomes (mainly male) who do not need to justify the long midday meal by calling it a Working Lunch.

FRENCH

The Berkeley Hotel Restaurant

Wilton Place, SW1 01–235 6000
⊖ Knightsbridge *Map C7*
Open 12.30–3 pm, 6.45–12 midnight; closed Saturday
Very expensive

- Access, Eurocard, Mastercharge
- Booking suggested

- Seats 80
- Jackets and ties required

There is no lack of real or symbolic effect in the grandiose restaurant of the Berkeley Hotel, which architecture critics described as 'all pudding outside and pastiche inside'. The decorative details are of bronze and marble and crystal and mirror. The carpet, the walls and the napery are all in a monotone of brownish-mauve. Icons of assurance converse with one another at large tables that seem to be set adrift in oceans of space.

Everything is served from a gleaming array of silver plate by impeccable, seemingly unflappable staff. The menu is long and very large, with many variations on classical French themes: *Ris de Veau Financière*, *Médaillon de Porc Calvados*, *Coquilles Saint-Jacques Bercy* and *Vol-au-Vent Régence*.
Late dinner; Sunday lunch

FRENCH
Café Royale the GRILL ROOM

68 Regent Street, W1 01–439 6320
⊖ Piccadilly Circus   *Map B70*
Open 12.30–3 pm, 6–10.45 pm; closed alternate Saturdays for lunch
Expensive

- Access, American Express, Barclaycard, Diners
- Booking suggested
- Seats 55

- Jackets and ties required
- ♿ Access to restaurant, WC by lift

No other public dining room in London has such a sense of overreaching extravagance in paint and gilding and carving. Few other restaurants can boast of such a remarkable wine cellar, and surely Carlo Ambrosini is the snappiest dressed and most attentive *maître d'* in town. From the 1890s until after the Second World War, this was *Bohemia*. The list of regulars sounds like a roll-call of the arts: James Whistler, Oscar Wilde, Aubrey Beardsley, Bernard Shaw, T. S. Eliot ... Over the years it has gone from arty to rich-arty to becoming a nostalgic reminder of bygone days.

The menu is long and provides ambitious choices such as *Scampis Oscar Wilde*, *Suprême de Volaille Guiliana* and *Côtelettes d'Agneau Farcies Brixham*. Unfortunately, the cooking standards are no longer up to the surroundings.
Pre-theatre; late dinner; Sunday lunch

FRENCH

The Capital Hotel Restaurant

22 Basil Street, SW3 01–589 5171
⊖ Knightsbridge *Map C11*
Open 12.30–2 pm, 6.30–10.30 pm, 7 days
Very expensive

- Access, American Express, Barclaycard, Carte Blanche, Diners
- Booking suggested
- Seats 30
- Parties catered for
- Pipe smoking not allowed
- Jackets and ties required
- ☍ Access to restaurant, WC

Behind a modest, modern façade in Knightsbridge is a small dining room, for about 30 only, with a deceptively simple appearance. The walls are decorated with silver fibreglass panels, the lighting is discreet, the colour of everything else is brown or beige. This is a place for people who find Château Lafite and Montrachet more to their taste than Muscadet and Côtes du Rhone. It helps to talk Cordon Bleu here.

The small, glossy menu is printed entirely in French, including a suggestion to diners to consider a short list of recommended wines, and an apology in case anything listed on the menu is not available. The only words in English explain about the two sets of prices against menu items. 'The charges in brackets are inclusive of 15% service charge and VAT'. The Swiss restaurant manager, Dieter Schuldt, sees to the dining room and the British chef Brian Turner produces *Mousseline de Coquilles Saint-Jacques* and *Terrine de Ris de Veau au Chou Vert* for starters, and *Filets de Canard au Chou Vert* or *Carre d'Agneau Persille aux Herbes de Provence.*
Pre-theatre; Sunday lunch

FRENCH

The Chelsea Room at the
Carlton Tower Hotel

Cadogan Place, SW1 01–235 5411
⊖ Sloane Square *Map C5*
Open 12.30–2.45 pm, 7–11 pm, 7 days
Very expensive

Let's Lunch in London

- Access, American Express, Barclaycard, Diners, Eurocard
- Booking suggested
- Seats 50

- Small parties catered for
- Live music
- Jackets and ties required
- Access to restaurant, WC by lift

The ceilings are high, the light is flattering, the sound is muted in The Chelsea Room, and the tables are arranged at discreet distances from each other, with views of Cadogan Gardens. Every meal created by the chef Bernard Gaume in this ritual theatre of eating is meant to be a multi-course masterpiece. Someone who knows about the finance of such efforts claims that it would cost the management less to give each customer a fiver and ask them to eat elsewhere.

Be that as it may, passionate palates abandon themselves to the sensation of taste at the mere perusal of the imaginative menu, and then must sample the specialities: *Salmon with Fish Mousse and Champagne Sauce, Roast Pigeon on a Bed of Macaroni with Crayfish, Duckling in Butter and Cream Sauce*, and for dessert, *Gratin de Fraises* (baked strawberries) or *Sorbets* made with fresh fruit in season.

Late dinner; Sunday lunch

ENGLISH/INTERNATIONAL

Grill Room at the Dorchester Hotel

Park Lane, W1 01–629 8888
⊖ Hyde Park Corner   *Map A31*
Open 12.30–3 pm, 6.30–11 pm, 7 days
Expensive

- Access, American Express, Barclaycard, Diners
- Booking suggested

- Seats 80
- Jackets and ties required
- Access to restaurant, WC

A Graham Greene sort of cast – Arab sheiks and their extended families, Colonel Blimp types and their wives, hard-up Harrovians and deal-making Americans – now frequents the Dorchester, a large gem of a hotel built with between-the-wars insouciance and character. The hotel's façade is irretrievably 1930s but recently the vast public rooms underwent renovations which have achieved an all too common style of undistinguished multi-national opulence.

Wisely, the Grill Room was left alone and remains a facsimile of a dining room in a Spanish castle. One feels grand, or grandee, here, amid the stucco and tapestries and wrought iron, amid the liveried waiters and the cuisine of Swiss culinary prizewinner, Anton Mossiman: *Rendez-vous de Fruits de Mer à la Crème de Ciboulette, Timbale de Sole Eugène Kaufeler, Entrecôte Sautée aux Quatre Poivres, Médaillons de Venaison à l'Orange.*
Pre-theatre; late dinner; Sunday lunch

FRENCH
A l'Ecu de France

111 Jermyn Street, SW1 01–930 2837
Θ Piccadilly Circus, Green Park *Map B86*
Open 12.30–3 pm, 6.30–11.30 pm, Monday to Friday; Saturday 6.30–11.30 pm; Sunday 7–10.30 pm
Very expensive

- Access, American Express, Barclaycard, Diners
- Bookings accepted
- Seats 120

- Parties catered for
- Taped music
- Jackets and ties required
- ⛀ Access to restaurant

This temple of *haute bourgeoisie* is just the place to entertain very rich and childless old uncles. Here you will find dark panelling and deep upholstered seating in a 1930s setting of serious posh, with attentive service by formally dressed staff: waiters *de rang*, who serve, wear dinner jackets, *commis* waiters, who clear, wear white jackets, and the ancient *sommelier* in velvet wears a thick gold chain and cup. There is a notable wine list, a dazzling buffet of hors d'oeuvres and a richly laden chariot of desserts. Main courses include *Beef Wellington, Sirloin of Veal Stuffed with Herbs, Filet of Bel Amour* (sole in white wine). However, the kitchen depends too much on those old gastronomic standbys: when in doubt, wrap it in puff pastry, or sentence it to be flambéed at the table.
Pre-theatre; late dinner

FRENCH
Le Gavroche

43 Upper Brook Street, W1 01–499 1826
Θ Marble Arch *Map A24*
Open 12–2 pm, 7.30–10.45 pm; closed Saturday, Sunday
Very expensive

Let's Lunch in London

- Access, American Express, Barclaycard, Carte Blanche, Diners
- Booking suggested
- Seats 70
- Parties catered for
- Jackets and ties required

For many years the most ecstatic 'ooh's' and 'ah's' for the 'Le's' and 'La's' of plush French eating houses have been uttered about the restaurants of the brothers Michel and Albert Roux whose business interests continue to expand. Naturally each new restaurant is eagerly awaited and must be better than the last, an exercise in culinary tight-rope walking.

The new Gavroche in Mayfair (designed by David Mlinaric) is somewhat larger than the former Michelin two-star Gavroche (now Gavvers) in Chelsea, and is also more luxurious, sober and traditional than its predecessor. No floor tiles here. The carpet was specially woven and looks like a forest floor in autumn. Tables are discreetly separated from one another and very comfortable, but try not to sit too close to the kitchen as you will hear the clatter of saucepans. The walls are covered with prints and watercolours from Albert Roux's collection.

M. Roux says he cooks first for the eye, then for the taste and his plate presentations are indeed artful, but delivered with a touch too much flourish à la silver service.

Cuisine is prepared under the close supervision of Albert Roux by a kitchen of journeymen encouraged by him in their ambitions for greatness. (Roux Brothers' alumni run La Tante Clair and L'Interlude de Tabaillau.) The menu states that the few classical dishes served have the hallmark of the Roux interpretation. Always there are two cold starters: *Smoked Salmon Wrapped Round Creamed Smoked Haddock with Gelée and a Truffle*, and *Foie Gras of Duck*. Entrees include *Caneton Gavroche, Tournedos Vigneronne, Fricassée de Turbotin au Porto*. Desserts are superb and there are always exceptionally good *Petits fours* served with coffee. Impressive wine list, very high prices.

Gavvers On the site of the old Gavroche at 61–63 Lower Sloane Street, SW1 (01–730 5983)
Open for dinner only.

FRENCH

Inigo Jones

14 Garrick Street, WC2 01–836 6456
⊖ Leicester Square *Map B52*
Open 12.30–2.30 pm, 6–11.45 pm; closed Saturday lunch, Sunday
Expensive

- Access, American Express, Barclaycard, Diners
- Booking suggested
- Seats 70
- Live and taped music
- ♿ Access to restaurant

Here you will find subtle lighting, stylish decor of calculated simplicity with pre-Raphaelite touches, deep carpeting and comfortable seating. The smartly dressed waiters are deft and friendly; the chef is inventive and reliable. The menu changes every six weeks, but these dishes are always available: *Lou Magret, Carré d'Agneau en Croûte Sauce à la Menthe, Oeufs de Caille Moscovite, Blinis au Saumon Fumé.*

Journalists, authors, publishers, opera singers and people who talk loudly about dogs and horses and sheep frequent the converted Victorian mission school that was named for the seventeenth-century architect of Covent Garden. This may be the only restaurant in London with *live* harpsichord music.
Pre-theatre; late dinner

FRENCH

Interlude de Tabaillau

7 Bow Street, WC2 01–379 6473
⊖ Covent Garden *Map B44*
Open 12.30–2 pm, 7–11.30 pm; closed Saturday lunch, Sunday
Expensive

- Access, American Express, Barclaycard, Diners
- Booking required
- Seats 45

On the corner of the Opera House and opposite the Bow Street Magistrates Court is Interlude de Tabaillau, a difficult name for Anglo-Saxon tongues, yet it quickly became known as one of London's most popular French restaurants. The chef/partner is Jean-Louis Taillebaud, formerly of Le Gavroche. Neither the lunch nor the dinner menu is large but there are many well-balanced and enticing possibilities, such as *Lamb en Croûte with Sauce Moelle, Barbue Karpinski, Suprême de Caneton Juliette.*

Designer Kennedy Sumner turned the ground floor of this old Covent Garden warehouse into an austerely handsome space, with large tinted windows that give a theatrical light in the daytime. The clientele is grand, assured and mainly of the top ranks in business and the arts.
Late dinner

ENGLISH
Lockets

Marsham Court, Marsham Street, SW1 01–834 9552
⊖ Pimlico, Westminster, then bus   *Map C55*
Open 12.15–2.30 pm, 6.30–11 pm; closed Saturday and Sunday
Moderate/Expensive

- Access, American Express, Barclaycard, Diners
- Booking required for lunch
- Seats 100
- Parties catered for

This large and discreetly pretentious restaurant, done up with gold and black patterned wallpaper, reproduction paintings and Regency-style furnishings, is near the Tate Gallery and within walking distance of the Houses of Parliament. It is often frequented by MPs, ministers, journalists and suchlike. It is where one would like to believe the finest intellects and wits of the political world come to talk and eat together, and brace themselves with a glass of fine port before the call of the division bell.

There is a distinguished wine list and the extensive menu is full of historic gastronomic quotations and recipes. Main courses include *Lamb and Leek Pie, Spiced Beef Cooked in Strong Ale, Aylesbury Duck with Black Cherry Sauce.*
Pre-theatre; late dinner

FRENCH
Mirabelle

56 Curzon Street, W1 01–499 4636
⊖ Green Park   *Map A33*
Open 1–2.30 pm, 7–11.15 pm; closed Sunday
Very expensive

- Access, American Express, Carte Blanche, Diners
- Booking suggested
- Seats 220
- Jackets and ties required

A decade or so ago, this kitchen and dining room set the tone and standard by which so many French restaurants in London were judged. In recent years, adventurous palates have gone elsewhere and the tables at lunchtime are filled mainly with those who spend corporate money. The food is no longer immortal, but tradition is worshipped here. Regular customers approach the experience with no doubt positive anticipation, expecting a safe and solid meal, with service rendered by a large cast – *maître d'*, *sommelier*, station headwaiter, waiter and *débarraseur* who takes away the plates that held the ambitious but sometimes heavy-handed cuisine of the chef, Jean Drees. Among his specialities, called *Les Plats des Gourmets*, are *Sole Mirabelle* (stuffed with lobster and scampi in a white wine sauce), *Quenelles d' Homard ou Brochet Nantua* (lobster or pike quenelles with crayfish sauce), *Médaillon de Boeuf Mirabelle* (beef with truffle sauce), *Meringue Glacée Chantilly* (with fresh berries).

The cellar holds many fine bottles. The dining room is, naturally, very grandly appointed and opens on to a charming, thickly planted garden where in good weather one may stroll, drink in hand, right in the heart of Mayfair.

Late dinner

FRENCH

Le Poulbot

45 Cheapside, EC2 01–236 4379
⊖ St Paul's *Map F14*
Open 12–2.30 pm; closed Saturday, Sunday, Bank Holidays
Expensive

- Access, American Express, Barclaycard, Carte Blanche, Diners, Visa
- Booking suggested
- Seats 45
- Parties catered for

Down a steep flight of stairs is Le Poulbot, a Gallic-inspired, super plush City chophouse, with high-back, upholstered booths and formal service. It is all done up in red and looks a bit like the inside of a sewing box. Here City gents repress boarding school desires for bangers and mash or Toad in the Hole and indulge in Roux Brothers' interpretations of classic French cuisine: *Pâté de Grousse au Porto, Boudin Blanc Sauce Perigueux, Filets de Sole Leonora, Chop d'Agneau Grillée Sauce Paloise, Entrecôte Mirabeau, Grenadins de veau Vallée d'Auge.*

On the ground floor is a pretty and cheerful little brasserie for non-expense account lunches and snacks, prepared in the Wandsworth kitchens of this large restaurant group: soups, *Confit de Canard, Blanquette de veau.* Or one can have omelets, bread and cheese and *pâtisseries.*

INTERNATIONAL
Ritz Restaurant at the Ritz Hotel

Piccadilly, W1 01–493 8181
⊖ **Green Park**   *Map B90*
Open 12.30–3 pm, 6.30–11 pm (Sunday 7–10 pm), 7 days
Expensive

- Access, American Express, Barclaycard, Carte Blanche, Diners
- Booking suggested
- Seats 100
- Parties catered for
- Live music
- Jackets and ties required

The Ritz is indeed ritzy. With only 142 rooms in the massive building, you know they are large. The architects (Mewes and Davis) had Versailles in mind when they designed the restaurant, an enormous room of marble columns and gilt under a cloud-flecked ceiling, with views of the actual sky, overlooking Green Park. Tables are large and widely spaced, service is distinguished and discreet, and the wines are very pleasant. Altogether this is an ideal spot for those who make an art form of the business lunch. The seller and buyer take cues from one another, pausing now and again for a bite of *Raie au Beurre Noir, Poussin Grillé en Crapaudine, Tournedos Périgourdin.*

At the time of writing, Michael Quinn had not yet left his three-star Gravetye Manor in Sussex to become *chef de cuisine* at the Ritz. He will be the first British head chef of this hotel.
Pre-theatre; late dinner; Sunday lunch

ENGLISH/FISH
Scott's

20 Mount Street, W1 01–629 5248
⊖ **Marble Arch, Hyde Park Corner**   *Map A27*
Open 12.30–3 pm, 6–11 pm; closed Sunday lunch
Expensive

- Access, American Express, Diners, Mastercharge
- Booking suggested
- Seats 100
- Jackets and ties required
- ♿ Access to restaurant

One feels cosseted here, among a clientele that is either very rich or is acting out its fantasies of being very rich. Although you can get any kind of food this is really a fish restaurant, originally established by John Scott in Coventry Street, Piccadilly, in 1851. The 'new' premises (c. 1969) are smaller but more spacious and luxurious with mirrored columns and crystal chandeliers, upholstered armchairs, commendable paintings, a large staff of waiters uniformed according to rank.

There is also an Oyster Bar which is bright and cheerful and less formal, where you can snack of course upon *Oysters*, or *Grilled clam claws, Lobster and Crab in Chablis Sauce* and *Seafood Vol-au-vent.* Or you can order from the main menu: *Délice de Sole Windsor, Petits Filets de Sole Lady Diana, Quenelle de Turbotin Royale.*
Pre-theatre; late dinner

PAKISTANI
Shezan

16–22 Cheval Place, SW7 01–589 7918
⊖ Knightsbridge   *Map C14*
Open 12–3 pm, 7–12 midnight; closed Sunday
Expensive

- Access, American Express, Barclaycard, Diners, Eurocard
- Booking suggested
- Seats 125
- Parties catered for
- Taped music

The setting of this below-stairs restaurant is one of restrained grandeur, achieved with elegant, modern decor. Recessed lights cast shadows on walls decorated with wooden shutters, racks of wine and Hola tiles from Pakistan. It is normally very quiet. Vague music plays in distant background. The tables are large and widely spaced. Service would be almost servile were it not for the genuine hospitality of the staff.

The menu has long explanations about Mughlai cuisine which has a high degree of richness and refinement attained during the reign of the Moguls in the sixteenth century. Try *Karahi Kabab Khyberi, Gosht Kata Masala, Murgh Tikka Lahori, Pulao Hijazi.*
Late dinner; take-away

JAPANESE
Suntory

72–73 St James's Street, SW1 01–409 0201
⊖ **Green Park** *Map B94*
Open 12–2.15 pm, 7–10.15 pm; closed Sunday
Very expensive

- Access, American Express, Barclaycard, Carte Blanche, Diners
- Booking required
- Seats 130
- Parties catered for

Lattice-work screens divide the two main sections of this large, luxurious restaurant on the St James's site of the former Mme Prunier's. In one section, waiters prepare *Teppan-Yaki*, which is meat and shellfish 'griddle cooked' on hot plates set into the wooden tables. In the other section, *Shabu-Shabu* is served. This is thinly sliced beef that you dip into boiling water, then into one or more of several sauces. Later vegetables and noodles are added and ladled out with the broth by kimono-clad waitresses. Service is exemplary, and apart from the lively sizzle of cooking sounds, an air of quiet calm pervades. The uninitiated may not know the proper style for eating this food, so copy the Japanese around you. Many of them are ministers from the Japanese Embassy and top-ranking business executives. They eat with their fingers and slurp their soup ... with delicacy and dispatch.

This restaurant is owned by Suntory Ltd, a £3 billion firm that produces and exports wines, beers and spirits. The company's growth has been so phenomenal that Japan is sometimes dubbed 'the Land of the Rising Suntory'.
Take-away

FRENCH
La Tante Claire

68 Royal Hospital Road, SW3 01–352 6045
⊖ **Sloane Square** *Map C72*
Open 12.30–2 pm, 7–11 pm; closed Saturday, Sunday
Very expensive

- American Express
- Booking required
- Seats 32
- Jackets required
- ♿ Access to restaurant

Two long rows of meticulously groomed gentlemen face their ladies sitting on striped velvet banquettes. The room is narrow.

The walls are padded and cloth-covered. There is a temple-like silence. No lip-smacking in this altar of gastronomy, only gentle murmurs and the soft tinkle of heavy cutlery on porcelain as worshipful regulars slowly savour such specialities as *Foie de Veau au Citron Vert, Pied de Cochon Farci aux Morilles* and *Canard aux Epices.*

Despite the formality, this is a mama and papa restaurant. Pierre Koffman does wonders in the kitchen and Mme Koffman sees to the upfront details with shy graciousness. Appreciation is appreciated and makes Madame smile.

Late dinner

ENGLISH/INTERNATIONAL

Walton's

121 Walton Street, SW3 01–584 0204
⊖ South Kensington, Knightsbridge   *Map C25*
Open 12.30–2.30 pm, 7.30–11.30 pm, 7 days
Moderate/Expensive

- Access, American Express, Barclaycard, Diners
- Booking required for dinner
- Seats 64
- Small parties catered for
- Taped music
- Jackets and ties preferred

Walton's is an exercise in fine design and serene taste which makes one wonder whether the effect is meant to be sumptuous simplicity or modest grandeur. The combination of Regency with modern furniture, of smoked mirrors with silk wall coverings and ingenious lighting is used throughout, but the mood of the front room is lighter and more cheerful than the more sombre back room.

The restaurant was designed by Michael Smith, who was consultant on the food featuring in the television series 'Upstairs, Downstairs' and 'The Duchess of Duke Street'. Walton's menu developed from his knowledge of eighteenth- and nineteenth-century English cookery and includes, *Noisettes of Welsh Lamb Béarnaise, Collops-in-the-Pan, Médaillons of Venison with Poached Pears* and *Breast of Pheasant Devonshire.* These are served at tables laid with Royal Copenhagen china and Georg Jenson flatware to *haute-cuisine* converts who grew up believing that it was a social crime to talk about food at the table.

Late dinner; Sunday lunch

FRENCH

The White House Restaurant

Albany Street, NW1 01–387 1200
θ Great Portland Street   *Map E9*
Open 12.30–3 pm, 6.30–11.30 pm; closed Saturday lunch, Sunday
Expensive

- Access, American Express, Barclaycard, Diners
- Booking suggested
- Seats 120
- Parties catered for

- Live music
- No-smoking area
- Jackets required
- Children over 8 allowed in dining room

You can't help but feel special in this spacious, club-like dining room where you get the agreeable sensation of being in a world of your own, as you do on a ship. Service is properly attentive, but the waiters sense when you want to be left alone so it is a very good place for serious discussion and serious eating.

The British chef, Ian Douglas Brown, produces classic French cuisine. Several dishes on the menu are changed daily. Perennial favourites include *La Quenelle de Brochet au Champagne, Salade de Foie et Champignons Sauvages, Le Carré d'Agneau Truffé Sarladaise* and *Les Rosettes sur Croûte au Salsifis*.

Pre-theatre; late dinner

Casual Elegant

These restaurants are the favourite stages of the moment for the super-successes of international business, films, recordings, racing and titled society, where the usually stared-upon rarely get an oblique glance of curiosity. They are settings of sophisticated innocence, intimate and luxurious, where the people seem to be the decorations.

The clientele turns up on schedules varying from a few times a year to a few times a week. They tip generously and often, yet even they sometimes compete fiercely for the best tables. Naturally an unknown, intending to impress a client with The Big Lunch, must first himself impress the staff in these elegant restaurants.

So, never phone for a reservation yourself, or if you do, pretend that you are your secretary. Then go to the same restaurant every day for at least two to three days, and always have a long and knowledgeable discussion about the cuisine with the manager and the headwaiter. Tell them what you liked and what you did not like. When they warmly greet you by name upon arrival, it is time to bring the guest you want to impress.

LEBANESE
Al-Amir

112–114 Edgware Road, W2 01–402 0087
⊖ Marble Arch *Map A10*
Open 12 midday–12 midnight, 7 days
Expensive

- Access, American Express, Barclaycard, Diners
- Booking suggested
- Seats 100
- Taped music
- Jackets and ties required
- ⟨ Access to restaurant, WC

Arabic music, trays of sweetmeats and scented dainties greet you as you enter Al-Amir (the Prince). It is a large restaurant with some alcoved tables, Eastern arches, fretted wood screens and very comfortable seating for the traditionally long and slow meals of many hors d'oeuvres and many glasses of potent arak.

This cuisine is subtle and immediately palatable to most people, so the clientele at lunchtime is a mix of local business people and many Near Eastern émigrés perhaps trying to recapture the tastes and culinary sensations of their native land.

The kitchen provides a large selection of cold and hot starters such as *Humous, Kabis* (a selection of pickles), *Makanek Sojok* (spiced sausages), *T'halat Meshwi* (a rather arcane dish of spleen, stuffed with parsley and garlic). There are also many charcoal grilled meats, served with rice.

Late lunch; pre-theatre; late dinner; take-away

FRENCH
Brasserie des Amis and Restaurant Mes Amis

27 Basil Street, SW3 01–584 9012
⊖ Knightsbridge *Map C13*
Open 11.30–3 pm, 6.30–11 pm, 7 days
Moderate/Expensive

- Access, American Express, Barclaycard, Diners
- Bookings not accepted for lunch in Brasserie
- Seats 40
- Parties catered for
- Taped music
- ♿ Access to restaurant

Facing one another in Basil Street are the rear windows of Harrods and the front windows of a brightly decorated brasserie filled with what appears to be a display of consummate shoppers at lunch. The seating is close. The decor is fresh and garden-like. The atmosphere is spirited. The staff are French and efficient, and the menu provides a selection of basic dishes: *Omelettes, Quiche Lorraine, Salade Niçoise, Goujons de Sole, Grilled Steaks* and *Chicken, Pissadaladière* (onion, cheese, tomato and anchovy tart).

Next door (same owners and executive chef who sees to two separate kitchens) is Mes Amis, a restaurant frequented by staff from the nearby embassies, and international businessmen who telex for reservations. Service and cuisine are more formal, elaborate and expensive. The dining room is done in *élégante-rustique* style à la Provence, with dark ceiling beams, tiled floors, much hanging greenery and a dazzling display of fresh

vegetables, cheeses, herbs and sausages. Entrees include *Suprême de Barbue Provençale, Cassolette Cap Ferrat* and *Caneton aux Cassis.* A la carte menu on weekdays, set price menu at weekends.
Pre-theatre; late dinner; Sunday lunch; outdoor eating

FRENCH
La Brasserie du Détour

5 Campden Hill Road, W8 01–937 9602
⊖ Kensington High Street *Map D19*
Open 8 am–11.30 pm, Sunday 11 am–11 pm
Moderate/Expensive

- Access, American Express, Barclaycard, Diners
- Booking suggested
- Seats 46
- Parties catered for
- ⅊ Access to restaurant

If you squint a little you can pretend that it is the Boulevard St Germain instead of Kensington High Street over the road. In this bright, gleaming brasserie, the aloof, all-French staff speak to the customers in dense Franglaise and to one another in French. *Tant pis!* A mixed crowd eyes itself in the big polished mirrors: distant Royals, journalists, architects, High Street merchants and shoppers, secretaries celebrating an important occasion. The atmosphere is usually lively. The menu is short but well constructed: *La Terrine de Truite Saumonée, Côte de Boeuf Grillé Sauce Béarnaise, Foie de Veau à la Façon du Chef* and *Noisettes d'Agneau à la Navaraise.* Although it calls itself a brasserie, du Detour offers only cold snacks between mealtimes.

Next door, and run in tandem with the brasserie, is the restaurant Le Détour where prices are considerably higher and the atmosphere is more formal – in fact, a touch formidable – and the food comes from the same kitchen.
Late lunch; pre-theatre; late dinner; Sunday lunch

FRENCH/INTERNATIONAL
Carrier's

2 Camden Passage, N1 01–226 5353
⊖ Angel *Map F22*
Open 12.30–2.30 pm, 7.30–11.30 pm; closed Sunday
Expensive

Let's Lunch in London

- American Express, Diners
- Booking required
- Seats 85
- ♿ Access to restaurant

Robert Carrier has had a profound influence on English gastronomy. A growing number of fine restaurants are run by alumni of his Camden Passage restaurant for a public that became food-wise and demanding after reading his books and sampling his 'great dishes of the world'.

The meals at Carrier's are quite heroic in size. The menu changes daily and with the seasons to include *Thai appetiser trio, Trio of Blinis à la Russe*, followed by main courses of *German Veal with Almonds, Calf's Liver with Avocado, Carpet Bag of Salmon with Oysters*, and 'Just Desserts' of *Amaretti soufflé*, and *Chocolate Soufflé*.

The restaurant, in a converted carriage house, consists of four separate dining rooms, each with a different mood. There are mainly tables for two in the lovely Garden Room. Also on the ground floor is the Beige Room, where you will see and be seen by everyone going to the other rooms. Upstairs is the Red Room, with mirrors, red walls and red napery. Next door is the Pink Room, all pastel chintz and over-blown flowers. Staff assume that women lunching together will prefer this room to all the others.
Late dinner

ENGLISH

Cowcross Restaurant

6–7 Cowcross Street, EC1 01–253 1140
ѱ Farringdon   *Map F1*
Open 12 noon–4.30 pm; closed Saturday and Sunday
Expensive

- Access, American Express, Barclaycard, Diners
- Booking suggested
- Seats 45
- Parties catered for
- Jackets and ties required
- ♿ Access to restaurant

You would not expect to find such a bright, modern, well-cared for restaurant so close to Smithfield Market. It is the inspiration and pleasure of Mr and Mrs Edward Anderson; he is a meat merchant with warehouses in the market.

Beef, glorious beef, charcoal grilled, and calves' liver, veal and chicken are simply prepared and accompanied by large amounts of bread, potatoes, greens and salads. Large groups of men, big in the wholesale meat and provision business,

themselves beefily filling out their wide-lapelled three-piece suits, seem to greatly enjoy late lunches together under the attentive service of slightly hovering staff.
Late lunch

SPANISH
Dulcinea

29 Ebury Street, SW1 01–730 4094
⊖ Victoria   *Map C47*
Open 12–3 pm, 6–11.30 pm; closed Saturday lunch, Sunday
Moderate/Expensive

- Access, American Express, Barclaycard, Diners
- Booking required
- Seats 85
- Parties catered for
- Taped music
- No-smoking area
- 👪 Access to restaurant

Fernand Point, who was to *haute cuisine* what Einstein was to physics, described success as 'the sum of a lot of small things correctly done', and this is the way at the Dulcinea: gracious reception, comfortable atmosphere, pleasing decor, friendly service and honest, well-prepared food. The cuisine is Spanish, with many original dishes by chef/owner and food writer Gino Benavides, who for many years had a highly rated restaurant (of the same name) in Weybridge.

Fish is a speciality here: *Sopa de Pescadores* (fish soup), *Zarzuela* (mixed seafood in brandy sauce), *Lubina Feria Mundia,* cooked with fennel (when sea bass is available) and *Paella Valenciana*, rice, chicken, pork and seafood with spices that bring out the flavour of each ingredient. There is an extensive list of Spanish, French, German and Californian wines.
Pre-theatre; late dinner

FRENCH/INTERNATIONAL
Eatons

49 Elizabeth Street, SW1 01–730 0074
⊖ Victoria   *Map C51*
Open 12–2 pm, 7–11.15 pm; closed Saturday and Sunday
Moderate

- Access, American Express, Barclaycard, Diners
- Booking required
- Seats 40
- Taped classical music
- 👪 Access to restaurant

Let's Lunch in London

Two partners, Dieter Vagtz and Shayne Pope (who were at Inigo Jones), and chef Santosh Bakshi wisely chose a simple but exceedingly apt name for their small restaurant where at lunchtime old aristos sit at tables very close to a new race of Englishmen in sales and electronics, and in the early evening hours MPs and other Belgravia residents come in for a light dinner before the Nine O'Clock News.

There is a rather short à la carte menu which includes *Blinis with Smoked Salmon and Sour Cream, Pâté Maison, Chicken Pancake with Curry Sauce* as starters, but they may be ordered as a main course and £1 will be added to the price. Specialities include *Pork Escalope Filled with Red Cabbage and Raisins, Trout Colbert with Herb Butter and Apple Slices, Lamb Fillet and Kidneys Sauté Provençale* and *Chicken Brochette with Bacon and Mushrooms.*

Late dinner

LEBANESE

Fakhreldine

85 Piccadilly, W1 01–493 8701
⊖ Green Park   *Map A36*
Open 12 noon–3 am, 7 days
Expensive

- All major credit cards accepted
- Bookings accepted
- Seats 180

- Parties catered for
- Taped music
- Jackets and ties required (except on Sunday)

Lebanese restaurants are true brasseries, serving food all the time they are open. Snacks, however, are not available during traditional mealtimes, when diners enjoy multi-course repasts. These usually start with *Mezze* or *Hors d'oeuvres*, of which there are 45 different sorts from *Hommos, Tabouleh, Felafel* and some bland Lebanese cheeses to the more exotic such as *Ncha'at Salatah* (brain salad) and *Haliwat* (fried sweetbread with lemon). Starters form the more interesting and varied part of a Middle Eastern meal but there are also charcoal grilled main courses to follow: *Shawarma* (slices of marinated beef, grilled on a spit) and *Bastorma* (smoked spiced beef fillets).

The restaurant, run by the Haddad brothers (one is chef), is elaborately decorated, with lots of mirrors, plants, a fountain and a wide wall of windows overlooking Green Park. It is named after the sixteenth-century founder of modern Lebanon, Fakhr El-Din

II, who distinguished himself both in battle and at the banqueting table.

Late lunch; pre-theatre; late dinner; Sunday lunch; take-away

FRENCH/NOUVELLE CUISINE

Four Seasons

69 Barnsbury Street, N1 01–607 0857
Θ Highbury and Islington   *Map F19*
Open 12.30–2.30 pm, 7–11 pm; closed Saturday lunch, Sunday
Moderate/Expensive

- Access, Barclaycard
- Booking suggested
- Seats 20

- Parties catered for
- No children under 12

This is a simply furnished restaurant with only seven tables in a modest house in a hard-to-find one-way street in Islington. It is run by Alain Bessemoulin, a former chef from Frederick's, and his wife Joyce who serves the food and makes the desserts. From a kitchen that may be smaller than the galley of a 747, they prepare *Smoked Mackeral Mousse, Mussels Provençal, Lamb sautéed with Bilberries, Veal with French Wild Mushroom Sauce* and *Duck with Marinade Liqueur Sauce.* Coffee is served with rum truffles.

The earnest graciousness of the Bessemoulins gives one the impression of being a guest in the home of generous but strict surrogate parents. At lunchtime the regulars are mainly businessmen from the City, drinking and discussing how to stabilise earnings by diversifying product line.

In warm weather the seven tables are placed under rafia umbrellas in a leafy back garden that is lit by candles at night.

Late dinner; outdoor eating

ITALIAN

Al Gallo d'Oro

353 Kensington High Street, W8 01–603 6951
Θ Kensington High Street, then bus   *Map D24*
Open 12–2.45 pm, 7–11.45 pm; closed Saturday lunch
Expensive

- Access, American Express,
  Barclaycard, Diners,
  Mastercharge
- Booking required

- Seats 65
- Small parties catered for

This all-white restaurant (designed by Enzo Apicella) looks like an elegant display-case for the abundantly arrayed chariots of hors d'oeuvres and sweets, and for the very decorative crowd – professional women who are also *sportives*, blokes who make bachelordom a religion, and other less intimidating types.

The white-jacketed staff are courteous and professional. Here, as in most Italian restaurants, it is possible to order items not listed on the menu and, so long as the ingredients are available, they will do them for you. Regular dishes include: *Paglia e Fieno alla Crema* (green and white noodles in cream sauce and bacon), *Involtino di Pesce Marilena* (pancakes filled with haddock, prawns, mushrooms, and cream sauce), *Filetti di Pollo 'Gallo d'Oro'* (sautéed fillets of chicken with wine sauce and tomato), *Medaglioni de Manzo alla Mostarda* (beef with mustard and brandy sauce).
Late dinner; Sunday lunch

CHINESE
I Ching

40 Earl's Court Road, W8 01–937 7047
⊖ **High Street Kensington, Earl's Court**   *Map D26*
Open 12 noon–11.30 pm, 7 days
Moderate/Expensive

- Access, American Express, Barclaycard, Diners
- Booking suggested for dinner
- Seats 80
- Parties catered for
- Taped music
- No-smoking area
- ♿ Access to restaurant, WC

The Chinese restaurant community is small and made up of the same people who tend to play a game like musical chairs with their best chefs, so just when you are learning your way round a particularly good menu, the chef moves on. I Ching, subtitled Fantasies of China, took its first name from the Taoist Manual of Cosmic Changes, and its chef direct from Hong Kong. Let us hope that he will stay a long time and continue to orchestrate the menu from his vast repertoire. For starters there are *Special Spring Rolls Wrapped with Lettuce* and *Stuffed Crab Claws with Minced Prawns*. Main courses include *Stuffed Chicken Pieces à la Kwong Nam, Chicken Fillet Sautéed in Oyster Sauce and Served in 'Yam Birds Nest'* and *Nam King Duck.*

The restaurant was designed in a sort of 'high tech' style and is decorated with fine paintings of Zodiac beasts by Ying Yang Lu, a Chinese artist who works in London.
Late lunch; pre-theatre; late dinner; Sunday lunch; take-away

CHINESE
Ken Lo's Memories of China

67–69 Ebury Street, SW1 01–730 7734
⊖ Victoria *Map C48*
Open 12–2.30 pm, 7–11.30 pm; closed Sunday
Expensive

- American Express,
  Barclaycard, Diners
- Booking suggested for
  dinner

- Seats 110
- Parties catered for
- ♿ Access to restaurant

Many Chinese restaurants in London subscribe to a double standard: one is for tourist customers whom the staff think dote on Wun ton soup, crispy spring rolls, sweet and sour pork, and other routine dishes; the other is for Chinese and those Westerners who have convinced the management that they want the Real Thing and get the kitchen's best efforts. No such double standard exists at Ken Lo's. The staff endeavour to please all their customers. Besides, even the *Wun Ton Soup* here is far from 'ordinary', with its multi-flavoured broth, transparent noodles, small meat-stuffed fish balls, cabbage and mushrooms, all in a pretty bowl decorated with Chinese characters of the restaurant's name. The menu changes with each new season, but some of the favourites are *Szechuan Hot-Fried Crispy Beef, Mongolian Lamb in Lettuce Puffs, Quick Fry of Three Sea Flavours in Black Bean Sauce* and *Peking Quick-Fried Diced Chicken in Garlic Sauce.*

The whitewashed walls are decorated with enlarged tracings of seals of old Chinese restaurants. Lattice-work screens divide the large, open dining room into several groupings of no more than four tables each, thus creating a sense of spaciousness and intimacy at the same time.
Late dinner

INDIAN/PAKISTANI
Kundan

3 Horseferry Road, SW1 01–834 3434
⊖ Westminster, Pimlico *Map C56*
Open 12–3 pm, 7–12 pm; closed Sunday
Moderate

Let's Lunch in London

- Access, American Express, Barclaycard, Diners
- Bookings accepted
- Seats 150
- Parties catered for

There are two basic types of Indian restaurant in London – those where the smell of spices greets you at the door, and those with kitchens large enough and distant enough from the diners to give no olfactory hint of what's cooking in the tandoori ovens. Kundan belongs to the latter group. It is in a spacious, modern basement, is thickly carpeted and luxuriously done up in shades of rich brown and warm cinnamon. Its proximity to Parliament makes it a popular haunt of those MPs and government officials who enjoy *Kundani Kebabs* of diced chicken grilled with Sarhadi spices in the traditional iron '*karahi*', or *Roghan Josh*, which is a lamb curry. *Vegetable Kebabs* are popular with non-meat eaters, as are *Dal* and *Dahi Raita* with unleavened breads.

Late dinner; take-away

INTERNATIONAL

Lanes at The Inn on the Park

Hamilton Place, Park Lane, W1 01–499 0888
⊖ Hyde Park Corner *Map A39*
Open 12–3.30 pm, 6–12 midnight; closed Sunday dinner
Expensive

- Access, American Express, Barclaycard, Carte Blanche, Diners
- Booking required for lunch
- Seats 90
- Parties catered for
- Live music
- Jackets and ties preferred
- ⴲ Access to restaurant

A cosseted international crowd enjoys the amenities of this glittering, Queen Anne-style dining room served by smooth, beige-uniformed staff who seem to appear effortlessly out of thick beige carpet when needed. An enormous hors d'oeuvres table laden with a cascade of prawns and a dozen other starters dominates the room. This is the first course of the special three-course lunches which are all-inclusive of service, VAT and as much house wine as you care to drink. Main courses may include *Prime Rib of Beef with Yorkshire Pudding, Grilled Plaice* or *Veal Vieux Manoir*. The price of the set meal determines the choice of main courses.

On Sundays, children's meals are half-price. Another unusual feature of Lanes is the bar, which provides everything a good barman can offer and a selection of Japanese snacks.
Pre-theatre; late dinner; Sunday lunch

FRENCH
Ma Cuisine

113 Walton Street, SW3 01–584 7585
⊖ South Kensington *Map C26*
Open 12.30–2 pm, 7.30–11 pm; closed Saturday, Sunday
Moderate/Expensive

- Diners
- Booking required
- Seats 30
- ♿ Access to restaurant

In a comforting, old-fashioned French arrangement, the owner, Guy Mouilleron, is in the kitchen and his wife Lucette in the dining room of this small, unpretentious restaurant. There are hanging copper pans, checked table clothes and little pots of flowers on the tables that are so close you can easily hear your neighbours' conversation. Everyone sits and talks about food . . . the food of Ma Cuisine where one's moderation dissolves upon exposure to *Lobster Bisque* and *Wine-pickled Vegetables*, and main courses such as *Chicken with Crabmeat*, *Lamb with Puréed Onions* or *Panache de Poisson*. Fortunately the desserts are displayed, so diners are alerted to save themselves for *Mousse Brûlée*, the tart of the day, or a taste of each of four or five daily offerings.

A restaurant's success is measured not only in the number of people it serves, but in the numbers it does not serve, and every day for years the Mouillerons have had to turn away many more people than they can feed. Advanced booking is *always* necessary.
Late dinner

PORTUGUESE
Os Arcos

44 Hugh Street, SW1 01–828 1486
⊖ Victoria *Map C54*
Open 12.30–2.30 pm, 7.30–11.30 pm; closed Saturday lunch, Sunday
Moderate/Expensive

Let's Lunch in London

- Access, American Express, Barclaycard, Diners, Mastercharge
- Booking suggested

- Seats 60
- Parties catered for
- Taped music

Os Arcos (The Arches) was opened about three years ago by importers of Portuguese wine, and the restaurant does have a good selection of bottles from Dao, Madeira and the Estoril.

There is a spacious and attractive bar on the ground floor. The dining room is in a white-washed and vaulted basement that is very simply decorated with greenery and has a colourful tile floor. It is deliberately reminiscent of the dining room of a posada ('pleasant inn') in the Estoril.

Fish is a speciality here: *Sopa de Marisco* (shellfish soup), *Salmonete Grelhado* (grilled red mullet) and *Bacalhau Assado* (salt cod in cream sauce), but there are also grilled meats and *Franco No Churrasco* (baby chicken grilled with *piri-piri*, a hot sauce of butter and chilli peppers).

Late dinner

ITALIAN

Tiberio

23 Queen Street, W1 01–629 3561
⊖ Green Park   *Map A32*
Open 12–3 pm, 7 pm–2 am; closed Saturday lunch, Sunday
Expensive

- Access, American Express, Barclaycard, Carte Blanche, Diners
- Booking suggested

- Seats 90
- Parties catered for
- Jackets required

After more than a decade Tiberio is still a regular setting for the high-powered lunch. Perhaps the tables are now more widely spaced than they were in the palmier days, but the place is always fashionably filled and the chefs in the *cucina* behind the translucent, red-tinted screen still produce reliable *Fettuccini alla Papalina, Insalata alla Calamari, Scalopini di Vitello a Sorrentino* and *Souvrana di Polla alla Vesuviana* (breaded chicken breast, eggplant, tomato, cheese *au gratin*).

This large, elegant Mayfair basement was designed by Enzo Apicella in the characteristic style that became the *sine qua non* of London trattorias and abetted the commercial success of the original Princes of Pasta, Mario and Franco: arches,

whitewashed walls, ceramic tile floors, witty artwork, well-directed lighting and those cane-seated chairs that have left their imprint on so many bottoms.
Late dinner

FRENCH
La Toque Blanche

21 Abingdon Road, W8   01–937 5832
⊖ Kensington High Street   *Map D27*
Open 12.30–1.45 pm, 7–10.45 pm; closed Saturday, Sunday
Expensive

- American Express, Diners
- Booking suggested for dinner
- Seats 38
- Parties catered for
- Taped music
- &. Access to restaurant

The decor here is crisply functional and French-restaurant-formal. The tables are close together but it is quiet even at peak dinner hours, and the regular clientele is soft-spoken and discerning.

It is never busy at lunchtime. A few tables only are taken by people in earnest discussion who at the same time seem capable of enjoying a prolonged, rich and bountiful meal. The menu includes many classical French dishes: *Crêpes aux Fruits de Mer, Ballotine de Volaille, Langoustines à ma Façon*. The owner and chef Charles Giovagnoli is from Nice, and his Provencal dishes are piquant. There are good vintages on the wine list and some pleasant inexpensive bottles.
Late dinner

Fashionable

In fashionable restaurants the type of food and the style of decor create a definite mood: art-deco Chinese, high-tech Japanese, Paris brasserie or Roman trattoria. The positioning of the tables, the manner of the staff, and the lighting are as carefully engineered as a theatre piece. And the customers respond as though they are part of the play.

Such restaurants are made for entrances ... to see who's where and wave. In the eyes of the locals, these restaurants are the best places in town; the places most mentioned in the gossip columns for their celebrated clients and decorative regulars. Those establishments that stay in vogue survive because they provide a good meal as well as a pleasing setting.

For most of the restaurants selected here booking is necessary, sometimes two to three days in advance.

ITALIAN
Apicella 81

4 Mill Street, W1 01–499 1308
⊖ Oxford Circus   *Map B25*
Open 12.30–3 pm, 7.30–12 midnight; closed Saturday lunch, Sunday
Expensive

- Access, American Express, Barclaycard, Diners
- Booking suggested
- Seats 64
- Live music (evening)
- Jackets required
- & Access to restaurant

Garlic is no more than a rumour in this strikingly handsome trattoria by Enzo Apicella, done all in white. The walls, the floor, the linened tables, the waiters' jackets are all crisply white, yet the place is warm and elegant, with an air of indefinable excitement. This is a beachhead to eclectic chic, frequented by the bachelor rogues of show biz, the precious babes of the fashion world, the heavyweights in the boardrooms of advertising.

Of course, many come here simply to eat, and the chef Bruno Piotto creates substance from fine ingredients: *Trenette Verdi alle Zucclini, Pollastella en Cocotte with Mushroom Sauce, Scampi Perseo, Carpaccio*; and for dessert there is *Chocolate Mousse Cake* and *Passion Fruit Mousse*. The tables are patrolled by waiters who are pleasant and helpful.
Late dinner

FRENCH/INTERNATIONAL
Bewick's
87 Walton Street, SW3 01–584 6711/2
⊖ South Kensington   *Map C27*
Open 12.30–2.30 pm, 7.30–11.30 pm; closed Saturday lunch, Sunday
Expensive

- Access, American Express, Barclaycard, Carte Blanche, Diners
- Booking suggested for dinner
- Seats 65
- Parties catered for

Pleasure is a big item in this plain 'n' fancy restaurant. The undistinguished decor in shades of green and white is 'dressed' by a lively and eclectic crowd: people who listen when social arbiters declare avocado with prawns or steak and kidney with oyster sauce 'in' or 'out', and people who come specifically to try the culinary skills of the young and talented chef, David Peake: *Cream of Pearl Barley Soup* in winter, *Strawberry and Cucumber Soup* in summer, *Smoked Salmon Mousse, Spiked Roast Lamb in Rosemary Crust, Pojarski de Veau à la Sauce Smitane*.

Oenophiles praise the wine list which includes many fine, reasonably priced bottles, as well as a Château d'Yquem 1869 for £1,725 and a Château Haut-Brion 1899 for only £1,150. The restaurant is owned by Julian Sacher and Richard Griggs who make it seem as though running a restaurant is a lot of effortless good fun.
Late dinner

FRENCH

Brasserie St Quentin

243 Brompton Road, SW3 01–589 8005
⊖ South Kensington, Knightsbridge   *Map C18*
Open 12–3 pm, 5–12 midnight, 7 days
Moderate

- Access, American Express, Barclaycard, Diners
- Booking suggested
- Seats 85
- Parties catered for (lunch only)
- Taped music
- ♿ Access to restaurant

A very busy place populated by those-who-are-always-first and by those-who-try-hard-to-be-second, plus a lot of other folks who drop in simply for the food – brasserie fare such as *Fish Soup*, *Oysters*, *Salads* and *Club Sandwiches*. These are served at the long bar in the front. At tables, waiters in long white aprons bring *Filet of Sole en Croûte*, *Veal with Morels*, *Salmon with Green Sauce*. The menu is entirely in French but staff do their best to explain. Service is meant to be swift and attentive but sometimes at peak hours, when St Quentin resembles the Paris Metro at rush hour, one may wait and wait.

The dining room downstairs has more space and is quieter. If you go downstairs notice the menus from La Coupole, Chez Allard and other Paris restaurants from the year 1967 (notice also the prices, of for instance a 1965 Chablis, 10 francs then . . .)
Pre-theatre; late dinner; Sunday lunch

INTERNATIONAL

Le Caprice

Arlington House, Arlington Street, SW1 01–629 2239
⊖ Green Park   *Map B91*
Open 12–2.45 pm, 6–12 pm; closed Saturday lunch, Sunday
Moderate/Expensive

- American Express, Barclaycard
- Booking suggested
- Seats 90
- Parties catered for
- Taped music
- ♿ Access to restaurant

This is a provocatively unpretentious place, totally coordinated in black and white, with touches of art deco, an urbane setting for the ritual lunch, frequented by the *haute-couture* hierarchy, theatre and art personages and lots of agents.

The menu has many tempting choices but is not divided into starters and main courses, and there is no minimum charge. You may order as much or as little as you want, and construct your own meal with such suggestions from the chef as: *Crudités Rafraichies, Salade Capricieuse, Charcuteries Assorties, Fettuccine al Pesto, Grillade de Canard Garnie, Beluga Caviar on Ice, New York Strip Loin Béarnaise.*
Pre-theatre; late dinner

FRENCH
Chanterelle

119 Old Brompton Road, SW7 01–373 5522
⊖ Gloucester Road   *Map D33*
Open 12–2.30 pm, 7–midnight, 7 days
Moderate

- Access, American Express, Barclaycard, Diners
- Booking suggested
- Seats 45
- Parties catered for
- ₳ Access to restaurant

This is a low-key restaurant frequented by many high-key people you might not expect to find lingering over long business lunches in the Old Brompton Road. Habitués park their fast cars in the little mews behind the restaurant, come through the back door, and sit at tables in the rear, assured of getting attentive service and the adventurous cooking of Fergus Provan. The seasonal menu changes every two days, and includes *Baked Brill with Crab Crust and Sorrel Sauce, Calves' Sweetbreads with Cream and Salsify, Fillets of Pork with Apple and Prune Stuffing* and *Salmon en Croûte*; salads and vegetables are extra. There is a well-chosen, small wine list that is reasonably priced.
Late dinner; Sunday lunch

ENGLISH/INTERNATIONAL
Drones

1 Pont Street, SW1 01–235 9638
⊖ Knightsbridge   *Map C23*
Open 12.30–2.45 pm, 7.30–11.30 pm, 7 days
Moderate

- Access, American Express, Barclaycard, Diners
- Booking suggested
- Seats 84
- Parties catered for
- Taped music

Let's Lunch in London

Drones is a beehive of social activity for the owners of small sports cars, usually illegally parked outside, who have time for long lunches. Stylishly coiffed tête-à-têtes are interrupted only long enough to order from the uncomplicated menu: *Smoked Salmon*, *Trout Amandine*, *Chili with Sour Cream*, *Lamb Kebab*, *Hamburgers*.

This attractive restaurant is on two floors. The main dining room is gardenlike, with a sky-light, trellises, lots of greenery and some fine American patchwork quilts on the walls. This is the room for those who care about their image. The room in the basement is quieter and less crowded, and very pretty in a vaguely Oriental style.

Late dinner; Sunday lunch; take-away

FRENCH
Du Rollo

20 Greek Street, W1 01-734 6991
⊖ Tottenham Court Road, Leicester Square *Map B33*
Open 12-3 pm, 6-11.15 pm; closed Saturday lunch, Sunday
Expensive

- Access, American Express, Barclaycard, Diners
- Booking suggested for lunch
- Seats 70
- Parties catered for
- Background music
- ⅄ Access to restaurant

The cuisine here is 'popular' French which means that it is not as sauce-y as *haute cuisine* yet more subtle than *cuisine bourgeoise*, and the menu is easy to understand. In fact, it contains admirably simple and concise translations of classic dishes: *Fillet de sole Amandine*, *Skate au Beurre Noir*, *Médaillon de Boeuf au Madère*.

The dining room is pretty and very well ventilated. The host/owner Peter du Rollo presides with a keen eye for detail and a warm welcome for both new and old customers.

Pre-theatre; late dinner

FRENCH/INTERNATIONAL
L'Escargot

48 Greek Street, W1 01-437 2679
⊖ Leicester Square, Tottenham Court Road *Map B32*
Open Rest: 12.30-2.30 pm, 6.30-11.00 pm; Brasserie 10 am-3 pm, 5.30-10.30 pm closed Sundays
Moderate

- Access, American Express, Barclaycard, Diners
- Booking required
- Seats 220

- Parties catered for
- Live music (evenings)
- &. Access to restaurant

The new Escargot replaces the old Soho favourite, L'Escargot Bienvenu, in the town house built for the Duke of Portland in 1740. Many fine architectural details have survived these two and a half centuries and cunningly adapted themselves to the present art deco decor, a suitable background for the chic clientele.

There is a ground-floor brasserie with a limited menu and three dining rooms on floors above serving a short but very tempting main list embellished with daily specialities: *Black Pudding with Apples*, *Vegetable Terrine Vinaigrette*, *Roast Guinea Fowl and Braised Garlic*, *Salt-beef 'Pot au Feu'* with its own vegetables. The dessert menu includes cheeses, sorbets and the pastry of the day.

The chef, Alistair Little, is a Cambridge graduate who trained in restaurants in Suffolk and Putney, and not a few of the waiting staff appear more accustomed to being served than serving. At the time of writing all the wines were from California and other western American states.
Pre-theatre; late dinner

ITALIAN
La Famiglia

7 Langton Street, SW10 01–351 0761
⊖ Sloane Square, then bus   *Map D38*
Open 12–2.45 pm, 7–11.45 pm, 7 days
Moderate

- Access, American Express, Barclaycard, Diners
- Booking required

- Seats 60
- Parties catered for
- &. Access to restaurant

In the early 1960s *grazie* and *ciao* crept into everyday conversation when Londoners crowded into Italian restaurants and ordered joyous meals in kitchen Italian, and carafes of *vino rossi* and cups of *caffe néro*. Host/owner Alvaro Maccioni was/is the golden boy of that charming fraternity of Italian restaurateurs casually dressed in light cashmere pullovers who greet their cherished customers with hugs, kisses and quips. If you are not known here do not be surprised if your greeting is the sort reserved for embarrassing relatives at a family reunion.

Let's Lunch in London

La Famiglia, at World's End, is the typically arched London trattoria with whitewashed walls and ceramic tile floors, a combination that makes conversation reverberate as if in an amplified echo chamber. The dining room is very noisy when full – every evening from about 9 o'clock to closing time. The regulars are both famous and not famous but mainly they are slim and fashionable. The best bets are the simpler offerings: *Fresh Agnolotti*, *Insalata of Avocado*, *Tomato and Mozzarella Cheese*, *Gamberoni allo Spiedo* (grilled prawns) and *Carpaccio* (thinly sliced raw beef). The regulars go there more for the ambience than for the sauces.

Late dinner; Sunday lunch

INTERNATIONAL

Foxtrot Oscar

79 Royal Hospital Road, SW3 01–352 7179
⊖ Sloane Square *Map C73*
Open 12.30–2.30 pm, 7.30–11.45 pm, 7 days
Moderate

- Access, American Express, Barclaycard, Diners
- Booking suggested
- Seats 55
- Taped music
- ৬ Access to restaurant

At lunchtime, but never much before 1.30, people mill two and three deep at the bar, cram themselves round tables, and sometimes even spill out into the street outside the Foxtrot Oscar. Everyone appears to be attractive and fashionably outfitted, and the age range is between 21 and 50. If you want to eat, be patient. It is hard for the waiters to get through the crowds.

The decor is ordinary-contemporary – mirrors and beige walls – and a spiral staircase connects the upstairs and downstairs dining rooms where big blackboard menus describe, in multi-coloured chalk, the variety of simple and reliable culinary offerings: *Veal T-Bone Steaks*, *Charcoal Grills*, *Eggs Benedict*, and a large selection of salads.

Late dinner; Sunday lunch; take-away

INTERNATIONAL

Foxtrot Qango

14 Hollywood Road, SW10 01–352 8692
⊖ South Kensington, then bus *Map D36*
Open 12.30–2.30 pm, 7.30–11.45 pm, 7 days
Moderate/Expensive

- Access, American Express, Barclaycard, Diners
- Booking required

- Seats 70
- Small parties catered for
- Taped music

Anybody may have a drink, something to eat, be treated politely, but to the crowds that overflow, it is knowing the staff, the host and half the customers by name that is the allure in this very attractive bar/restaurant, patterned after those glittering watering holes on New York's upper East Side.

The menu offers both light snacks of *Hamburgers*, *Pâtés*, *Eggs Benedict* and various salads as well as more fortifying main courses such as *Boeuf Bourguignon*, *Stuffed Boned Quail*, *Trout Amandine*, *Mussels Marinière*.

Late dinner; Sunday lunch

JAPANESE
Fuji

36–40 Brewer Street, W1 01–734 0957
⊖ Piccadilly Circus   *Map B66*
Open 12–2.30 pm, 6–10.45 pm; closed Saturday lunch, Sunday
Expensive

- Access, American Express, Barclaycard, Diners
- Bookings accepted
- Seats 54

- Parties catered for
- Taped music
- ♿ Access to restaurant

At lunchtime the Fuji is sometimes sparsely populated, making for relaxed, unhurried, almost hushed dining, the right atmosphere in which to dabble in the mysteries of Japanese cuisine. Don't be put off by the garish plastic food displays in the window. These are meant to help the undecided. The dining room is simple and elegant, in a tranquil mixture of Eastern and Western design, with bamboo screens between black-topped tables.

A nice way to begin the meal is with a glass of chilled plum wine. *Ishi Yaki* is a house speciality. This beef, vegetable and seafood dish is cooked on a heated stone at the table. The kitchen provides a full range of Japanese specialities: *Shabu Shabu*, *Sushi*, *Sashimi*, *Tempura* and *Sukiyaki*.

Pre-theatre; take-away

CHINESE/PEKING

Gallery Rendezvous

53 Beak Street, W1 01–734 0445
⊖ Piccadilly Circus, Oxford Circus *Map B29*
Open 12–3 pm, 6–11 pm, 7 days
Expensive

- Access, American Express, Barclaycard, Diners
- Booking suggested
- Seats 130
- Parties catered for

There is a palpable sense of privacy between widely spaced tables in this flag-ship restaurant of the Rendezvous group. The high-ceilinged dining room is done up in warm colours, browns and aubergine, yet the modern decor has a cool, impersonal feeling. The pictures and calligraphy on the walls are worth close inspection. At lunchtime the patrons, collectively, are smooth, very well turned out and tend to blend with the background.

The courteous *maître d'* sees that the formally dressed waiters give good service without hovering as they bring *Shark's Fin Soup, Soft Noodles with Minced Pork and Cucumber, Pancakes with Pork and Spring Onion, Spare Ribs* or *Peking Duck.*
Pre-theatre; late dinner; Sunday lunch; take-away

INTERNATIONAL/ENGLISH/FRENCH

Langan's Bistro

26 Devonshire Street, W1 01–935 4531
⊖ Regent's Park *Map A4*
Open 12.30–2.15 pm, 7–11.15 pm; closed Saturday lunch, Sunday
Expensive

- Credit cards not accepted
- Booking suggested
- Seats 44
- ♿ Access to restaurant, WC

This is Peter Langan's first London restaurant. He went there as chef in the mid sixties and bought it soon after. It has a short, inventive menu that changes often and sometimes includes such starters as *Jamaican Avocado* (blended with rum, fresh ginger and raisins) or *Goats' Cheese and Artichoke Salad with a Herb Vinaigrette.* Main courses may be *Poussin Roasted with Honey, Whiskey and Pine Kernels, Fillet of Pink Trout Baked in Foil with Spinach and Cream,* and always there is *Mrs Langan's Chocolate Pudding.*

The small restaurant is served by a small staff who are usually friendly and efficient. The walls of the dining room are heavily laden with old photographs and amusing prints. The ceiling is hung with inverted paper parasols and the table cloths are covered with brown wrapping paper, bistro-style. The people who eat here tend to look chic and self-possessed.

Late dinner

FRENCH

Langan's Brasserie

Stratton Street, W1 01–493 6437
ϴ **Green Park** *Map B80*
Open 12.30–2.45 pm, 7–11.45 pm; closed Saturday lunch, Sunday
Expensive

- Access, American Express, Barclaycard, Diners
- Booking suggested

- Seats 200
- Live music
- ⓘ Access to restaurant

This big, mirrored, white linened and columned restaurant has much the same spirit as La Coupole in Paris, and is peopled by an endless procession of major, minor and non-celebrities, most of whom fit its mood of glitter and tarnished splendour. It is fun to go there with pals, preferably a famous film star or a fashionable designer.

Service tends to be erratic but the food is good. Everything on the menu looks tempting and what the waiters bring to the nearby tables looks terrific, particularly when you are waiting for your own *Petit Tournedos avec Poivre Vert*, *Quenelles de Brochet* or *Carré d'Agneau avec Herbes de Provence*.

The pretty first-floor dining room is more formal and less frenetic, but in the evenings the live music is downstairs. On Thursday evenings there is foot-tapping to the jazz clarinet of art dealer Eric Lister.

The drawing by David Hockney on the menu cover is of the chef, Richard Shepard, and co-owners, restauranteur Peter Langan and actor Michael Caine.

Late dinner

INDIAN

Last Days of the Raj

22 Drury Lane, WC2 01–836 1628
⊖ Covent Garden *Map B28*
Open 12–2.30 pm, 6–11.30 pm; closed Sunday lunch
Moderate

- Access, American Express, Barclaycard, Diners
- Booking suggested

- Seats 65
- Parties catered for
- ♿ Access to Restaurant

A cooperative of eight partners (six from Bangladesh, a Nepali and an Indian) created this de luxe, modern, well-attended Covent Garden restaurant that makes a serious effort to produce the cuisine of the major regions of both Northern and Southern India. There is *Raj Lamb Roast Special* (for four, give 24 hours' notice), *Tandoori Lamb Chop*, *Murgh Makhani*, *Chingiri Buna* (Bengal seafood), and moderate to incendiary curries.

The number of nationals eating in an ethnic restaurant is a well-known clue to authenticity; here the food is as authentic as any you will find west of Suez yet the midday crowd are mainly Anglo-Saxon children of happy families from the Home Counties, wheeling and dealing together.

Pre-theatre; late dinner; take-away

FRENCH/INTERNATIONAL

Monkeys

1 Cale Street, Chelsea Green, SW3 01–352 4711
⊖ South Kensington *Map C62*
Open 12.30–3 pm, 7.30–12 midnight; closed Saturday and Sunday
Moderate

- Credit cards not accepted
- Booking suggested

- Seats 49
- ♿ Access to restaurant

The most prominent decorative detail of this little Chelsea *relais* is the stately-home-type wood panelling on the walls. Tables are placed so close together that this is indeed an intimate place, frequented by people who, when in doubt, keep their car engines running while they check out the scene. There are two seating areas. Try for a table upfront: it is brighter and airier than the rear section.

Here you never need know gastronomic indecision, for the offerings are very few. The menu changes weekly and is well chosen and well prepared. There are soups of the day, *Cheese Beignet*, *Cassolette of Shellfish*, *Frogs' Legs*, *Poached Turbot with Caviar*, *Caviar and Egg Mousse*, and game in season.
Late dinner

CHINESE/PEKING

Mr Chow's

151 Knightsbridge, SW1 01–589 7347
⊖ Knightsbridge *Map C1*
Open 12.30–2.45 pm, 7–12 midnight, 7 days
Expensive

- Access, American Express, Barclaycard, Carte Blanche, Diners
- Booking suggested
- Seats 120
- Parties catered for
- ⅋ Access to restaurant

Mr Chow's is always in vogue with those who believe that you are *where* you eat. The spare but sparkling setting was designed for entrances and exits. To be seated properly, one should request the main floor at lunch, upstairs at dinner. There is not a touch of chinoiserie nor an Asian waiter either. They are all impeccably Occidental here, as in Mr Chow's New York and Beverly Hills establishments.

The noise level is high. The tables are close together and pristinely set with snowy white cloths and fresh flowers. The food is basically a mix of Northern Chinese adapted to English tastes: *Peking Duck*, *Fresh Lobster with Ginger*, *Steamed Sea Bass*.
Late dinner; Sunday lunch; take-away

ITALIAN

La Nassa

438 King's Road, SW10 01–351 0761
⊖ Sloane Square, then bus *Map C65*
Open 12–2 pm, 7–12 midnight, 7 days
Moderate

- Access, American Express, Barclaycard, Diners
- Booking required
- Seats 60
- Parties catered for
- ⅋ Access to restaurant

Let's Lunch in London

Just 1½ miles from Sloane Square, at the Fulham end of the King's Road where rents are lower and parking is easier, is La Nassa, done up in shades of green and yellow, with hanging plants and the familiar (La Famiglia) mock arches, starched napery and cane-seated chairs. There are home-made pastas, *Chicken al Mattone*, *Saltimbocca alla Romano*, *Trout with Mint*.

The well-designed menu promises rather more than it delivers but it does not much matter because, like most successful restaurateurs, Alvaro of the twinkling blue eyes and sardonic smile always makes his patrons feel as though they are all together at the best party in town.
Late dinner; Sunday lunch

ENGLISH
Newport's

Knightsbridge Green, 22 Brompton Road, SW1 01–589 8772
⊖ Knightsbridge   *Map C3*
Open 12–3 pm, 7–12 midnight; closed Sunday
Moderate/Expensive

- Access, American Express, Barclaycard, Diners
- Booking suggested
- Seats 70
- Parties catered or
- Taped music

This is a coolly elegant place where the sleek and fashionable appear like silhouettes seated at tables on a stage minimally set as a restaurant. Actually, the 7th Earl of Bradford, formerly Viscount Newport, urbane veteran of the restaurant game, has used this address twice before. His previous effort was a caviar restaurant and, as long as the supply lasts, *Caviar* and trimmings here are somewhat reasonably priced: one ounce of *Sevruga* is £7.50, one ounce of *Beluga* £9.50. The other offerings on the menu will not be an anti-climax either: *Noisette of Lamb with Rosemary*, *Sea Bass Meunière*, *Pork Charcutiere* and *Steak, Kidney and Mushroom Pie*.
Late dinner

CHINESE/CANTONESE
Poon's of Covent Garden

41 King Street, WC2 01–240 1743
⊖ Covent Garden   *Map B54*
Open 12 noon–12 midnight; closed Sunday
Moderate/Expensive

- American Express, Diners
- Booking required for dinner

- Seats 120
- Parties catered for

It is best to go to Poon's with at least four people to be able to sample as many different dishes as possible. Over 350 are listed in the 24-page menu. One page is almost entirely devoted to exotic soups: *Shark's Fin*, *Bird's Nest*, *Fish Maws*, *Silver Mushrooms*. Another page lists *King Prawns* served in twenty different ways. *Wind-dried Meats* and *Sausages* are Poon's specialities. They taste remarkably different from other smoked or air-dried sausages, ducks and chickens.

A stylish, modern clientele, dressed in suits from the warm-up to the three-piece variety, adorns the simple but very stylish modern dining room built round a see-through kitchen where chefs slice, stir-fry and steam with balletic ebullience.

Late lunch; pre-theatre; late dinner; take-away

FRENCH

The Restaurant and Brasserie

Dolphin Square, Chichester Street, SW1 01-828 3207
⊖ Pimlico *Map C75*
Open: Restaurant 12–2.30 pm, 7–11.30 pm; Brasserie 7.30 am–11.30 pm, 7 days; pub and cocktail bar 11–3 pm, 5–11 pm
Moderate

- Access, American Express, Barclaycard, Diners
- Booking suggested

- Seats 90 (Restaurant and Brasserie)
- Parties catered for
- Live music

Alain Lhermite's small and intimate Covent Garden bistro, Mon Plaisir, has been a London favourite for many years, and now he also presides over the very large dining rooms in Dolphin Square which he has turned into a sparkling venue that resembles the grand salon of a luxury liner, circa 1930s. Wide stairs flanked by art deco handrails lead to the Restaurant, where many of the original decorative details have been faithfully restored and where an ambitious young French chef, trained in both tradition-al and Nouvelle Cuisine, provides a comprehensive menu that includes *Hot Smoked Salmon with Butter Sauce*, *Fillet Steak with Cream Sauce and Five Peppers* and *Breast of Duck with Black-currant Sauce*.

41

Let's Lunch in London

The Brasserie, in the same style as the Restaurant, provides meals and snacks all day: *Brochette of Mixed Lamb*, *Beef and Pork*, *Grilled Steaks* and *Fish*, *Chef's Salad*. A large cocktail lounge and a pub are also part of this ship-shape complex.
Late lunch; pre-theatre; late dinner; Sunday lunch

JAPANESE

Sakura

9 Hanover Street, W1 01–629 2961
⊖ Oxford Circus   *Map B24*
Open 12–3 pm, 5.30–10 pm, 7 days
Moderate

- Access, American Express, Barclaycard, Diners
- Booking suggested
- Seats 100
- Parties catered for
- Taped music
- ⅋ Access to restaurant

A mixed crowd comes here: lots of Japanese art dealers and business people with their families, and also slim, fashionable young habitués of Mayfair eating with tentative chopstick skills. The atmosphere is somewhat less formal and the decor rather more colourful than one sees in most Japanese restaurants.

One of the specialities is *Sushi*, made of rice with vinegar and larded with tiny cubes of fish, vegetables and condiments. The preparation is more craft than cookery. The ingredients are spread thinly on pre-toasted seaweed rolled tightly together using a little bamboo mat as a guide. The roll is sealed with a few sticky grains of rice and cut into bite-sized pieces – an acquired taste. There is also *Tempura*, *Sukiyaki* and *Teriyaki*.
Pre-theatre; Sunday lunch

ITALIAN

Sambuca

6 Symons Street, SW3 01–730 6571
⊖ Sloane Square   *Map C32*
Open 12.30–3 pm, 7–12 midnight; closed Sunday
Moderate/Expensive

- Access, American Express, Barclaycard, Diners
- Booking required
- Seats 70
- Parties catered for
- ⅋ Access to restaurant

This is not your ordinary London trat. It was originally designed by David Hicks and the present owners changed very few details of the trellised-gazebo-in-a-summer-garden look when they moved into it. A very pretty place, and very lively, particularly in the evening when *tutti* London go there to show off their new clothes and talk about where they have been and where they are going. It is more *piano* at lunchtime. People tend to stay in their seats then and pay closer attention to their own table-mates and to the menu offerings: *Spaghetti Ciocara* (with ham, peas and mushrooms), *Animella 'Mare e Terra'* (sweetbread with cream, brandy and lobster sauce), *Pollastrino 'Sambuca'*, *Mixed Seafood Salad*.

Late dinner

FRENCH/FISH

Le Suquet

104 Draycott Avenue, SW3 01–581 1785
⊖ South Kensington, Sloane Square *Map C30*
Open 12.30–2.30 pm, 7.30–11.30 pm; closed all day Monday, Tuesday lunch
Expensive

- American Express
- Booking suggested
- Seats 35
- Taped music

Le Suquet is a few blocks of expensive real estate surrounding the old port of Cannes and an apt name for M. Martin's pretty replica of a South of France restaurant on a corner of Old Chelsea. Dufy-like coastal scenes brighten the whitewashed walls, and there are tiles on the floor and bright patterned cushions on the café chairs.

A confident crowd orders the seafood platters, working hard to peel the shrimp, to get the meat out of the crab's claws, to ferret the little winkles from their shells. The *fruits de mer* are wonderfully fresh, from French waters: *Langoustines*, *Grilled Sole*, *Lotte à la Niçoise*, served by waiters in tight blue shirts.

Late dinner; Sunday lunch

CHINESE/HUNAN/PEKING/SZECHUAN

Tai Pan

8 Egerton Gardens Mews, SW3 01–589 8287
⊖ South Kensington *Map C19*
Open 12–3 pm, 7–12 midnight, 7 days
Expensive

Let's Lunch in London

- Access, American Express, Barclaycard, Diners
- Booking required for dinner
- Seats 80
- Taped music

If you like quiet, uncrowded places and enjoy hot and spicy Hunan cuisine, the Tai Pan is your kind of place at lunchtime. It is in a deep basement in a Chelsea mews, very pretty, mirrored, horticultured, with roomy seating and elegant table settings. There is a limited lunch menu: *Hot and Tangy Hunan Lamb Slices, Spicy Szechuan Beef, Peking Duck, Prawns in Garlic and Black Bean Sauce.*

The à la carte dinner menu includes over 81 items, many that are very hot indeed, and many with lyrical names.

There is no chance of getting a table in the evenings unless you book. This restaurant is owned by a peer of the realm. It was designed by a well-known decorator, and is frequented by the people marketing consultants think do all the trend-setting and expensive product buying.

Late dinner; Sunday lunch; take-away

INTERNATIONAL

Tapas

30 Winchester Street, SW1 01–828 3366
⊖ **Pimlico** *Map C74*
Open 12.30–2.15 pm, 7.30–11.15 pm; closed Saturday lunch, Sunday
Moderate/Expensive

- Access, American Express, Barclaycard, Diners
- Bookings accepted
- Seats 55
- Parties catered for
- Taped music

Tapas is a lush setting for snacking. Its name derives from the Spanish idea of having a variety of hors d'oeuvres with drinks. It is also similar to the Chinese Dim Sum meals. But here the menu is cross-cultural to an almost infinite degree. Cold starters include *Turkish Chicken and Walnut Pâté, Ceviche* and *Gravad Lax,* and there are hot *Chinese Pancake Rolls, Calamares alla Romana, Indonesian Satays* and *Portuguese Fish Balls.* If you are not jet-lagged by the end of the first course you can go on to main dishes which are large enough for two to four, so bring friends to this elegant looking restaurant which is run in a friendly, informal way that will appeal to people who enjoy the best of all worlds.
Late dinner

Traditional

Many of London's traditional restaurants are as familiar a part of the landscape as Big Ben and the Tower of London. They have survived fame, fickleness, facelifts and bad reviews. Some are among the last strongholds of the conservative, meat-eating male, serving dishes which never vary and of which the customers seem never to tire. Others represent a definitive style: a vintage Chinese restaurant in the City; elegant, Edwardian English; typical Japanese regional restaurants; classic renditions of French cuisine and ambience. These are places where ethnic and social traditions are maintained.

ENGLISH
Baron of Beef

Gutter Lane, Gresham Street, EC2 01–606 6961
⊖ St Paul's   *Map F6*
Open 12–3 pm, 6–9 pm; closed Saturday, Sunday
Expensive

- Access, American Express, Barclaycard, Diners, Grand Met
- Booking required for lunch, suggested for dinner

- Seats 60
- Parties catered for
- Taped music (evenings)

This eponymously named restaurant caters to the eating habits of the stockbroking male: *Roast Sirloin of Prime Scotch Beef with Yorkshire Pudding* from the trolley; *Beefsteak and Kidney Pie*, *Roast Suckling Pig* and *Jugged Hare with Redcurrant Jelly*. Even if you finish everything on your plate, you will not get rich puddings here: the choice is fruit or cheese. In City restaurants the vegetables are overcooked but the meats here are prime. The decor is modern-baronial done with lots of wood panelling, plus upholstery, polished tables and Alfred Munnings sporting

45

prints. Service tends to be solemn.

The clientele are chaps who may still refer to a successful businesswoman as a 'rare bird'. Ladies are presented with a flower by the management.

Pre-theatre; take-away

ENGLISH

The Carlton Tower Hotel
The Rib Room

Cadogan Place, SW1 01–235 5411
⊖ **Sloane Square**   *Map C5*
Open 12.30–2.45 pm, 6.30–10.45 pm, 7 days
Expensive

- Access, American Express, Barclaycard, Diners, Eurocard
- Booking suggested
- Seats 130
- Parties catered for
- Live music
- ♿ Access to restaurant, WC

The Rib Room is large in scale and strongly masculine in design, a place for serious meat-eating. Waiters wear tartan jackets as a reminder that the giant-sized ribs of beef, cut thick off the bone in the American style, are prime Aberdeen Angus, from Scotland. And from the grill and roast come *Thick Steaks*, *Double Lamb Cutlets with Rosemary*, *Calf's Liver*, *Steak American*, and 10 oz *Hamburgers*.

The front page of the menu, possibly the largest double-page spread in town, has a description of the feeding, ageing and marbling of ribs and loins. Despite all this attention to the cow, the kitchen (supervised by Bernard Gaume) also provides fodder for cholesterol counters: soups, *Poached Turbot*, *Fried Sole* and a good selection of fresh vegetables.

Pre-theatre; Sunday lunch

CHINESE/CANTONESE

City Friends

34 Old Bailey, EC4 01–236 7141
⊖ **St Paul's**   *Map F11*
Open 12 noon–11.15 pm; closed Sunday
Moderate

- American Express, Barclaycard, Diners
- Bookings accepted
- Seats 140
- Parties catered for
- Taped music

This is a quiet, well established Cantonese restaurant with a loyal clientele of Asian and Occidental businessmen in dark suits and of unscrutable demeanor. The decor is very restrained, except for a large, back-lit photo mural of Hong Kong against the rear wall. Formally dressed waiters walk silently on thick carpet, bearing subtle and delicately prepared *Roast Duck*, *Beef with Cashew Nuts*, *Sweet and Sour Pork*, *Sautéed Sole with Vegetables* in a light sauce, and *Special Rice*.

Late dinner; take-away

FRENCH

The Restaurant at Claridge's Hotel

Brook Street, W1 01–629 8860
⊖ Bond Street *Map A22*
Open 12.30–3 pm, 7–11.30 pm, 7 days
Expensive

- Access, Eurocard, Mastercharge
- Booking suggested
- Seats 150
- Parties catered for
- Live music
- Jackets and ties required
- ⅙ Access to restaurant

In Claridge's Restaurant, haunt of Greek ship owners and ex-kings, it is as if nothing at all in the world has changed since before the assassinaton of the Archduke Ferdinand in Sarajevo. Each day, at 12.30 precisely, valets in red waistcoats open the great art deco iron gates to the pastel-hued dining room as the Hungarian String Quartet plays nostalgic tunes in the foyer.

Felix-Jean Soubrand, an English chef of French extraction, presides over the kitchen. Fresh menus are printed for each meal, but there is little variation among the traditional selections: *Sole Meunière*, *Grillé or Colbert*, *Game Pie Sandringham* and *Perdreau Roti sur Canapé*. Claridge's has a reputation for serving particularly good breakfasts and is one of the foremost bastions of the sweet trolley. The *Bread and Butter Pudding* is justly famous.

Every three to four tables has its own waiting staff, the *maître*, the *chef de rang* (station waiter), *commis* waiter (busboy or trainee), and this vast dining room has three *sommeliers* with whom to discuss selections from the notable wine cellar. The most eminent guests are usually seated at the most prominent tables, at the front of the room.

Late dinner; Sunday lunch

FRENCH

Restaurant and Grill at the Connaught Hotel

Carlos Place, W1 01–499 7070
θ Bond Street   *Map A28*
Open: Restaurant 12–2.30 pm, 6.30–10.30 pm, 7 days; Grill
12.30–1.30 pm, 6.30–10 pm; closed Saturday and Sunday
Very expensive

- Access, Eurocard, Mastercharge
- Booking required

- Seats: Restaurant 80; Grill 35
- Jackets and ties required

'There's a small hotel . . .' with only 89 rooms, and it turns away more people than it can accept and does not even advertise. It is a legend, with a reputation as unassailable as a safety-deposit box. Service and patina polishing are still performed largely by the old-guard, grey-haired, avuncular staff, and chef Michel Bourdin still produces high style cooking: *Croustade d'Oeuf de Caille Maintenon* and *Feuilleté d'Oeufs Brouillés Magda*, for starters. Main courses include *Coulibiac de Saumon*, *Hâtelet de Coquilles Saint-Jacques* and *Paillard de Saumon à l'Oseille*. And for dessert, *Bread and Butter Pudding* or *Crème Brûlée aux Fraises de Bois*; and much more.

There are two dining rooms.

The Restaurant is the larger of the two, with polished mahogany screens and dado, cream-coloured walls and crystal lights. In both rooms the tables are arranged to give a sense of privacy. The settings make everyone appear distant and courteous – what newspaper diarists usually refer to as being 'formidable'.

Sunday lunch (Restaurant)

JAPANESE

Defune

61 Blandford Street, W1 01–935 8311
θ Marble Arch, Baker Street   *Map A9*
Open 12–2.30 pm, 6–11 pm; closed Sunday
Moderate

- American Express, Diners
- Bookings accepted for dinner only

- Seats 20
- Taped music

The main feature here is a long, immaculately clean Sushi bar of natural wood behind which the chef works. There are also a few tables, but serious Sushi and Sashimi eaters prefer to sit at the counter to be close to the display of raw fish and vinegared rice titbits in order to make their educated selections. In Japan, fish buyers want to look the fish in the eye, they say, to 'see if it has sincerity', a most cherished Japanese quality.

This is a very small and friendly place frequented by many slim and ascetic Westerners who are dab-hands with chopsticks. The decor is simple, elegant and serene. Although raw fish is the speciality, the set lunch menus also offer *Beef Yasai* (beef cooked in Teriyaki sauce with vegetables), *Pork Teriyaki* and *Tempura* (prawns and vegetables crisply deep fried with Tempura sauce).

Pre-theatre; late dinner; take-away

FRENCH

Le Français

259 Fulham Road, SW3 01–352 4748
⊖ South Kensington *Map C59*
Open 12–1.45 pm, 5–10.45 pm; closed S⁰nday
Moderate

- American Express, Barclaycard
- Booking suggested for dinner

- Seats 60
- Taped music
- ⅍ Access to restaurant

Bernard Caen and his chef/partner were apprenticed with the redoubtable Mme Prunier in her Paris and London restaurants. Two or three generations of captains, waiters and *sauciers* trained with Mme Prunier but very few have their own restaurants, and this tough headmistress gave her nod of approval when she visited Le Français soon after it opened in 1967.

The decor is comfortable, elegant and understated in this restaurant, which produces a different regional menu each week of the year. The second week of March, for instance, is devoted to cuisine of the Loire valley: *Mussels Rochelaise* is one of the starters, and there are *Quenelles de Veau* and *Timballe de Fruits de Mer*. The week before, specialities were from the Périgord: *Canard Sauvage* and *Carré d'Agneau Sarladais*. The wines of each region are always available, as are *eaux-de-vie* of plum, pear or raspberry. There is also a fixed carte of well-chosen French dishes.

Pre-theatre; take-away

ENGLISH

The Guinea Grill

30 Bruton Place, W1 01–629 5613
⊖ Green Park, Bond Street *Map A26*
Open 12.30–2.30 pm, 7–11 pm; closed Saturday lunch, Sunday
Very expensive

- Access, American Express,
  Barclaycard, Diners
- Booking suggested
- Seats 90

Simple offerings are temptingly displayed at the entrance to the
maze of little dining rooms at the Guinea Grill: *Smoked Salmon*,
Asparagus and other seasonal starters; *Steaks*, *Chops* and *Mixed
Grill*. The chef cooks the meat of your choice to your liking. The
cooking staff is deft but it is the choice of raw ingredients that
keeps the regulars coming back again and again. The grill, in the
heart of the executive zone, is filled with striped-suited carnivores at lunchtime.

As in many English restaurants, the staff is Spanish, headed by
the sometimes moody *maître d'*, Dominguez. If you happen to be
a Greek ship owner or a celebrity of international fame, you will
put him in a good mood.
Late dinner

FRENCH

Mijanou

143 Ebury Street, SW1 01–730 4099
⊖ Victoria *Map C52*
Open 12.30–2 pm, 7.30–10 pm; closed Saturday and Sunday
Expensive

- Access, American Express,
  Diners
- Booking suggested
- Seats 30
- Parties catered for
- No-smoking area

Those on the gourmet circuit, ever searching for the culinary
equivalent of Shangri-la, carefully watch the development of self-
taught French chef, Sonya Blech. The Blech's ran the Michelin
one-star Crown Inn in Wales, and now have a small restaurant
seating 30 in a terraced house in Belgravia where Mrs Blech
creates what she calls 'cuisine artisinal'. It is eclectic, inventive
and sometimes too complicated. The simpler offerings are usually the most successful: *Dodines de Foie et Ris de Veau au Porto
Blanc*, *Cailles au Riz Sauvage de Mon Amie Pearl*, *Mignonettes*

de Chevreuil au Sureau, Paupiettes de Suprême de Volaille Homardine.

The two dining rooms are both neatly furnished in reds, blacks and white, decorated with an assortment of maps and prints of France. The upstairs room is reserved for smokers, downstairs for non-smokers. Mr Blech is host and sees to the wine list which, at the time of writing, included only French wines.

JAPANESE
Mima

4 Queen's Gate, SW7 01–581 3832
⊖ Gloucester Road   *Map D20*
Open 12–2.30 pm, 6–11 pm, 7 days
Moderate/Expensive

- Access, American Express, Barclaycard, Diners
- Booking suggested
- Seats 30
- Taped music
- ⅙ Access to restaurant

In recent years Japanese cooking has had a considerable influence in the West, as many chefs of Nouvelle Cuisine acknowledge. At Mima, one can watch what seems to be a very simple style of cooking: vegetables and meat grilled with wines and sauces very quickly on a sizzling hotplate built into your table. The skill is in the preparation of raw ingredients. There are ten different ways of cutting every vegetable, and Japanese master chefs usually have a set of 30 precious knives which they often pass on to their favourite disciples when they retire.

Mima is a traditional grill house. The lunch menu is limited to soups, pickles, *Rice and Teppen Yaki, Beef, Chicken* and *Seafood* cooked at the table. At dinner *Shashimi, Tempura* and *Yakitori* are also available. This is a quiet spot with neat and functional decor. At the entrance is a big Japanese drum and a sign inviting each guest to beat it once, for good luck.
Pre-theatre; late dinner; Sunday lunch

ENGLISH
Rules

35 Maiden Lane, WC2 01–836 5314
⊖ Covent Garden, Charing Cross   *Map B59*
Open 12.15–3 pm, 6–11.15 pm; closed Saturday lunch, Sunday
Expensive

Let's Lunch in London

- Access, American Express, Barclaycard, Diners
- Booking required
- Seats 150
- Parties catered for
- Jackets and ties preferred
- ♿ Access to restaurant, WC

First-time visitors go to Rules because, like Mount Everest, it is there and has been since 1798. Regulars, mainly pin-striped City gents, go there because they always have, not because they are particularly impressed by its long history and decorative memorabilia of England's literary and theatrical world, or by the legendary antics of Edward VII and Lily Langtry, for whom a special niche was built in a corner of the upstairs dining room. Some people have felt that the gentlemen who lunch at Rules are apparently not bothered by the over-cooked vegetables and generally mediocre quality of its high-priced meals, or by the sometimes cavalier service that those unknown to the staff may sometimes experience in this quaint, clubby and historic landmark.

Pre-theatre; late dinner

FRENCH

Savoy Hotel The Grill Room

The Strand, WC2 01–836 4343
⊖ Charing Cross   *Map B63*
Open 12.30–2.30 pm, 6.30–11.30 pm; closed Saturday and Sunday
Very expensive

- Access, American Express, Barclaycard, Eurocard
- Booking suggested
- Seats 120
- Jackets and ties required
- ♿ Access to restaurant

Since renovations several years ago, the Savoy Grill has lacked the classy authenticity it had when champagne corks popped for Edward VII and Lily Langtry, for Winston Churchill, Noel Coward and Gertrude Lawrence, to name but a few vaunted names. Those who remember it well say there was nothing to match the room's lavish, old-world elegance. Well, what does any longer? Nevertheless there is still the illusion of pomp and panoply in the marble, the pale woods and the smoked mirrors despite an inappropriate choice of chandeliers. The waiting staff are as professional and discreet as one can reasonably expect of mere mortals.

The kitchen may not be innovative but it continues to send forth worthy offerings of classic dishes: *Les Filets de Sole Veronique, Le Médaillon de Turbotin Waleska, Le Coq au Vin de Chambertin, Les Noisettes d'Agneau Castillane.*

FISH

Sheekey's

29 St Martin's Court, WC2 01–240 2565
⊖ **Leicester Square**   *Map B79*
Open 12–3 pm, 5.30–11.30 pm; closed Sunday
Moderate

- Access, American Express, Diners, Mastercharge
- Booking suggested
- Seats 100
- Taped music

Sheekey's was opened by Mrs Sheekey, and her daughter, Mrs Williams, ran it until a few years ago when the owners of Scott's Fish Restaurant took the place over. They fancied it up a bit too much, particularly in the area of the old oyster bar, but generally the dining rooms still maintain the serious demeanour of a traditional London fish restaurant: wooden floors, small tables close together, a good wine list at fair prices, and big *Oysters, Turtle Soup, Fish Salad. Sole* and *Brill* can be had with the roll-call of inevitable sauces, the *Mornays, Véroniques, Florentines* and *Bonne Femmes*, but the best bets are the plain grills which attest to the freshness of the fish.
Pre-theatre; late dinner

ENGLISH

Simpson's-in-the-Strand

100 The Strand, WC2 01–836 9112
⊖ **Charing Cross**   *Map B64*
Open 12–3 pm, 6–10 pm; closed Sunday
Very expensive

- Access, Barclaycard, Mastercharge
- Booking suggested
- Seats 400
- Parties catered for
- Jackets and ties required

On weekdays the ground floor of this famous institution with an authentic Edwardian club atmosphere is still reserved for men only. The cashiers, however, are female, and women are allowed to eat upstairs and even reserve their own tables there, in the vast, rather characterless South Room and in the smarter West Room.

For well over a century solid, soberly suited men of great jaw and vigour, in chartered accountancy, law and insurance, have come here to eat their chop and read their book and/or talk about business in between talk of leaping salmon and of grouse moors.

The veg are reminiscent of the overcooked boiled cabbage, bubble and squeak *et al.* served in public-school dining rooms but higher marks for the *Roast Sirloin of Beef, Roast Aylesbury Duck with Apple Sauce* and *Roast Loin of Pork.*

The wine list is good. The Stilton cheese is reliable, and there is always vintage port by the glass to drink with it.

Pre-theatre

ENGLISH

Simpson's of Cornhill

38½ Cornhill, EC3 01–626 9985
⊖ **Bank** *Map F25*
Open 11.30–3 pm; closed Saturday and Sunday
Inexpensive/Moderate

- Access, American Express, Barclaycard, Diners
- Bookings not accepted
- Seats 140
- Jackets and ties preferred

This is a picturesque bow-windowed tavern where stock brokers come early, metal brokers arrive later and their assistants are gone before the bosses order their first pint. The sole purpose of the tavern or chop house is to provide food and drink to City gents during the frantic lunch hour. Service is speedy. The vegetables are pre-cooked and kept hot in steam tables, likewise the meats which are reheated over an open fire.

There is lots of atmosphere though, and hail-fellows-well-met at communal tables. There are high-backed 'horse boxes', with brass hat stands, from the days when captains of industry wore silk toppers.

There are two bars and two dining rooms. The Grill is on the ground floor and has more olde charm than the Restaurant upstairs. The fare is simple: *Steak and Kidney Pie, Roast Foreribs of Beef, Liver and Bacon, Bubble and Squeak, Chips, Steamed Jam Roll.*

ENGLISH/FISH
Sweetings

39 Queen Victoria Street, EC2 01–248 3062
θ **Bank** *Map F17*
Open 11.45–3 pm; closed Saturday and Sunday
Inexpensive/Moderate

- Credit cards not accepted
- Bookings not accepted
- Seats 75

This old City seafood restaurant, now run by former fish merchant Graham Needham, still has many of the jolly staff who have
been opening oysters, sousing herring and jellying eels for
countless years in an authentic Victorian corner in the shadow of
that modern monster Bucklersbury House.

There are a few tables in the back room, but most people sit
or stand at the counters enjoying their Muscadet or Blanc de
Blancs with *Smoked Haddock*, and a full cast of fish fresh from
Billingsgate Market.
Take-away

INDIAN
Veeraswamy's

99–101 Regent Street, W1 01–734 1401
θ **Piccadilly Circus** *Map B69*
**Open 12 noon–3 pm, 5.30–10.30 pm, 7 days (Sunday dinner open-
ing 7 pm)**
Expensive

- Access, American Express,
  Barclaycard, Diners
- Booking suggested
- Seats 90
- Parties catered for
- Taped music

This is one of London's oldest Indian restaurants, where Kipling
would have felt on familiar ground. The decor is strictly pukka,
at once both exotic and sturdy, with relics of things past such as
a great tiger skin and an old cloth ceiling fan that needs to be
pulled by strong hands to stir the air that air-conditioning now
cools.

Genial light-footed waiters bring large portions of *Veeraswamy Special Biryani* (tandoori chicken and lamb cooked with
rice and garnished), *Chicken* or *Lamb Vindaloo* (very hot curry),
Maharaja Tandoori Mix and *'Vegetable Delights'* – various vegetables cooked in traditional spices.
Pre-theatre; late dinner; Sunday lunch; take-away

FRENCH/FISH

Wheeler's

12a Duke of York Street, SW1 01-930 2460
Θ Piccadilly Circus   *Map B93*
Open 12–2.30 pm, 6–10.45 pm; closed Sunday
Expensive

- Access, American Express, Barclaycard, Carte Blanche, Diners
- Booking suggested
- Seats 47

If one ate at Wheeler's seafood restaurants exclusively, it would be reasonable to believe that *Dover Sole* (prepared in 25 different ways) are caught off English waters swimming in *Sauce Véronique*, *Mornay*, *Colbert*, *Antoine*, *Egyptienne*, etc. But one would be wrong, and it is far better to eschew these bland and undistinguished sauces and tuck into the *Oysters*, *Smoked Salmon* and the fresh fish in season that is simply grilled or fried.

Wheeler's reputation was established many years ago by oysterman Bernard Walsh, the late founder, who developed the particular style of cooking and ambience. The chefs are Chinese. The sauces are French. The decor is pub-like, cluttered and quite cheerful. Tables are very close together in attractive old buildings of rabbit-warren dimensions. The concept was so successful that the name Wheeler's, at one time, was synonymous with fish restaurant. Unfortunately, the places themselves are not always so reassuringly reliable.

Wine is by the glass (5½ fl.oz) and is very expensve: £1 for white, £1.50 for red (1981 prices).
Pre-theatre

There is another good branch, called **Wheeler's Antoine's**, at 40 Charlotte Street, W1 (01–636 2817)
Open 12–2.30 pm, 6–10.45 pm; closed Saturday

GREEK/MEDITERRANEAN

The White Tower

1 Percy Street, W1 01-836 8141
Θ Tottenham Court Road, Goodge Street   *Map B11*
Open 12.30–2.30 pm, 6.30–10.30 pm; closed Saturday and Sunday
Expensive

- American Express, Barclaycard, Diners
- Booking required
- Seats 80
- Parties catered for
- &. Access to restaurant

John Stais has presided over this gem-like Edwardian restaurant since shortly before the Second World War, and he never closed it for one evening during all the bombings. If he has kept a guest-book it must include the name of every twentieth-century celebrity who ever dined in London. This gleaming room is the epitome of very expensive *haute-cuisine* theatricality: fresh flowers on starched linen cloths, a surgical line-up of flatware, experienced and attentive waiters who know their ageing clientele. Some early customers remember that in The White Tower's opening months, a three-course lunch cost 1*s* 6*d*.

John Stais introduced *Taramasolata* (still the best in town), *Shaslik, Kebab of Turbot* and *Moussaka* to London long before the proliferation of Greek, Cypriot and Turkish restaurants made souvlaki as commonplace as chips with vinegar. The restaurant was once unique for its unfamiliar cuisine, and is still unique as a worthy period place.

Pre-theatre

ENGLISH/FISH/GAME

Wilton's

27 Bury Street, SW1 01–930 8391
⊖ Green Park *Map B92*
Open 12.30–2.30 pm, 6.30–10.30 pm; closed Friday dinner, Saturday, Sunday
Very expensive

- American Express, Diners
- Booking suggested
- Seats 64
- Jackets required, ties preferred

Wilton's is a clubland of oysters and Blanc de Blancs, of game and claret, of loyal confidants and inspired amateurs, many with an irresistible stammer or lisp. The decor is irresistible too: polished mahogany, art nouveau glass, Mucha posters and candid photos of the Royal Family; discreetly private, high-backed boothes upholstered in gold velvet underneath a cheery skylight.

Tourists may find the service and ambience a bit self-conscious but the place has a lot of class. The simple menu rarely changes: *Grilled Steaks* and *Grilled Fish, Salads of Duckling and Smoked Turkey, Game in Season.*

Romantic

As no two earlobe nibblers and under-the-table intimates are alike, so restaurant retreats for affairs of love must be especially varied – exotic, South Pacific or desert-tent settings; places that are slightly seedy and vulgar; others that are coolly elegant, or charming and provincial; and yet others that are mysterious with dark, flashy interiors.

SPANISH/INTERNATIONAL

Alonso's

32 Queenstown Road, SW8 01–720 5986
⊖ None nearby; 137 bus   *Map C78*
Open 12.30–2 pm, 7.30–11.30 pm; closed Saturday lunch, Sunday
Expensive

- American Express, Diners
- Booking suggested
- Seats 80
- Parties catered for
- Taped music
- Jackets preferred

Starched pink napery, deep purple carpets, fuchsia-coloured felt-covered walls, red Magestretti chairs, lighting that flatters every pallor . . . a romantic setting; lunchtime regulars are mainly brokers, bankers and businessmen involved in the nearby Nine Elms Market, but the nights are made for love.

One must ring the front doorbell to be admitted to this Battersea outpost owned by Alonso Galvez, who is the chef, and his wife Carmen. Alonso concocts cuisine for adventurous eaters: first courses may be *Seafood Pancake in Lobster and Pernod Sauce* or *Avocado and Kipper Mousse*. Main courses include *Oxtail in the Pot in the English Manner, Rack of Lamb with Cherries and Tangerines* and *Classic Spanish Ajillo*.

Atuchaclass, two doors away at 24 Queenstown Road, SW8 (01–622 7800), is a simpler, less expensive restaurant run by the Galvez family.
Open evenings only, 7–11.30 pm.

INTERNATIONAL

Blakes in Blakes Hotel

33 Roland Gardens, SW7 01–370 6701
⊖ Gloucester Road   *Map D34*
Open 12.30–2.30 pm, 7.30–11.30 pm, 7 days
Expensive

- Access, American Express,
  Barclaycard, Diners,
  Eurocard
- Booking suggested for
  dinner

- Seats 45
- Taped music

The engineering of images dramatically implemented with the
sure line and clarity of an Utamura print creates a most stylish and
comfortable dining room. But what does it look like? Basic black
and white in art deco style with track lights illuminating a well-
chosen collection of tribal costumes, ethnic art and over-blown
photos. There is a black and white bar, and an alcove done in
Oriental splendour with great multi-coloured cushions on black
sofas in front of a stunning lacquered Indian screen. All very in
and *outré*. At black-linened tables, people with gossip-column
names are hardly stared at by unimpressible neighbours.

The chef is inventive and versatile. Among the main dishes for
dinner are *Kao Lu Duck, Rack of English Lamb Roasted with
Herbs, Yakitori, Dutch Calf's Liver Grilled on Lava Rock*. At the
time of writing, the lunch menu had not been fully developed, but
choices included *Soups, Freshly made Pasta, Roast Rack of
Lamb, Salads, Sandwiches* and various desserts.
Late dinner

FRENCH

Boulestin

25 Southampton Street, WC2 01–836 7061
⊖ Covent Garden   *Map B58*
Open 12–2.30 pm, 7–11.15 pm; closed Sunday
Expensive

- Access, American Express,
  Barclaycard, Diners
- Booking suggested

- Seats 65
- Small parties catered for
- Jackets required

It is a few years since Mrs Maxwell Joseph resurrected this
venerable restaurant that bears the name of the famous

gastronome who cooked and advised the British on matters of food. The gilded and brocaded decor of this Edwardian landmark were refreshingly restored. Service, particularly to familiar faces, is reminiscent of by-gone days. And the culinary skills of Welsh chef/manager Kevin Kennedy keeps the tables filled with the patrician and with those who write articles about them. Do not ask for a corner table: Fleet Street occupies them all at lunchtime.

Marcel Boulestin would no doubt have asked for seconds of Mr Kennedy's *Eventail de Turbot et de Loup sous Cloche à la Crème de Basilic*, *Noix de Carré d'Agneau sur un lit d'Oignons Blancs*, *Suprême de Faisan aux Ecrivisses en Subric*.
Late dinner

LEBANESE
Al Bustan

215 Brompton Road, SW3 01–584 9388
⊖ **South Kensington, Knightsbridge**   *Map C17*
Open 12 noon–12 midnight, 7 days
Moderate

- Access, American Express, Barclaycard, Diners
- Booking required

- Seats 70
- Parties catered for
- Taped music

Lebanese newspapers are provided in the small up-front bar, and snacks and meals are served throughout the day with gracious formality at Al Bustan (The Garden). Photographs of Lebanon in the last century add a touch of nostalgia to the setting, which is colourful and comfortable.

Although the Near East is very mixed in racial origins, in religion and nationalities, the Lebanese, Turks, Syrians and Persians all claim similar national dishes as their own. There are many choices for vegetarians. The most subtly delicate examples of this cuisine appear in the hors d'oeuvres, an array of salads, spreads and dips meant to be eaten with hot and grainy pitta bread. *Hommos*, *Tabbouleh*, *Falafel* and *Arayes*, which is Lebanese steak tartare, are served as starters, but you can also order small portions of main dishes such as *Kibbeh Bil Seneyeh*, *Sharama* and *Chicken Kebab*.
Late lunch; pre-theatre; Sunday lunch; take-away

FRENCH
Café Jardin

10 Lancashire Court, 122–123 Bond Street, W1   01–493 2896
⊖ Bond Street   *Map A23*
Open 12–2.30 pm, 7–11.30 pm; closed Saturday lunch, Sunday
Expensive

- Access, American Express,
  Barclaycard, Diners
- Booking suggested
- Seats 100

- Parties catered for
- Live music
- ঙ Access to restaurant

This is a new restaurant at the time of writing, which looks like
fulfilling its promise. The cuisine, by noted chef Alan Bird, is
neither totally classic nor bizarrely nouvelle, and it expresses his
preference for fish: *Paté of Turbot and Lobster*, *Cloche de Fruits
de Mer*, in pastry, among the starters. *Turbot Roti au Beurre
Nantais* and *Lotte à la Macon* are among fishy main courses, and
there is also *Petit Filet au Poivre Vert* and *Médaillon de Veau
Sauté Catherine*.

It is located in a meandering mews just off Bond Street in what
had previously been an elaborately done-up disco. The dance
floor has been carpeted over and tables put into the long narrow
basement dining room where there is a fireplace, coloured glass
murals of palm trees and cats, alcoves and many tables for two,
at which sit couples who seem to be in love, against a cheerful
and flashy background with the glow of romance.
Late dinner; outdoor eating

AFGHAN
Caravan Serai

50 Paddington Street, W1   01–935 1208
⊖ Baker Street   *Map A7*
Open 12–3 pm, 5.30–11.30 pm, 7 days
Moderate

- Access, American Express,
  Barclaycard, Diners
- Booking suggested for
  dinner

- Seats 54
- Parties catered for
- Taped music

You walk through an ordinary door in Paddington Street, but
once over the threshold you are hit by a sense of authentic
exotica. The staff greet you as though you were long-awaited

guests stopping at their desert tent. Actually the decor is by the owner's Italian wife. The walls are white and hung with Afghan artifacts, some intended for the table, others – such as strangely shaped muscats and effective looking daggers – for the battlefield. The seats are cushioned with brightly woven little carpets.

The cuisine has influences both from the Arab world of the East Mediterranean and from the Balkans and Asia. *Murgh Beryon* is marinated chicken barbecued in a clay oven and served with tomatoes and onions. *Lamb* is done the same way, or as *Bara Mosi* it is cooked in yoghurt sauce with onions, or with hot chilli sauce when it is called *Bara Kuner*. *Brienge-E-Moukamel* translate as 'complete rice dishes' and these have flavours that are unique to Afghanistan.

Pre-theatre; late dinner; Sunday lunch; take-away

THAI
Chaopraya

22 St Christopher's Place, W1 01–486 0777
⊖ Bond Street   *Map A16*
Open 12–3 pm, 6.30–11 pm; closed Sunday
Moderate

- Access, Barclaycard, Diners
- Booking required
- Seats 55
- Parties catered for
- Taped music
- Jackets and ties required

The evening menu here would take months to know, but there are set lunch menus that provide a good introduction to the contrasting textures and the spicy and aromatic flavours of Thai cuisine. *Rice Noodle Crispy Fried with Pork and Shrimp* is the traditional *Mee Krob* sold in Bangkok street stalls: fine, golden, crisp noodles tossed with pork and shrimps and sweet and sour sauce. This is not hot, but many other dishes are seasoned with chilli, lemon grass and coriander in combinations that can set little fires under the tastebuds. Soups are served in a *tom po t'ek*, a funnelled brass pot with a flame in the centre.

The main dining room is downstairs, with tables for two in recesses behind peaked arches. Background Thai music and a shyly gracious and efficient staff contribute to the simple yet exotic atmosphere. There is Thai dancing on Friday and Saturday evenings, after 9.30 pm.

Pre-theatre; late dinner; take-away

INTERNATIONAL
Coconut Grove

3–5 Barratt Street, W1   01–486 5269
ϵ Bond Street   *Map A17*
Open 12 noon–1 am (closes at 12 midnight Sunday)
Moderate

- Access, American Express, Barclaycard, Diners
- Booking required
- Seats 200
- Parties catered for
- Live and taped music

This 'American' restaurant is run by two English lads, who have adapted style and substance culled from hamburger joints to fancy supper clubs all across the USA and come up with their own lively formula ... and menu: *Potato Skins with Sour Cream*, *Steak on a Stick*, *Crab's Claws*, *Fish Kebab* and big salads.

Cocount Grove is a big, shiny-bright, art deco style cocktail-bar/restaurant, where the real and the fantastic mix as happily as the sloe gin and orange juice that make the Sloe Screw. Cocktails are a big item here, so is make-believe. It may only be your lunch hour, yet you feel like an extra in a 1930s Hollywood extravaganza, waiting for your cue to get up and dance as soon as Fred and Ginger finish their big production number.

Late lunch; pre-theatre; late dinner; Sunday lunch; outdoor eating

FRENCH/FISH
La Croisette

168 Ifield Road, SW10   01–373 3614
ϵ Earl's Court, South Kensington, then bus   *Map D35*
Open 12.30–2.30 pm, 8–11.30 pm; closed Monday, Tuesday lunch
Expensive

- American Express
- Booking suggested for dinner
- Seats 45
- Taped music

The name, La Croisette, evokes warm feelings of sea, sand and sex, of film-people longing for awards during Cannes Festivals. This pretty little basement restaurant in Fulham is just the place you'd expect to find in the hills above the Côte D'Azur. Fish is sent from the Mediterranean three times a week, for the pleasure of the classy, gastronomically sophisticated clientele who start their meal with a glass of kir. *Plateau de Fruits de Mer* follow. Then

the choices include *Moules, Cold Langoustines, Loup Grilled over Fennel, Baked Dorade or Rouget Cooked in Provençal Herbs*, served by waiters in tight summery garb to tapes of Piaf and Aznavour.
Late dinner; Sunday lunch

ENGLISH
The English House

3 Milner Street, SW3 01–589 3002
⊖ South Kensington, Sloane Square   *Map C29*
Open 12.30–2.30 pm, 7.30–11.30 pm; closed Sunday
Expensive

- Access, American Express, Barclaycard, Diners
- Booking suggested for lunch, required for dinner
- Seats 30
- Small parties catered for
- Taped music
- ♿ Access to restaurant

Ladies from a Jane Austen novel would not feel out of place in this little restaurant in a little house in a little street in Chelsea. It is elegantly furnished with appropriate antiques, padded walls covered with flowered fabric, brass candle-holders and fresh flower arrangements. There are places for about 30 people at a time, and they are almost always the sort who can afford to 'look like a million dollars'.

Colin Livingstone (formerly at Carrier's) is the charming host. The chef works from a wide spectrum of English court and country cooking: *Chilled Stilton Soup, John Farley's Veal, Collops of Venison with Juniper Berries* and *Steak, Kidney and Mushroom Pie*. Vegetables and salads are offered with all main courses.
Late dinner

FRENCH/INTERNATIONAL
Frederick's

Camden Passage, N1 01–359 2888
⊖ Angel   *Map F21*
Open 12.30–2.30 pm, 7.30–11.30 pm; closed Sunday
Expensive

- Access, American Express, Barclaycard, Diners
- Booking suggested
- Seats 165
- Parties catered for
- Taped music
- ♿ Access to restaurant

Frederick's is a lesson in the theatre of dining. The stage is elegantly set. You enter, and there are two levels ... the upper level is more formal and private, with the tables widely spaced. Here the clientele is made up of bankers and solicitors from the City, and local publishers and antique dealers. This area opens to the light and airy conservatory, which overlooks a walled-in garden used for outdoor dining in the summer.

The staff are well cast. The menu gives cues for an enjoyable performance and includes an invitation to visit the kitchens where the *brigade de cuisine* is preparing *Deep Fried Breadcrumbed Mushrooms*, *Smoked Salmon Garnished with Lumpfish*, and such main courses as *Loin of Porc Périgourdine*, *Lamb with Crèpes*, *Veal Carême*, vegetables and salads. The wine list contains good burgundies and clarets at reasonable prices.

Late dinner; outdoor eating

CHINESE/PEKING

The Gallery Boat Chinese Restaurant

Opposite 15 Prince Albert Road, in the Cumberland Basin, NW1
01-485 8137
⊖ Chalk Farm, then 74 bus *Map E5*
Open 12–2.30 pm, 6–11.30 pm, 7 days
Moderate

- American Express
- Booking required for dinner
- Seats 80
- Parties catered for
- Taped music

The next best thing to a festive meal aboard a sampan in Typhoon Shelter Bay, Hong Kong, is to climb aboard London's first floating Peking restaurant, captained by Mr Wong, the friendly and active host/owner. The surroundings enhance one's appetite for: *Lobster with Spring Onions and Ginger Sauce*, *Crispy Aromatic Duck Served with Pancakes and Spring Onions and Plum Sauce*, *Grilled Lemon Chicken*.

This converted river barge (the old Barque and Bite) is now pleasingly decorated with Laura Ashley prints. It is permanently moored, and so still that you wouldn't believe you had left terra firma were it not for views of the canal's opaque waters from portholes at each table in the below-deck Captain's Saloon. There are also a few tables on the Upper Deck, facing the Zoo and the Snowden aviary.

Pre-theatre; late dinner; Sunday lunch; take-away

Mr Wong also owns **The Welcome Chinese Restaurant** at 68 Belsize Lane, NW3 (01–794 9217)
Open 12–2 pm, 6–12 midnight, 7 days

ITALIAN
Meridiano

169 Fulham Road, SW3 01–589 8815
⊖ South Kensington *Map C35*
Open 12.30–3 pm, 7–12 midnight, 7 days
Expensive

- Access, American Express, Barclaycard, Diners
- Booking suggested
- Seats 150

- Parties catered for
- Live music
- ঌ Access to restaurant

Meridiano is Enzo Apicella's own restaurant, opened after he had designed Terrazzo, Tiberio, San Frediano, Pontevecchio *et al.* during London's Great Italian Restaurant Renaissance. Apicella has designed 35 restaurants in Great Britain, all in his enduring style of sexy sophistication.

This arched, tile-floored, white-walled trattoria is the perfect setting for the stars and supporting cast of London's langorous late lunchers who greet each other in Italian, kiss hands, kiss cheeks, nibble ears and, in summer, bask in South Kensington sunshine on the first-floor terrace. It is family time at the weekend, when children are given ice-cream freely, and for free.

The menu offerings are classic Italian: *Fettucine with Ricotta and Mushrooms*, *Melon with Parma Ham*, *Veal Scaloppine* and *Veal Chop alle Sassi.*
Late dinner; Sunday lunch; outdoor eating

ITALIAN
Montpeliano

13 Montpelier Place, SW7 01–589 0032
⊖ Knightsbridge *Map C9*
Open 12–3 pm, 7–12.30 am; closed Sunday
Moderate/Expensive

- Credit cards not accepted
- Booking suggested

- Seats 65
- Parties catered for

Montpeliano should be, and probably has been, the setting for adverts for San Pelligrino or Cinzano. It is chic, lively and romantic, and it can feed you well. It is no surprise that it remains popular with those who know the correct way to pronounce the jojoba bean (hohoba) and who use its oil to shampoo their lustrous hair.

The discriminating and the slimming find a lot to order from the varied menu, which includes *Spaghetti Vongole*, *Fresh Crab Mornay*, *Veal Montpeliano* and *Nodino Divetello Burro e Salvia*.
Late dinner; outdoor eating

FRENCH
Odette's Restaurant and Wine Bar

130 Regent's Park Road, NW1 01-586 5486
⊖ Chalk Farm   *Map E2*
Open 12.30–2.30 pm, 7.30–10.30 pm, 7 days
Moderate/Expensive

- Access, American Express, Barclaycard, Diners
- Booking required
- Seats 45
- Parties catered for
- Taped music
- ໄ Access to restaurant

One hundred gilt-edged mirrors cover the walls of this pretty ground-floor dining room, thus the see-and-be-seen lunch crowd hardly need to move to be reflected from every angle. This is a meeting place frequented by photographers, models, artists and artisans from nearby studios; some are well known, others are trying for that. They come to talk to one another, as well as for the *Gravad Lax*, *Calves' Liver with Sage and Avocado*, *Chicken Brochette* and *Crab Salad*.

In warm weather, tables are put on the pavement in front and the roof slides open on the Garden Room in the rear.

Odette's Wine Bar is downstairs, in a vaulted basement that manages to be light and airy and contains a fine collection of photographs, lent by the clientele, and a few appropriately biting cartoons by John Glashan. Here you may have *Salads*, *Charcuterie*, *Soups*, *Salmon Trout Mousse* and various desserts.
Sunday lunch; outdoor eating

ENGLISH

The Palm Court at the Ritz Hotel

Piccadilly, W1 01–493 8181
⊖ **Green Park**   *Map B90*
Open 3.30–5.30 pm for tea; drinks served during licensing hours
Moderate

- Access, American Express,
  Barclaycard, Carte Blanche,
  Diners
- Bookings not accepted

- Seats 60
- Parties catered for
- Jackets required, ties
  preferred

The carpeted Long Hall and wide marble stairs leading to the Palm Court were designed for grand entrances and graceful exits, or graceful entrances and grand exits. Here is glorious, burnished Edwardian kitsch beneath rose-tinted ceiling lights that make everyone look romantic and healthy. Tea is still served ritually by tail-coated waiters while a piano trio plays such numbers as 'Fascination' and a medley from 'The Student Prince'. The set tea includes a plate of wafer-thin sandwiches filled with smoked salmon, cucumber and suchlike, and a selection of French pastries.

The Ritz champagne cocktail is one of the best in town: iced non-vintage bubbly with just a dash of brandy, a drop of bitters, one lump of sugar and a twist of orange peel.

INTERNATIONAL

Pomegranates

94 Grosvenor Road, SW1 01–828 6560
⊖ **Pimlico**   *Map C76*
Open 12.30–3 pm, 7.30–12 midnight; closed Saturday lunch, Sunday
Expensive

- Access, American Express,
  Barclaycard, Diners
- Booking suggested for
  dinner

- Seats 60
- Parties catered for
- Taped music

There is an almost fictional grandeur about this rather small basement restaurant where pinpoint lights play softly on tawny walls and lots of glittering mirrors in gilded frames – a setting romantic enough for a love triangle in an Auteuil garden.

The menu is for serendipitous eaters, for people who enjoy the pleasures of *Burek* from the Near East, and *Saté* from the Far East, Spanish *Gazpacho* and *Gravad Lax* from Norway, for starters. Entrees are just as multinational: *Provençal Gigot with Flageolets*, *Szechuan Pork with Rice*.

Late dinner

FRENCH

La Pomme d'Amour

128 Holland Park Avenue, W11 01–229 8532
⊖ **Holland Park**   *Map D12*
Open 12.30–2.15 pm, 7–10 pm; closed Saturday lunch, Sunday
Expensive

- Access, American Express, Barclaycard, Diners
- Booking suggested

- Seats 68
- Parties catered for
- ⅙ Access to restaurant

A suave international crowd frequents this restaurant with a calm atmosphere and a reverential attitude toward cuisine and service that at times becomes a touch pretentious. But, *vive la* french cuisine. It is a pretty place, with a conservatory dining room that looks summery all the year round, and a more elegant and intimate room for dinner only.

The daily set lunch offers simple fare: *Poisson du Marche* (depending on available fresh ingredients the poisson may be halibut one day and cod the next), or *Poulet Chasseur* or *Entrecôte Poivre Vert*. The evening choices include *Canard Sauvage au Chou Rouge*, *Game in Season*, *Turbot Braisé aux Langoustines* and *Carré d'Agneau aux Aromates*.

FRENCH

La Poule au Pot

231 Ebury Street, SW1 01–730 7763
⊖ **Victoria**   *Map C53*
Open 12.30–2.30 pm, 7–11.15 pm; closed Sunday
Moderate

- Access, American Express, Barclaycard, Diners
- Booking suggested

- Seats 50
- Parties catered for
- Taped music

Let's Lunch in London

There is a friendly, authentic atmosphere in this provincial-type bistro. Basic, bourgeois food is well turned out here: *La Poule au Pot* (chicken in the pot), *Le Jambon Braisé, Le Lapin aux deux Moutardes, Le Canarde Roti aux Citrons Verts, Carbonnade de Boeuf.*

Although there is a blackboard menu as well as printed menus, the waiting staff are inclined to recite the daily specialities. Perhaps that is why service tends to be slow, but no one seems to be in a hurry. Public relations people woo editors, decorators and their clients talk about colour and mood, starry-eyed couples touch a lot at tables for two before or after shopping expeditions at Peter Jones or Casa Pupo.

Late dinner

FRENCH/FISH

Au Quai St Pierre

7 Stratford Road, W8 01–937 6388
⊖ **High Street, Kensington** *Map D28*
Open 12.30–2.30 pm, 7.30–11.30 pm; closed Tuesday lunch, Monday
Expensive

- Credit cards not accepted
- Booking required for dinner
- Seats 36
- Taped music

Restaurateur Pierre Martin is the patron saint of this fish place in a Kensington backwater. Even if you do not speak French, you will think it 'charmant' as you enter. There is a rough and ready stall for the sale of fresh Mediterranean fish, and just beyond is a pair of art nouveau doors to a rapturously authentic quai-side bistro, complete with the sound of (too) loud French popular music.

There are only 6 tables upstairs and seats for 12 at the counter downstairs. This is the smallest of M. Martin's London restaurants; the others are Le Suquet and La Croisette. The cuisine is similar: *Plateau de Fruits de Mer* to start, and *Turbot in Champagne and Cream Sauce, Grilled Sea Bass with Fennel* or in a *Bordelaise Sauce, Grilled Red Mullet.*

Late dinner; Sunday lunch; take-away

PAKISTANI
Salloos

62 Kinnerton Street, SW1 01–235 4444
⊖ Knightsbridge *Map C6*
Open 12–3 pm, 7–12 midnight; closed Sunday
Expensive

- Access, American Express, Barclaycard, Diners
- Booking suggested for dinner
- Seats 70
- Parties catered for
- Taped music

Over twenty years ago the host/proprietor Mr Salahuddin (known familiarly as Salloo) left the insurance business to open Salloos in Lahore, where he developed a team of chefs to create specialities from recipes that had been in his family for generations. With some of the same chefs, Salloos of London presents the clean, sharp flavours of exotically spiced Muglai dishes such as *Shekh Kebab* (hot and spicy lamb sausages barbecued in charcoal Tandoor), *Bhuna Gosht* (lamb with spinach cooked in onions and spices), *Pulao* (Basmati rice), *Alu Zeera* (potatoes cooked in 9 spices).

Indian food takes a long time to cook, to serve, and to eat. For this last reason, Salloo searched far and wide for what may be the most comfortable chairs in a London restaurant. The surroundings are rather formal but they are also light and airy, with typical Mughal horseshoe arches and ornamental lattice work. Contemporary Indian paintings and Baluchi embroidery add splashes of colour to the all-white decor.
Late dinner; take-away

ITALIAN
San Lorenzo

22 Beauchamp Place, SW3 01–584 1074
⊖ Knightsbridge *Map C22*
Open 12.30–3 pm, 8–11.30 pm; closed Sunday
Expensive

- Credit cards not accepted
- Booking required
- Seats 100
- Jackets and ties required (evening)

Since it opened in the early 1960s Lorenzo and Mara's pretty *osteria* has been urgently chic, noisy and jam-packed with people who for the most part make their living in fashion, advertising and the arts. Towards the end of the lunch hour a few tousle-haired late risers, looking as they they'd just rolled out of satin sheets, arrive for their 'breakfast'. The menu offers *Spaghetti Integrali al Funghi*, *Organically Grown Rice with Mushrooms*, *Italian Bouillabaisse*, *Veal Piccata al Limone*. The wines are well chosen.

An abundance of plants, wicker chairs and sunny murals create a garden-like setting. A collection of small drawings on the wall near the bar is worth noticing. Service is deft and typical of Italian waiters, who seem longing to be loved despite their somewhat condescending manner.

Late dinner

FRENCH

Thierry's

342 King's Road, SW3 01–352 3365
⊖ Sloane Square, then bus *Map C68*
Open 12.30–2.45 pm, 7.30–11.45 pm; closed Sunday
Moderate

- American Express,
  Barclaycard, Diners
- Booking suggested

- Seats 60
- Taped music
- ⅃ Access to restaurant

This is the sort of place you think twice before recommending, lest it become too popular. Yet for ten years the same owner has maintained a warm and competently served atmosphere for a staunch following, and the same chef from Lourdes has miraculously produced consistently good cuisine: *Quenelles de Brochet*, *Magret de Canard*, *Poulet en Manteau Vert*, *Aiguillettes de Canard Sauvage*.

Outside in the King's Road (near World's End), the parade keeps marching to a different drummer. Inside, Piaf, Aznavour and sometimes Rampal are played softly and intermittently in the dimly lit, narrow dining room in which you will not want one candle, picture, mirror, plant, chair or table to be changed.

Late dinner

Frequent Haunts

Between sixty and eighty per cent of a restaurant's regular lunchtime clientele can be counted on for at least one visit a week. The dinner crowd is not so steady in its patronage.

Every successful lunchtime restaurant is frequented by regulars who work within easy walking distance, and its character is therefore largely defined by its location. There is a distinctly different ambience and clientele between restaurants located in, say, the City and those near the vegetable or meat markets, and between those close to the Houses of Parliament and those in the West End near the offices and studios of the rag trade, the advertising and entertainment worlds.

The following are renowned hangouts in all parts of London, where people go to talk shop, flirt with new job opportunities and new colleagues, to establish their status, to be seen – and to eat their lunch.

ITALIAN

La Barca

80–81 Lower Marsh, SE1 01–928 2226
ө **Waterloo** *Map F34*
Open 12–2.30 pm, 7–11.30 pm; closed Saturday lunch, Sunday
Moderate/Expensive

- Access, American Express, Barclaycard, Diners
- Booking required for lunch, suggested for dinner
- Seats 70
- Parties catered for
- ら Access to restaurant

La Barca (The Boat) in Lower Marsh (The Cut) sounds very nautical, but what you see outside is a lively street scene, with stalls and full-voiced vendors selling fresh fruit and vegetables in a busy neighbourhood near the South Bank arts complex and the Young Vic and Old Vic theatres. Predictably the restaurant draws a theatre crowd from both sides of the footlights, and there are also people there who work in publishing, oil and television.

The restaurant is owned by Luciano Ferrari and Pasquale Fini. Pasquale is the ambitious chef from Lucca, Italy. His kitchen does honour to *Spaghetti La Barca, Pappardelle all 'Vera', Gameroni Pasquale* and *Pulcino Pasquale*. Luciano, who looks after the dining room, has that sultry self-assurance of Italian restaurateurs which overwhelms with its balance of charm and commerce.

Late dinner

ENGLISH/FISH

Bentley's

11 Swallow Street, W1 01–734 4756
Piccadilly Circus   *Map B83*
Open 12–2.45 pm, 6–10.30 pm; closed Sunday
Moderate

- Access, American Express, Barclaycard, Diners
- Booking required for lunch
- Seats 120
- Parties catered for

During the lunch hours Bentley's is as lively as a boys' school at break-time. Many of the regulars (who all seem to know one another) are in the wine trade, or in art and antiques, and there are also many who take a keen interest in horses. Between courses, they often nip over the road to the betting shop.

Customers want nothing changed in this Edwardian Oyster Bar and Restaurant, so the wood panelling, the lamp shades, the hunting pictures and even the colour of the walls are kept exactly as they were in the days of Bill Bentley, the barrow boy turned actor who, in 1916, founded this long-popular fish restaurant.

Standards will inevitably vary somewhat over a 66-year period, and there have been some ups and downs in the quality of food and service. However, the *Oysters* from Bentley's West Mersea beds, the *Dressed Crab* and the fresh *Fish, Grilled, Poached* or *Fried* are the best bets. Bentley's Reserve or Selection is a fine choice for house wine.

Pre-theatre; take-away

INTERNATIONAL
Bertorelli Bros Restaurant

19 Charlotte Street, W1 01–636 4174
Θ Goodge Street   *Map B10*
Open 12–2.30 pm, 6–10 pm; closed Sunday
Moderate

- Access, Barclaycard
- Booking suggested
- Seats 200

- Parties catered for
- &. Access to restaurant, WC

The four Bertorelli brothers opened their first restaurant in Charlotte Street in 1913 and in those good old days, when a plate of smoked salmon cost 10 pence and a big bowl of minestrone was half that price, young students from the nearby medical, art and drama schools could afford to eat there, alongside members of the Bloomsbury Set and many other notable and nice people.

Since then, little has changed but the prices in this unflaggingly popular, homely, family-run restaurant where waitresses tend to treat favourite customers like naughty schoolchildren and everyone enjoys the banter. The portions are large. The menu is long. One can have anything from *Irish Stew* to *Welsh Rarebit*, *Fillet of Sole Bertorelli*, *Beef Stroganoff*, *Roast Guinea Fowl*, *Cassoulet of Duck*, *Pasta*, etc., which means that too much is pre-cooked or comes from the freezer, but none of the regulars seem to mind at all.
Pre-theatre

ITALIAN/INTERNATIONAL
Bianchi's

21a Frith Street, W1 01–437 5194
Θ Tottenham Court Road, Leicester Square   *Map B31*
Open 12–2.30 pm, 6–11 pm, 7 days
Moderate/Expensive

- Access, American Express, Barclaycard, Diners
- Booking suggested

- Seats 100
- Parties catered for
- &. Access to restaurant

Outside, a blue plaque marks the building where John Logie Baird invented television. Inside is a big, non-fussy, family-run restaurant where for thirty years Elena Salvoni (not a family member) greeted everyone and made them feel at home. Then Ms Salvoni left, to work for a new competitor over the road, and the

media people among her regulars wondered aloud in their newspaper columns whether all the trade would go with her. But old lunch habits die hard, and the old crowd is still often in the same seats (upstairs, not in the downstairs dining room) discussing advertising campaigns, theatre ventures, novel plots and such subjects, over working lunches of *Fegato alla Veneziana*, *Filetti di Sogliola Veronica*, *Escalope di Vitello alla Valdostana*, and molti carafes of plonk.
Pre-theatre; late dinner; Sunday lunch

INTERNATIONAL/FRENCH
La Brasserie

70 New Bond Street, W1 01–629 2272
⊖ Bond Street   *Map A21*
Open 10 am–11 pm; closed Sunday
Moderate

- Access, American Express, Barclaycard, Diners
- Booking suggested
- Seats 100
- Parties catered for
- Taped music
- ⅋ Access to restaurant

There is a lived-in feeling and a sense of domesticity in this brasserie frequented by diverse shoppers, art dealers, auctioneers and aristos, who repair here after they have been down to the local 'hock shop' (Sotheby's) with a picture or two under the arm, to boost the coffers. The art work on the walls is less than inspired, as is often the case when restaurants are frequented by the art trade.

Service is helpful, friendly and quick, but you are not rushed if you want to tarry. The kitchen produces both French and Italian dishes: *Noisette d'Agneau with Herbs*, *Salmon Trout Mousse*, *Lasagne*, *Involtini with Parma Ham and Cheese*, *Scampi Wrapped in Cabbage and Fried*.
Late lunch; pre-theatre; late dinner

ITALIAN
Cecconi's

5a Burlington Gardens, W1 01–434 1509
⊖ Piccadilly Circus, Green Park   *Map B68*
Open 12–2.30 pm, 7.15–11 pm; closed Saturday lunch, Sunday
Moderate/Expensive

- Access, American Express, Diners, Eurocard, Mastercharge
- Booking suggested

- Seats 100
- Jackets and ties required
- ♿ Access to restaurant

One would be surprised to smell the pungent thrust of garlic at Cecconi's (pronounced Checkoni). This is a restaurant of character; quiet, dignified, with an air of calm superiority, reflected by the two impeccable host/partners who know not to make minor stirs with seating, not to sit an ex-husband next to an ex-wife, or ex-business partners within earshot of one another. People of substance come here to talk about property, art, banking and money.

Everything in the spacious and elegant dining room looks as fresh as showroom samples. Service is attentive. The pastas are home cooked – *vero*: *Pagliolili Verbi Gratilati*, *Tagliatelle*, *Ravioli*, *Filetto Carpaccio* (wafer-thin slices of raw beef).
Late dinner

FRENCH/NOUVELLE CUISINE
Didier's

5 Warwick Place, W9 01–286 7484
⊖ Warwick Avenue *Map D1*
Open 12.30–2.30 pm, 7.30–10.30 pm; closed Saturday and Sunday
Moderate/Expensive

- American Express
- Booking suggested
- Seats 84

- Parties catered for
- ♿ Access to restaurant

You can easily pretend that you are having a meal in a friend's home in this pretty, domesticated restaurant, presided over by a genial host and an inspired amateur chef. It is located in a tiny tree-lined street in Little Venice.

Service tends to be slow, but the lunchtime clientele seem in no hurry to leave. Many stay well past 3 o'clock, talking about themselves and their deals in advertising, publishing and the music business while affable staff serve *Mushrooms with Coriander*, *Scandanavian Slid Marinated in Aquavit*, *Truite Meunière*, *Grilled Lambs' Kidneys with Bacon*. Muscat de Baumes de Venise, the house dessert wine, is a nice finale to a leisurely meal.

Let's Lunch in London

Gay Hussar

2 Greek Street, W1 01–437 0973
⊖ Tottenham Court Road, Leicester Square *Map B27*
Open 12.30–2.30 pm, 5.30–11 pm; closed Sunday
Moderate/Expensive

- Credit cards not accepted
- Booking required for lunch
- Seats 40
- Small parties catered for
- ♿ Access to restaurant

Whoever said, 'Nobody goes there anymore, it's too crowded', could have been talking about the Gay Hussar, where there is never an empty place at lunchtime and the tables are so close together it would seem that everyone must sit down and get up at the same time. This Hungarian bistro is frequented by Literary London, the literary leftwingers and peers of the Labour party, and anyone who has ever gone there and fallen under the spell of Victor Sassie, a host who takes pleasure in introducing his guests to one another, touring his restaurant floor to fill a glass here, provide a fresh plate there, and make suggestions about the hearty cuisine: *Cold Sour Cherry Soup, Serbian Chicken with Barley, Stuffed Cabbage with Dumplings, Goose Gizzard Goulash* (which is *Zusza Porkolt Galuskaval*) and rich, rich desserts.

Most people drink Hungarian Bull's Blood after studying the wine list, which also includes some very good clarets at moderate prices and plenty of Tokay.
Pre-theatre, late dinner

Ginnan

5 Cathedral Place, EC4 01–236 4120
⊖ St Paul's *Map F13*
Open 12–2.30 pm, 6–10 pm; closed Saturday and Sunday
Moderate

- Access, American Express, Barclaycard, Diners
- Booking suggested
- Seats 56
- Parties catered for
- Taped music

The secret in Japanese restaurants is to develop a meaningful relationship with the Sushi chef and explore the exotica of the day. The cognoscenti hug the counter, improvising a lunch of raw bits of tuna, octopus, salmon, sea urchin and imported Japanese shellfish and molluscs. In between, they may eat a slice of pickled ginger, as a palate cleanser. Satisfaction comes from the different colours, textures and flavours of 5 or 6 courses, which can become quite an expensive habit. There is a set lunch of *Sashimi*: appetiser, soup and rice. And there are wholesome noodle dishes, *Yakitori* (skewered barbecued chicken) and *Tempura* (deep fried prawns and vegetables).

The restaurant is decorated in dark woods and olive green formica in a tranquil style. Staff are helpful and get people in and out quickly. It is populated mainly by Japanese city-gents and quite a few Japanese women in business.

There is a tatami room for private parties: £10 minimum per person, advance booking required.

Pre-theatre

FISH

The Golden Carp

8A Mount Street, W1 01–499 3385
⊖ Marble Arch, Hyde Park Corner   *Map A29*
Open 12–3 pm, 6–11 pm; closed Saturday lunch, Sunday
Expensive

- Access, American Express,
  Barclaycard, Carte Blanche,
  Diners, Euro
- Booking suggested

- Seats 62
- Parties catered for
- Taped music

There is a superabundance of decoration here, and some mad keen polisher keeps a mirror-like shine on the wood panelling of walls and vaulted ceilings, on the buttoned leather banquettes, on the wide stairs and the flamboyant fish motif of this aptly named restaurant which serves carp along with other fresh fish dishes such as *Scampi à la Caesar*, *Salmon in Champagne Sauce*, *Turbot Poché (Hollandaise)*.

Efficient, almost obsequious staff attend to financial people in advertising, cosmetics and the rag trade. Pocket calculators are often brought out between courses.

Pre-theatre; late dinner

FISH

Grahame's Sea Fare

38 Poland Street, W1 01–437 0975
⊖ Oxford Circus   *Map B21*
Open 12–3 pm, 5.30–8.45 pm; closed Sunday, Monday lunch
Moderate

- Credit cards not accepted
- Booking suggested
- Seats 90
- Small parties catered for
- ♿ Access to restaurant

The fish come fresh from the Channel and the North Sea. The customers come from all over to this seventeen-year-old family-run restaurant that looks like a tarted up fish-and-chip shop but is much more. When the maternal waitresses put down a plate in front of a customer, they believe he or she is going to like the crisp flavour of the *Sole Meunière*, *Sweet and Sour Halibut*, *Potato Latkes* and *Fried Plaice*.

It is always very busy at lunchtime and has a loyal following of local business people, many of whom work in film, fashion and pop music.
Pre-theatre; take-away

ENGLISH/INTERNATIONAL

The Grange

39 King Street, WC2 01–240 2939
⊖ Covent Garden   *Map B56*
Open 12.30–2.30 pm, 7.30–11.30 pm; closed Saturday lunch, Sunday
Expensive

- American Express
- Booking required
- Seats 60

The simple, somewhat austere environment in autumnal colours, devised by David Hicks over eleven years ago, reminds us of the residence of a gentleman farmer. One can easily imagine the three-piece suited bankers, solicitors and publishers who regularly lunch here with gun under arm and dog at heels. Yet the decor (big baskets of fruit and vegetables, Victorian portraits, the tracery of an oak church confessional) is also an appropriate setting for the evening's performers and audiences from the opera and ballet.

The hum of civilised conversation is interrupted only by gentle crunching of *Crudités* chosen from those beautiful baskets of fresh vegetables (served only at dinner). The German chef, Jurgens Boldt, has a way with *Beef Wellington*, *Shrewsbury Lamb* and *Veal and Mushroom Pancakes*, and creates unexpected taste marriages with *Brochette of Pork in Peanut Sauce* and *Braised Ox Tongue with Peaches*.

Late dinner

ENGLISH/INTERNATIONAL

The Greenhouse

27a Hays Mews, W1 01–499 3331
⊖ **Green Park**   *Map A30*
Open 12–2.30 pm, 7–11 pm; closed Saturday lunch, Sunday
Expensive

- Access, American Express, Barclaycard, Carte Blanche, Diners
- Booking required
- Seats 84
- Small parties catered for

The Greenhouse is at the Waverton Street end of T-shaped and cobbled Hays Mews, and you walk through a long courtyard to reach the restaurant where you can imagine that you have abandoned city life for a while. There is a slightly affected air of a country inn trying to out-do the London competition in the light and leafy dining room peopled by the ubiquitous lunch crowd in cosmetics, fashion, advertising and the record businesses.

The menu offers a good assortment of simple dishes: *Charcoal Grilled Steaks*, *Pigeon and Mushroom Pie*, *Salmon and Langoustine Rolls*, *Roast Rack of Welsh Lamb*.

Late dinner

AMERICAN

Joe Allen

13 Exeter Street, WC2 01–836 0651
⊖ **Covent Garden, Charing Cross**   *Map B61*
Open 12 noon–1 am, 7 days
Moderate/Expensive

- Credit cards not accepted
- Booking required
- Seats 100
- Taped music

Let's Lunch in London

Joe Allen's stylish, informal theatre-land restaurant has been playing to standing room only since its New York City début several years ago. Now Paris, Los Angeles and Toronto also have replicas of the original, with lots of theatre posters on red brick walls, wooden floors and blackboard menus. The food is all-American: *Black Bean Soup*, *Chef's Salads*, *Chili*, *Barbecued Ribs*, *Pecan Pie* and *Ice Cream with Hot Fudge Sauce*. In addition to these, at lunchtime only, there is a long omelet menu.

Service is by usually affable staff who are meant to resemble the actor/waiters or waiter/actors (depending on their latest credits) of the New York parent. They act 'laid-back' while trying to be efficient. The chef's role may be even less clearly defined, by the rather mediocre taste of much of the fare. Nevertheless or in spite of all this, everyone seems to be having a terrific time, even the 'extras' who often have a long wait for a table.

Late lunch; pre-theatre; late dinner; Sunday lunch

FRENCH

Legends

29 Old Burlington Street, W1 01–437 9933
⊖ Piccadilly Circus, Green Park   *Map B67*
Open 12.30–3 pm, 8–12.30 am; closed Saturday lunch, Sunday dinner
Expensive

- Access, American Express, Barclaycard, Diners
- Booking suggested

- Seats 60
- Parties catered for
- Taped music

Legends is the setting for wheelings and dealings, introductions and seductions, where more *caché* is attached to a hairdresser or a punk designer than to a Jay Gatsby of British finance. The decor, by Nicholas Hills, is hard-edged, chrome and mirror, with big photographs of Legend-ary film stars. This is no gastronomic mecca but the kitchen staff seem to try with offerings such as *Scampis Flambés*, *Suprême de Volaille Cordon Rouge* and *Steak Tartare*.

In the evenings there is a discotheque downstairs, in a room designed to make you feel that you're dancing inside a kaleidoscope. (No membership required.)

Late dinner; Sunday lunch; outdoor eating

INTERNATIONAL
Neal Street Restaurant

26 Neal Street, WC2 01–836 8368
⊖ Covent Garden   *Map B39*
Open 12.30–2.30 pm, 7–11 pm; closed Saturday and Sunday
Expensive

- Access, American Express,
  Barclaycard, Diners
- Booking suggested

- Seats 70
- Parties catered for
- ♿ Access to restaurant

In this restaurant designed by Terence Conran, whose walls are hung with modern pictures chosen by art dealer John Kasmin, every detail is contrived with such elegant simplicity that you may feel as though you are part of a prize-winning habitat, and wonder if it is true that the chic will inherit the earth while all around you about-to-be-published novelists play the interview game with journalists from the glossy magazines. This is a lively place from lunchtime until the last after-theatre diner leaves late in the evening.

The menu is illustrated by David Hockney. The offerings depend very much upon the season: you may find *Sorrel Soup* or *Asparagus in Chervil Butter* to start, and then *Escaloped Salmon en Papillotte* and a game menu of grouse, partridge or pheasant cooked '*à la main*', to order.
Late dinner

FRENCH
Odins

27 Devonshire Street, W1 01–935 7296
⊖ Regent's Park   *Map A3*
Open 12.30–3 pm, 7–12.30 am; closed Saturday lunch, Sunday
Expensive

- Credit cards not accepted
- Booking suggested
- Seats 60

- Small parties catered for
- ♿ Access to restaurant, WC

Odins is a large, voluptuous place, with walls covered in some very fine pictures, crisp linened tables at which sit some of London's best dressed eaters, and people from television and the advertising and recording industries. It is handsomely decorated in a *fin-de-siècle* style, with memories of slower, more gracious days.

The menu is for adventurous palates: *Mushroom Pâté in Brioche*, *Scallop Pâté with Fennel Sauce*, *Noisettes of venison with Green Peppercorns*, *Pink Trout Quenelles with Julienne of Vegetables*, *Fresh Fruit Sorbets* and *Mrs Langan's Chocolate Pudding* (which costs 75p more here than it does next door in Langan's Bistro).

Late dinner

FRENCH/FISH

Poissonnerie de l'Avenue

82 Sloane Avenue, SW3 01–589 2457
⊖ South Kensington *Map C37*
Open 12.15–3 pm, 7–11.30 pm; closed Sunday
Expensive

- Access, American Express, Barclaycard, Diners
- Booking suggested
- Seats 80

- Parties catered for (less than 10 people)
- ♿ Access to restaurant

Back in the early 1960s, when Peter Rosignoli opened Le Poissonnerie, it was a little fish restaurant. Now it is a big fish restaurant, seating almost a hundred, yet it has lost none of its friendliness or intimacy. There is a polished mahogany oyster bar upfront for quick meals. The dining room is plushly tailored, with fishy details and some reasonable seascapes. Staff are polite and professional, as are the customers. Estate agents come here a lot at lunchtime. Evening brings in local French people whose children go to the nearby Lycée, and middle-aged couples living during the week in Chelsea *pieds-à-terre*.

The menu changes often: there are *Oysters*, *Raie au Beurre*, *Saint-Jacques Maison*, *Filets de Sole Véronique*, *Haddock Fumé Poché Beurre Blanc*. Meat dishes are also available.

Late dinner; take-away

FRENCH

The River Restaurant at the Savoy Hotel

The Strand, WC2 01–836 4343
⊖ Charing Cross *Map B63*
Open 12.30–2.30 pm, 7.30 pm–1 am, 7 days
Very expensive

- Access, American Express, Barclaycard, Eurocard
- Booking suggested
- Seats 150
- Live music
- Jackets and ties required

The Savoy was built by the music impresario Richard D'Oyly Carte in 1889. César Ritz was its first general manager. For the grand opening, George Auguste Escoffier prepared the banquet and Johann Strauss led the orchestra, and after all these years the melody still lingers on in its two famous restaurants.

Although the best seats in the River Restaurant are at the windows, one can see the river without and the activity within from almost any table in the beautifully proportioned but now rather innocuously decorated room, in true grand-hotel style. On weekdays between 1.20 and 2.10 pm (and you can set your watch on these times) nabobs in commerce, industry and government take their usual tables for The Big Business Lunch while heavy bylines in the press take notes and waiters serve *Grilled Halibut with Anchovy Butter*, *Jugged Hare* and *Poached Turbot Sauce Divine*.

At weekends this is a frequent haunt of foreign tourists and suburban shoppers. In the evening there is dinner dancing to big-band music.

Late dinner; Sunday lunch

ENGLISH/STEAK

Rowley's

113 Jermyn Street, SW1 01–930 2707
⊖ Piccadilly Circus, Green Park *Map B87*
Open 12 noon–11.30 pm; closed Sunday lunch
Moderate

- Access, American Express, Barclaycard, Diners
- Booking suggested
- Seats 70
- Parties catered for
- Taped music
- ♿ Access to restaurant

With sensibly few changes, this hundred-year-old Mayfair butcher's shop was transformed into an elegant bistro/steak house where the one and only main course is *Entrecôte au Beurre Epice* with *Pommes Frites* and salad. These are not your ordinary steak and chips though. The Scotch beef is charcoal grilled in a spicy butter sauce. The crisp and soft-centred golden chips are worth every calorie. Decisions are not necessary until it is time for dessert: *Home-made Cakes*, *Ice Cream*, *Sorbet* or cheese. Coffee is extra but a large glass of house wine is included in the set price meal.

The idea here is speed and efficiency, quick turnover and quick profit, yet no one who wants to have a leisurely meal is rushed. At lunchtime chic and sleek carnivores, mainly working in the glamour industries, eye one another and themselves in the mirrors that line the original Victorian tiled walls of the old shop. In the evenings, a lively crowd sustains itself on its way to and from the theatre, films and clubs.

Late lunch; pre-theatre; late dinner

FRENCH

RSJ

13a Coin Street, SE1 01–928 4554
⊖ Waterloo *Map F28*
Open 12–2.30 pm, 7–11.30 pm; closed Sunday
Moderate

- Credit cards not accepted
- Booking required
- Seats 48
- Parties catered for
- Taped music
- ⅙ Access to restaurant

The modestly priced and ambitious menu at RSJ changes every month, to the delight of the regulars from nearby office blocks that house Shell Oil, International Press Corporation and other assiduous lunch eaters who for years had almost nowhere other than staff canteens to go to in their neighbourhood. Now they can eat beyond necessity of the *Fillet of Salmon Trout Mille Feuilles, Lamb with Honey and Mint, Calves' Liver with Avocado* and other dishes that reflect the Chinese and French influences of Peter Waller, the Savoy-trained English chef.

After a portion of such tasty sustenance any editor should be able to revise two thoughtful essays and a feature article.

Both dining rooms are simply designed, comfortable and friendly, yet everyone prefers to sit upstairs, at tables beside the windows.

Late dinner

ITALIAN

Rugantino

26 Romilly Street, W1 01–437 5302
⊖ Leicester Square, Tottenham Court Road *Map B34*
Open 12–3 pm, 6–12 midnight; closed Sunday
Moderate

- Access, American Express, Barclaycard, Carte Blanche, Diners
- Booking suggested
- Seats 50
- Parties catered for
- Taped music

Conditions in less pleasant surroundings would seem crowded, but in this friendly ristorante, they are 'snug'. The chairs also look more comfortable than they are yet this does not deter the faithful clientele (lots of voluble people in the media and show business) from spending their long lunch hours at small, neatly laid tables where portions are large, well prepared and served by amiable and well-trained staff.

The menu offers a variety of regional Italian dishes: *Petto di Pollo Livornese, Agnello al Rosmarino, Piccata al Funghetto, Fegato alla Veneziana.*
Pre-theatre; late dinner

ITALIAN
Rugantino East

109 Fleet Street, EC4 01–235 2680
⊖ Chancery Lane, Temple *Map F8*
Open 12–3 pm; closed Saturday and Sunday
Moderate

- Access, American Express, Barclaycard, Carte Blanche, Diners
- Booking suggested
- Seats 125
- Parties catered for
- Taped music

Restaurants where the food is noteworthy are scarce in this part of the world, so this cellar *ristorante* near Ludgate Circus is busy and lively. A frequent topic of conversation among the regulars (journalists and lawyers) is the drinking capacity of absent companions.

The dining room is large, carpeted and brightly lit, with substantial fittings and fixtures. Service is attentive. The menu is rather brief but includes a good selection of the cooking of Italy: *Petto di Pollo Favorita, Piccata all Dionisio, Medaglione di Cervo alle Ciliege, Quaglie alla Pergola.*

Let's Lunch in London

ITALIAN

Santa Croce

112 Cheyne Walk, SW10 01–352 7534
⊖ South Kensington, Sloane Square, then bus *Map C70*
Open 12.30–2.30 pm, 7–12 midnight; closed Sunday
Moderate

- Access, American Express,
  Diners
- Booking suggested

- Seats 120
- ⅗ Access to restaurant

Santa Croce, on a picturesque corner beside the Thames, is a prototypical, Apicella-designed trattoria. It is not as noisy as other trats, however, or perhaps the business lunchers here speak softly. They come from the Nine Elms Market across the river, from Millbank and from the City. Many are drivers of impatient Porsches and Lotuses that they park just outside the door.

The place is run by Walter Tessera and Mino Parlanti, whose grandmother owned a trat in Tuscany. Service is attentive and friendly. *Pastas*, *Game* (in season), *Chicken* and *Veal* dishes prepared in light sauces are among the Tuscan specialities. For dessert, try the *Chocolate Covered Ice Cream* in the shape of an apple that is cracked open and covered with Strega. An interesting wine list includes lesser-known Italian wines.
Late dinner; outdoor eating

ENGLISH/INTERNATIONAL

South of the Border

8 Joan Street, SE1 01–928 6374
⊖ Waterloo *Map F31*
Open 12–2.30 pm, 6–11.30 pm, 7 days
Moderate/Expensive

- Access, American Express,
  Barclaycard, Diners
- Booking suggested

- Seats 85
- Parties catered for

Several years ago Paul Tutton turned a solid mattress factory into a two-storey-with-roof-terrace, farmhouse-like restaurant in a business neighbourhood that was a virtual desert for expense account lunching. It became an instant success, and despite some recent competition is still popular with editors from IPC and executives from the many engineering firms up and down the Blackfriars Road.

The paintings and photographs on the walls are changed every six weeks and are for sale. The menu changes every six weeks also. Specialities include *Duck Pancake*, *Kidneys in Port*, *Red Mullet* and *Roast Rib of Beef.*

Joan Street is a very short street not far from the South Bank arts complex and the Young Vic and Old Vic theatres.

Pre-theatre; late dinner; Sunday lunch; outdoor eating

INTERNATIONAL

Summit Restaurant at St George's Hotel

Langham Place, W1 01–580 0111
⊖ Oxford Circus   *Map B9*
Open 12.30–2.30 pm, 6–10 pm, 7 days
Expensive

- Access, American Express, Barclaycard, Diners
- Booking suggested

- Seats 90
- Live and taped music
- ᕕ Access to restaurant, WC

The aptly named Summit Restaurant is high up on a central but secluded West End corner, with panoramic views of London from every table and close-ups of its neighbours, Broadcasting House and the Church of All Souls, designed by John Nash.

People from the BBC, the rag trade, and the music and film businesses find it a quiet place for a working lunch. The dining room is spacious and crisply maintained. Service is formal and efficient. There is always a lunchtime carving trolley, and *Halibut Steak* (pan fried in butter with lemon and parsley), *Duck with Orange and Black Cherries*, *Egyptian Bamia* and *Roast Beef.*

Pre-theatre; Sunday lunch

AMERICAN

Surprise

12 Great Marlborough Street, W1 01–434 2666
⊖ Oxford Circus   *Map B20*
Open 12–3 pm, 6–11.15 pm; closed Sunday dinner
Moderate/Expensive

- Access, American Express, Barclaycard, Diners
- Booking required for lunch

- Seats 125
- Parties catered for
- Taped music

Let's Lunch in London

This lively, attractive and lavishly tailored American-style restaurant is a mere frisby throw from Carnaby Street and very close to London's fashion and film worlds, thus it is a popular spot for those members of the Working Lunch set who seem to spend their days in New York and their nights in London, and vice versa.

There is a very big cocktail bar, and in the dining room the walls are covered with a good selection of contemporary graphics, but the centrepiece is the Salad Bar, a long refrigerated still-life of an enormous array of crispy, crunchy greens, dressings and garnishes. Main courses include *Club Sandwich*, *Corned Beef Hash*, *10 oz Steak with Broiled Mushrooms*, *Sautéed Onions and Cole Slaw and Calves' Liver with Onion*.

Do not be surprised to find a questionnaire on your table asking about your attitude towards some non-controversial current issue, or, if you are lucky, to receive a bottle of champagne as a prize for carrying a theatre programme that is their 'theatre of the day'. The owners are marketing consultants and must think they 'gotta have a gimmick', when, in fact, the place has great appeal without any of the extras.

Pre-theatre; late dinner; Sunday lunch

FRENCH

Thomas De Quincey

36 Tavistock Street, WC2 01-240 3972
⊖ Covent Garden *Map B51*
Open 12.30–3 pm, 6–11.15 pm (Saturday 7–11.30 pm); closed Saturday lunch, Sunday
Expensive

- Access, American Express, Barclaycard, Carte Blanche, Diners
- Booking suggested
- Seats 50
- Parties catered for
- Taped music
- &c. Access to restaurant, WC

This is an attractive restaurant, not especially original in design, with brick walls, lots of greenery, mirrors and a very good collection of paintings, yet a curious mood pervades, rather like that of an old sepia print with definite edges and long shadows. This feeling may be evoked by the spirit of Thomas De Quincey, the nineteenth-century essayist and critic who once lived here, and aspired to become 'the intellectual benefactor of mankind' (his words), best known for his *Confessions of an English Opium-eater*. The present-day crowd that frequent the nicely laid tables are a wholesome looking lot, from all the glamour industries and the music and dance world.

'*La grande cuisine exige beaucoup de temps*' ... thus the menu advises or warns the unwary not to expect quick service for the chef's specialities: *Paupiette de Turbot Loverdos, Filets de Sole en Feuilletage Pascale, Cotelettes d'Agneau Surprise.*

Pre-theatre; late dinner

Informal and More Informal

These are, for the most part, small to medium-sized restaurants, seating about thirty to one hundred people. They are amiable, unpretentious, inviting, and usually run by a family or by a group of compatible people who take full responsibility for the tedious as well as the enjoyable aspects of restaurant management. There is a feeling of comfort and congeniality among the staff and the clientele.

Such restaurants are friendly places to which the regulars remain faithful, and where newcomers immediately feel welcome.

Informal

JAPANESE
Ajimura

51–53 Shelton Street, WC2 01–240 0178
⊖ Covent Garden   *Map B40*
Open 12–3 pm, 6–11 pm; closed Saturday lunch, Sunday
Moderate

- Access, American Express, Barclaycard, Carte Blanche, Diners
- Booking suggested
- Seats 55
- Parties catered for
- Taped music
- ♿ Access to restaurant, WC

This restaurant is owned by four English Japono-philes with a serious desire to provide fresh, authentic food in a traditional provincial setting. The style and menu can satisfy both the initiated and those who are beginners to the mysteries of this cuisine.

A Japanese chef, Susumu Okada, supervises the preparation of a wide range of dishes such as *Tonkatsu* (loin of breaded pork that is deep-fried), the quick fried *Prawn and Vegetable Tempuras*, *Yakinku* (steak grilled in a special sauce). The chic and bookish regulars seem to fancy the low calorie, low cholesterol *Sushi* and *Sashimi*, but heartier customers may cook for themselves such dishes as *Shabu Shabu* or *Sukiyaki* at their table. Illustrated recipe cards are provided with the ingredients.
Pre-theatre; late dinner; take-away

ITALIAN
La Barca

541 King's Road, SW7   01–731 0039
⊖ Sloane Square, then bus   *Map D39*
Open 12–2.30 pm, 7–11.30 pm; closed Sunday
Moderate/Expensive

- Access, American Express, Barclaycard, Diners
- Bookings accepted
- Seats 65
- Parties catered for
- ♿ Access to restaurant

La Barca at World's End is a bright and cheery trattoria, with trolleys of myriad hors d'oeuvres and puddings displayed against its whitewashed walls. The place is, to borrow a musical expression, *animato*; service is performed *con brio* (with dash), and when the dining rooms are very busy the sound becomes *crescendo*.

The chef performs *con spirito*: specialities include *Spaghetti La Barca en Papillon*, with seafood sauce, *Gamberoni La Barca*, *Spring Chicken* (*Pulcino*) *with Herbs and Garlic in Wine Sauce* and *Trotta Pescatora*, with prawns, capers and tomato sauce.
Late dinner

FRENCH
Bubb's

329 Central Markets, EC1   01–236 2435
⊖ Farringdon, Chancery Lane   *Map F3*
Open 12.15–2 pm; closed Saturday and Sunday
Expensive

- Credit cards not accepted
- Booking suggested
- Seats 55

Let's Lunch in London

This is a charming little bistro near the Smithfield Market run by Peter and Catherine Bubb with the super-serious nature of many Parisian restaurants. The dominant feature is the flavour of natural ingredients, bought fresh from the markets daily. The short menu changes with the seasons and includes: *Ris de Veau au Safran*, *Brochette de Fruits de Mer and Magret de Canard au Citron Vert*.

Wooden floors, painted walls, a few posters and lace curtains at the windows create a no-nonsense decor. Tables are set close together in two dining rooms (the one downstairs is quieter). There is a long wait between courses as everything is cooked to order, so one has time to relax and enjoy the house wine which is good and reasonably priced.

MALAYSIAN

Bunga Raya

107 Westbourne Grove, W2 01–229 6180
⊖ **Notting Hill Gate** *Map D7*
Open 12–3 pm, 6–11.30 pm, 7 days
Inexpensive/Moderate

- Access, Barclaycard
- Booking suggested at weekends
- Seats 90

- Parties catered for
- Taped music
- ⅙ Access to restaurant

Three Malaysian partners look after this warm but starkly simple environment in beige and dark brown, where food of little pretension and considerable character is served in abundant helpings by friendly staff.

None of the dishes contains pork, in deference to the Mohammedan customers. Vegetarians also are catered for, so mention it when you order if you are of that persuasion, and the sauces served will be vegetable-based. Specialities include *Satays*, *Crab Soya* and *Crab Sambal with Spicy Sauce*. The curries, and there are many kinds, cannot be made not-so-spicy, but generally Malaysian curries are not as hot as those of Southern India.
Pre-theatre; late dinner; Sunday lunch; take-away

THAI
Busabong

331 Fulham Road, SW10 01–352 4742
⊖ South Kensington, then bus   *Map C63*
Open 12–3.30 pm, 6.30–12 midnight, 7 days
Moderate

- Access, American Express, Barclaycard, Diners
- Booking accepted
- Seats 150

- Parties catered for
- Taped music
- ♿ Access to restaurant, WC

The Busabong is a flashy bit of exotica that may not appeal to every taste, but it certainly gives a lot of options. There are three dining rooms in this large family restaurant. At lunchtime, in the Fast Food Room, a small selection of *noodle dishes*, each a meal on its own, is displayed in the hot cabinet. However, additional dishes may be ordered from the traditional dining room in the basement. This room is all in red – red carpet, red brick walls, red tablecloths and napkins. Next door is the Khan Tok Room, with low tables and cushions on the floor, and sword fighting and classical Thai dances performed on Friday and Saturday evenings only. (£12 per person for a set meal with entertainment.)

The cuisine is influenced by India in the use of spices and herbs, and by China in its quick stir-frying and steaming methods. These techniques result in a large and diverting selection, including: *Clear Soup with Lemon Juice and Chilli, Chicken with Chilli and Cashews, Fried Fish Sweet and Sour Sauce* and *Fried Beef with Curry Paste.*
Pre-theatre; late dinner; Sunday lunch; take-away

FRENCH
Le Chef

41 Connaught Street, W2 01–262 5945
⊖ Lancaster Gate   *Map A14*
Open 12.30–2.30 pm, 7.30–11.30 pm; closed Sunday and Monday
Moderate

- Access
- Booking required
- Seats 48

- Parties catered for
- Taped music
- ♿ Access to restaurant

Nothing at all changes at this twelve-year-old bistro where Alan King does the cooking in an open kitchen and Mrs King sees to the customers. At least 80 per cent of the clientele turn up regularly and often for the few simple and reliable daily offerings. *Soupe de Poisson with Rouille, Terrine au Chef, Sauté de Veau Provençal, Coq au Vin*, and a very good cheese board.

None of those flimsy bentwoods here. The seating is sturdy and the decor is unaffectedly French.
Late dinner

FRENCH
La Corse

362 King's Road, SW3 01–352 0074
⊖ Sloane Square, then bus   *Map C66*
Open 12–2.30 pm, 7–11.30 pm; closed Sunday
Moderate

- Credit cards not accepted
- Bookings accepted
- Seats 36

- Taped music
- & Access to restaurant

The customers seem happy at La Corse. The waiters are friendly. The owner hops from table to table. People nod and smile at one another.

Food comes from the spotlessly clean open kitchen: *Snails 'Bergère', Eggs à la Corse, Cassoulet Maison, Chicken with Herbs, Entrecôte with Shallots Grilled over Charcoal.*

The owner François Merluzzi is a Corsican, thus the name of the restaurant, which is very pretty, comfortable and filled with memorabilia to his fellow countryman, Napoleon Bonaparte. The house wine is a robust Figarella, an *appellation contrôlée* French wine from Corsica.
Late dinner

ENGLISH/NOUVELLE CUISINE
Dan's

119 Sydney Street, SW3 01–352 2178
⊖ South Kensington, Sloane Square   *Map C60*
Open 12.30–2.30 pm, 7.30–11.30 pm; closed Sunday evening
Moderate

- American Express, Barclaycard
- Booking required
- Seats 50

- Parties catered for
- Taped music
- & Access to restaurant

An inspired chef and a charming host is as unbeatable a combination as Butch Cassidy and the Sundance Kid. Thus the partnership of chef Tony Worrell-Thompson and ex-stockbroker Dan Whitehead, who together aspire to having the first Michelin three-star restaurant in England, bodes well for London food lovers. The chef, influenced by French Masters and Nouvelle Cuisine, is developing his own English style with such dishes as *Red Mullet Marinated in Orange and Herbs*, grilled and served with fresh limes and butter sauce, *Home-made Sausages 'Father and Son' Beef and Veal*, *Grilled Breast of Duck with Hot Walnut Vinaigrette*, *Wiltshire Pink Trout*, rolled in almonds, sautéed, served with Sorrel Sauce. The price of the main course includes vegetables and either a starter or a pudding.

The restaurant is small and pretty, with perhaps a few too many potted plants.

Late dinner; Sunday lunch; outdoor eating

CREOLE

Le Dodo Gourmand

30 Connaught Street, W2 01–258 3947
⊖ Lancaster Gate, Marble Arch *Map A13*
Open 12.30–2.30 pm, 7.15–10.30 pm; closed Saturday lunch, Sunday
Moderate

- Access, American Express, Barclaycard, Diners
- Booking suggested

- Seats 32
- Parties catered for
- Taped music

The chef/owner, Bernard de Rosnay, created this friendly little restaurant to introduce Londoners to the Creole cuisine of his native Mauritius, the island south-east of Madagascar in the Indian Ocean. The difference between the Creole cuisine of Louisiana and that of the West Indies is that the latter has been influenced by the spices and curries of Southern India, using basically the same seasonings but with a lighter touch. Creole specialities include *Vindaye de Poisson aux Gros Piments*, which is fish marinated with coriander and saffron and served with rice; and *Rougaille de Saucisses*, which is black pudding served with lentils and rice. *Chatini* (chutney) accompanies these dishes. A selection of French dishes is also available.

ENGLISH

Drakes

2a Pond Place, SW3 01–584 4555
⊖ South Kensington   *Map C36*
Open 12.30–2.15 pm, 7.30–11 pm, (Sunday 12.30–2.45 pm, 7.30–10.15 pm)
Expensive

- Access, American Express, Barclaycard, Diners
- Booking suggested
- Seats 75
- Parties catered for

Drakes in Pond Place sounds like a country idyll, and this eight-year-old interior by Robert Lush indeed maintains a fresh and salubrious air with its genuine old oak beams and brick walls and floors, leather chairs, polished wood tables and an open kitchen whose centrepiece is a revolving spit.

Ducks, Pork, Lamb, Chicken and Suckling Pig and game (when available) are featured among a short list of traditional English offerings: *Pancake of Finnan Haddock, Grilled Salmon Trout with Hazelnuts, Calves' Liver with Onions and Fresh Herbs.* Wines are well chosen and affordable, with a good selection of half-bottles. One can have a hearty joint with all the trimmings, or a light lunch.
Late dinner; Sunday lunch

TURKISH

Efes Kebab House

80 Great Titchfield Street, W1 01–636 1953
⊖ Oxford Circus   *Map B5*
Open 12 noon–11.30 pm; closed Sunday
Inexpensive/Moderate

- American Express, Barclaycard
- Booking suggested
- Seats 60
- Parties catered for
- Taped music
- ⅃ Access to restaurant, WC

Turks say farewell beautifully, *Guleyh*, 'Go with a smile', which is just what you will do after a meal at this popular and undemanding restaurant. In the front is a glass enclosed counter behind which the chef works. It is filled with a munificent array of food that may be taken away or served at tables in the back. The dining room is brightened by Byzantine colours and memorabilia.

Portions are not only generous but artfully arranged on the plates. *Soguk Mezeler* (hors d'oeuvres) are a real test of the chef's skills. Try the *Special Meze* which includes *Tahini, Tarama, White cheese with Chilli, Stuffed Vine Leaves with Rice and Pine Kernels* and *Aubergine Stuffed with Onion, Tomatoes and Parsley.* There is also a large selection of meat kebabs and grills such as *Rolled and Marinated Breast of Chicken* skewered with peppers and mushrooms and cooked on charcoal, *Doner Kebab* and *Spicy Minced Lamb,* charcoal grilled.

Late lunch; pre-theatre; late dinner; take-away

FRENCH

Le Gamin

32 Old Bailey, EC4 01–236 7931
⊖ St Paul's *Map F10*
Open 12–2.30 pm; closed Saturday and Sunday
Expensive

- Access, American Express, Barclaycard, Carte Blanche, Diners
- Booking suggested
- Seats 100
- Parties catered for

Le Gamin (The Waif) is in a basement near the Central Criminal Courts. Its harsh lighting and garish floor tiles, marble-topped tables, cane café chairs, art-nouveau-style wall sconces (all imports from France) evoke the setting of a tarted-up brasserie in the old Boulevard des Italiens in Paris. The food has an authentic flavour too: *Feuilleté d'Huitres aux Radis, Boudin Noir aux Pommes, Suprême de Perdix Grand-Veneur, Coquilles Saint-Jacques à la Crème d'Ail.*

Upstairs is an inexpensive little fast food stop where the queue forms from noon and moves with the speed of the micro-wave oven heating up the *Soups, Sole with Lemon Sauce, Boeuf Bourguignon, Quiches* and other daily specials from the Roux Brothers' Wandsworth kitchens. Counter service only.

FRENCH

Les Halles

57 Theobald's Road, WC1 01–242 6761
⊖ Holborn *Map B13*
Open 12–2.30 pm, 7.30–10.30 pm; closed Saturday and Sunday
Moderate

Let's Lunch in London

- Access, American Express, Barclaycard, Diners
- Booking suggested

- Seats 60
- Taped music
- ♿ Access to restaurant

Les Halles could be a winner for those who liken finding a good restaurant in Holborn to an Outward Bound experience. This is an authentic brasserie, with noisy charm, an old pewter bar, marble-topped tables, art nouveau tiles, lamps and polished brass fittings, all transplanted from an old café in Les Halles, Paris.

The setting makes everyone look worldly and pleased to be at their tables, eating the simple, well-prepared cuisine. Fish is a speciality here: *Grilled Sole with Herbs*, *Monkfish with Prawns*, *Brill with Cream Sauce and Beetroot*. *Pour les viandes* there is *Entrecôte with Parsley and Lemon Butter* and *Roast Lamb*. The menu changes daily, and one of the nicest desserts is *Tarte Tatin*, flambéed with calvados and served with cream.

Just next door is a small wine bar under the same management.

JAPANESE
Hiroko at the Kensington Hilton

179 Holland Park Avenue, W11 01–603 5003
⊖ Holland Park, Shepherd's Bush   *Map D11*
Open 12–2 pm, 6–10 pm; closed Monday lunch
Expensive

- Access, American Express, Barclaycard, Diners
- Booking suggested for dinner
- Seats 60

- Parties catered for (lunch only)
- Taped music
- ♿ Access to restaurant, WC

With conditioning, palates raised on shepherd's pie and roast beef and Yorkshire pudding can get excited about a single carrot curl or a lone sprig of watercress floating in a bowl of clear broth. Then they should go to Hiroko, where the charming and helpful Mr Shoji understands English preferences and caters to them with a large repertory of traditional Japanese dishes: *Shabu Shabu*, thin slices of beef cooked fondue-style at the table, then dipped into sauces, *Deep Fried Bean Curd* done with spring onion and soy sauce, and *Chicken Yakitori* ... delicious with Kirin beer.
Pre-theatre; Sunday lunch

FRENCH
Jacaranda

Walton House, Walton Street, SW3 01–589 0075
⊖ South Kensington, Knightsbridge *Map C28*
Open 12.30–2.30 pm, 7–11.30 pm; closed Sunday
Moderate

- Access, American Express, Barclaycard, Diners
- Bookings accepted
- Seats 60
- Parties catered for
- Taped music

This is not the sort of place you dress up to go to. It is a neighbourly restaurant in a prime location (just behind Harrods) and has always attracted a rich and loyal trade from locals who use it as if it were at the end of a little lane close to their country cottages.

It is just off the main street, in Lord Walton's old house, and the restaurant is situated in what was the squash court. The interior decor is unresolved, but there is a big fireplace with roaring fires in winter, and a garden for use in summer. The staff are few and friendly. The menu is simple: *La Suprême de Volaille Jacaranda*, *La Courgette Nantua*, *L'Escalope de Veau Concorde*, *L'Escalope de Veau Arlisienne*.
Late dinner; outdoor eating

CHINESE
Joy King Lau

3 Leicester Street, WC2 01–437 1133
⊖ Leicester Square, Piccadilly Circus *Map B75*
Open 11 am–11.30 pm Monday to Saturday, 10 am–10 pm Sunday
Inexpensive

- American Express, Carte Blanche, Diners
- Bookings accepted for dinner
- Seats 200
- Parties catered for
- Taped music
- No-smoking area

This big, family-run restaurant is presided over by Norman Han, a third-generation Liverpudlian who created a sedate and classy architectural setting, muted colours, chrome and glass, starched napery, and smooth service by friendly staff, where gastronomes by chopsticks possessed enjoy an explosion of flavours and textures. There are also many simple dishes for the less adventurous.

Let's Lunch in London

Tim Sums are served between 11 am and 5.30 pm: *Duck Web in Black Bean Sauce*, *Meat Ball with Chinese Dumpling*, *Spareribs in Black Bean Sauce*. There is the usual contingent of *Cantonese Soups*, plus *Fish Lips with Duck Broth* and *Fish Head with Bean Curd*. There is chicken and duck, and lots of eel and abalone dishes, and much more.

Joy King Lau is very close to the half-price ticket kiosk in Leicester Square.

Late lunch; pre-theatre; late dinner; Sunday lunch; take-away

AUSTRIAN

Kerzenstüberl

9 St Christopher's Place, W1 01–486 3196
⊖ Bond Street   *Map A18*
Open 12–3 pm, 6 pm–1 am; closed Saturday lunch, Sunday
Moderate

- Access, American Express, Barclaycard, Diners
- Booking suggested
- Seats 48
- Parties catered for
- Taped music
- ♿ Access to restaurant

The owners, Ilse and Herbert Rauscher, smile as brightly as the shine on the copper and brass cooking utensils that decorate the white stucco walls of this folksy and friendly restaurant specialising in robust Austrian fare. Among the *Hausspezialitaten* are *Herring and Apple Salad*, *Calves' Liver with Onion*, *Sauerbraten*, *Venison with Red Cabbage*, and *Pancakes* and *Apfelstrudel* for dessert. There is a good wine list of German and Austrian wines.

It is busy but quiet at lunchtime although yodelling, solo and group singing are encouraged in the evening.

Pre-theatre; late dinner

INDIAN

Khan's

13–15 Westbourne Grove, W2 01–727 5420
⊖ Bayswater, Queensway   *Map D8*
Open 12–3 pm, 6 pm–12 midnight, 7 days
Inexpensive/Moderate

- Access, American Express, Barclaycard, Diners
- Booking suggested for dinner
- Seats 100
- Parties catered for
- ♿ Access to restaurant

Khan's prepares Muglai dishes from North and Central India based on mutton and chicken, rice and bread (nan), and also does *Tandoori* cooking over charcoal in clay ovens kept at a constant high temperature. In these they cook *Chicken Tikka* (diced chicken and spices), *Tandoori Chicken* and the spicier *Tandoori Boti Kabab*. There are also curries with exotic names, but the thing to consider is the base, usually meat, vegetables or prawns. Ask the waiter for a meat or a vegetable curry that is 'not too hot' or 'quite hot', and begin to sample that way. *Rogan Josh* and *Pasanda* are Southern Indian dishes recommended by the chef.

This was once (six years ago) an ABC cafeteria. Now plastic palm fronds grow out of plastic columns under puffy white clouds on a blue ceiling. Eastern arches divide the front room from the back room, where often at weekends there are traditional Indian wedding parties.

Late lunch; late dinner; take-away; Sunday lunch

RUSSIAN

Luba's Bistro

6 Yeoman's Row, SW3 01–589 2950
⊖ South Kensington   *Map C20*
Open 12–3 pm, 6–12 pm; closed Sunday
Inexpensive/Moderate

- Access, Barclaycard
- Bookings not accepted
- Seats 58
- Parties catered for
- Unlicensed
- ᶑ Access to restaurant

Luba has retired and in her place is Anna Kogan, a young, winsome and very capable cook from Moscow. This is the sort of restaurant you get sentimental about, with its dripping candles, coloured overhead lights, tables on the street when the weather is good. Strangers exchange innocent banter with one another here.

The cuisine has old country authority and strong flavours. It is basically Russian with Slavic touches of French and Italian. Among the starters are *Kapoostniak* (braised cabbage with prunes and sour cream) and *Piroshki* (minced beef and egg wrapped in a pancake and deep fried). Main courses include *Pojarsky* (veal cutlet with mushroom sauce) served with salad and chips, and *Lasagne with Spinach and Meat Sauce*. Bring your own wine (no corkage charge).

Pre-theatre; late dinner; outdoor eating

CHINESE/PEKING/SHANGHAI

Luxuriance

40 Gerrard Street, W1 01–437 4125
⊖ **Leicester Square, Piccadilly Circus**   *Map B72*
Open 12 noon–12 midnight; closed Sunday
Moderate

- Access, Barclaycard,
  Diners, Mastercharge
- Bookings accepted during
  the week only

- Seats 60
- Parties catered for
- ♿ Access to restaurant

Despite its name, Luxuriance is an unassuming and friendly place, freshly decorated in bright colours and an unobtrusive contemporary style. A variety of Shanghai and Peking dishes are offered. These are mildly sweet and aromatic, and even savory and spicy dishes are rarely hot. Specialities include *Sole in Sweet and Sour Sauce*, *Quick Fried Sliced Eel*, *Crispy Aromatic Duck*, the legendary Mandarin delight, *Peking Duck*, and a wide assortment of *Dim Sum*. The steaming of these dumplings derives from an ever-present scarcity of energy in China, from earliest times. The multi-shaped Dim Sum are stacked in bamboo containers and cooked over a single steam source that penetrates 8 or 10 levels of different preparations at a time.
Late lunch; pre-theatre; late dinner; take-away

ENGLISH

Maggie Jones

6 Old Court Place, W8 01–937 6462
⊖ **Kensington High Street**   *Map D17*
Open 12.30–2.30 pm, 7–11.30 pm, 7 days
Moderate

- Access, American Express,
  Barclaycard, Diners
- Booking suggested

- Seats 50
- Parties catered for
- Taped music

This small, rustic-styled restaurant, in a narrow lane that winds between Kensington High Street and Kensington Church Street, is the sort of place that feels like 'your place' even on a first visit. Maybe the nostalgia comes from the music; old gramophone records of popular ballads from the twenties to the fifties. More likely it is that owner/restaurateur Neil Ware knows how to create an attractive, lived-in atmosphere with a few scrubbed pine tables, candles and flowers. Then add a friendly staff and good plain English cooking, and the customers keep coming back.

The menu changes daily. Specialities include *Steak and Kidney Pie*, *Beef Olives*, *Boiled Beef Dumplings*, *Chicken and Cucumber Sauce*.

Late dinner; Sunday lunch

CHINESE/CANTONESE

Man Fu King

30 Leicester Square, WC2 01–839 2939
⊖ Leicester Square *Map B88*
Open 9 am–1 am, 7 days
Moderate

- Access, American Express, Barclaycard, Diners
- Booking suggested on Sunday

- Seats 350
- Parties catered for
- Taped music
- ♿ Access to restaurant

Ardent devotees of Chinese food maintain that the origins of sauces, pastas, sauerkraut and almost everything that is good to eat can be traced back to their favourite cuisine which must be the most varied in the world. Thus in big restaurants like Man Fu King ('Palace of Ten Thousand Good Fortunes'), the length of the menu can be intimidating and confusing. However, in this gilded, tasselled, boisterous red lacquer box, you can sit at a table and choose from an elaborate array of *Dim Sum* wheeled by on trollies. At the end of the meal the bill is added up from the number of plates stacked on your table.

Dim Sum ('heart's delight') are hot dumplings stuffed with meats, seafood and vegetables, and you can make a meal of them, or have a few as a starter and sample some main courses from the hundred specialities on the menu.

Late lunch; pre-theatre; late dinner; Sunday lunch; take-away

FISH

Manzi's

1–2 Leicester Street, WC2 01–437 4864
⊖ Leicester Square *Map B74*
Open 12–3 pm, 5.30–11.40 pm, 7 days
Inexpensive/Moderate

Let's Lunch in London

- Access, American Express, Barclaycard, Diners
- Booking suggested
- Seats 115
- Small parties catered for
- ♧ Access to restaurant

Few of Manzi's regulars ask to have their fish filleted. They do it themselves, deftly lifting the backbone off round fish like trout or herring, or eating the meat off the bone of flat fish like sole.

Some of the best fried fish is sold in this old seafood restaurant. More consistent sauces and somewhat less cooking of vegetables would improve things, but apart from these flaws Manzi's offers a wide choice of *Fish*, well grilled, fried or sautéed; and for first courses there are robust *Soups* and big and tangy *Whitstable Oysters*.

Downstairs there is a bistro atmosphere, with wooden floors, checked table clothes and a counter for those in a hurry. It is lively and animated at lunchtime, but service gets a bit brusque before theatre. Upstairs is the Cabin Room, which is plusher and with a more extensive menu. Those who eat upstairs are hardly aware that the ground floor dining room exists, and vice versa.

Children under five years are not welcome.

Pre-theatre; late dinner; Sunday lunch

FRENCH

Mon Plaisir

21 Monmouth Street, WC2 01–836 7243
⚙ **Covent Garden, Leicester Square** *Map B35*
Open 12–2 pm, 6–11 pm; closed Saturday and Sunday
Moderate

- Credit cards not accepted
- Booking required
- Seats 78
- Parties catered for
- Taped music

More than 80 per cent of the lunchtime crowd at Mon Plaisir are regulars, but something about the place makes you feel like a regular even if you go there only occasionally. Nothing much can change in this forty-eight year old Covent Garden bistro because the building is under a preservation order. Therefore the same travel posters, from the time *plat du jour* cost only a few shillings, go right back in the same places each time the walls are painted the same shade of nicotine-yellow. On a cold day the small back room, with beamed ceilings, a roaring fire and Piaf tapes softly playing, must be the cosiest lunch spot in the West End. Book ahead as there are only a few tables in this room.

The menu reads like *Leçon Un* for ordering basic French cuisine: *Assiette de Hors d'oeuvres*, *Truite Meunière*, *Poulet Rôti aux Champignons*, *Entrecôte Mon Plaisir*.
Pre-theatre; late dinner

CYPRIOT

Nontas

16 Camden High Street, NW1 01–387 4579
⊖ Mornington Crescent *Map E6*
Open 12–3 pm, 6–12 midnight; closed Sunday
Inexpensive

- Access, Diners
- Booking required
- Seats 50

- Parties catered for
- Taped music
- & Access to restaurant

Everyone comes here – prosperous painters and starving art dealers, the richly dressed and the shabby, family groups celebrating happy events – because Nontas fulfils the popular expectation of what a small, family-run restaurant should be.

The dining room is simply furnished but comfortable and intimate. On your second visit you will be remembered by the friendly staff. A small open kitchen produces a good range of this cuisine: *Home-made Smoked Sausage*, *Jugged Hare*, *Halloumi* (cheese toasted on charcoal), meatloaf called *Roullo*, and *Kleftiko*, lamb cooked slowly in its own juices in the oven. *Kleftiko* means 'stolen', and the dish got its name long ago when shepherds cooked their stolen sheep underneath the ground, very slowly.
Pre-theatre; late dinner; take-away

BRAZILIAN

Paulos (A Taste of Brazil)

28 Wellington Street, WC2 01–240 1919
⊖ Covent Garden *Map B50*
Open 12.30–3 pm, 6.30–12 midnight; closed Sunday
Inexpensive

- Access, American Express, Barclaycard, Diners
- Booking suggested
- Seats 120

- Parties catered for
- Taped music
- & Access to restaurant

Let's Lunch in London

Walk through a rather stark modern coffee bar (*si, si*, there's lots of coffee in Brazil) and go downstairs to a setting of paper butterflies and parrots in flight across sky-blue ceilings and murals of jungle foliage. Here, authentic Brazilian food is prepared under the guidance of Senhora Wanda Torres who started serving this beguiling national cuisine to a few friends and neighbours in a little snack bar in Hammersmith in 1975. Now lots of South Americans and Covent Garden denizens go to this *cozinha* for *Camarao no Espeto*, (grilled jumbo prawns on a skewer with fresh limes), served with *Farofa* which is cassava flour fried with eggs, onions and peppers.

On Saturdays, there is *Feijoada*, a traditional dish of beans, with sausages, meats, rice, fried greens, oranges and *Farofa*.
Pre-theatre; late dinner

ITALIAN
Pontevecchio

256 Old Brompton Road, SW5 01–373 9082
⊖ **Earl's Court**   *Map D32*
Open 12.45–3 pm, 7–11.45 pm, 7 days
Moderate

- Access, American Express, Barclaycard, Diners
- Booking required
- Seats 120
- Parties catered for
- ♿ Access to restaurant

The Pontevecchio is popular because it serves many needs. You can relax in a comfortable and undemanding spot where you can eat well and where you can also be seen. Since it opened in the late 1960s this classic, Apicella-designed trattoria (quieter than many of the others) has attracted a wholesomely fashionable crowd. It is particularly busy and *animato* on Sundays as it is just about the only *trat* to stay open.

The staff is well trained and the kitchen is reliable.
Late dinner; Sunday lunch; outdoor eating

CEYLONESE
Sri Lanka

19 Child's Place, SW5 01–373 4116
⊖ **Earl's Court**   *Map D29*
Open 12–3 pm, 6–12 midnight, 7 days
Moderate

- Access, American Express, Barclaycard
- Booking suggested for dinner

- Seats 75
- Parties catered for
- Taped music
- &. Access to restaurant

This brightly caparisoned restaurant close to the Earl's Court tube station was named Sri Lanka (Resplendent Island) years before Ceylon changed its name and became an independent Republic in 1972. The menu is long. The kitchen prepares both Indian and Ceylonese dishes. If it is your first time, you might like to go along with the suggestions of Mr Chowdhury: *Devilled Prawn and Pittu or Rice*, *Nee Goreng*, *Nasi Goreng*, *Tandoori Chicken*, *Biriyani* dishes.

Pre-theatre; late dinner; Sunday lunch; take-away

SWISS

Swiss Centre

1 New Coventry Street, Leicester Square, W1 01-734 1291
⊖ Leicester Square   *Map B77*
Open 11.30 am–12 midnight
Inexpensive/Moderate/Expensive

- Access, American Express, Barclaycard, Diners
- Booking suggested for the Chesa

- Seats 365
- Parties catered for
- Taped music
- No-smoking areas

Think Swiss ... cow bells, edelweiss, Heidi, yodelling, cheese and chocolate, efficiency ... all are an intrinsic part of this lively 'chalet' in Leicester Square which includes five separate and distinctive eating areas.

The Chesa is the most up-market and the only one in which bookings are taken. Chairs, tables, menus, portions are all bigger in this dark wood-panelled dining room. Le Menu Gourmet Suisse changes monthly. In autumn, there are many game dishes such as *Pheasant on Salad with Wild Mushrooms* or *Venison in Red wine*. All the year round there is *Raclette Valaisanne* (melted cheese with boiled potato), *Veal Steak in Creamy Lemon Sauce* and *Fried Fillet of Sole with Sauce Mousseline*.

The Rendezvous sounds as though it would be French but actually the style and the cuisine are more Swiss-German. There is both counter service and tables where snacks and meals are served throughout the day. *Toggeburgers* are among the specialities: these are chopped beef steak, grilled and served with various toppers such as *Edelweiss* (pear and herb cheese butter) or *Alpenrose* (peach and spicy butter).

The Locanda shows influences of Swiss-Italian in decor and cuisine: *Antipasto Ascona*, *Filetti de Sogliola Fritti* (fried sole) and *Pastas* (made on the premises in giant, super-modern kitchens): *Ravioli alla Panna*, *Tagliatelle Valle Verzasca*, *Spaghetti con Carciofi e Peperone*.

The Taverna is very reminiscent of Alpine *après-ski* and is the venue for *Cheese Fondues*. The Imbiss (with its own entrance in Wardour Street) is as reliable as a St Bernard, providing sustenance in the form of chocolate croissants, sausages, flans and Swiss wines seven days a week.

Late lunch; pre-theatre; late dinner; Sunday lunch; take-away

INTERNATIONAL
The Tent

15 Eccleston Street, SW1   01–730 6922
⊖ **Victoria**   *Map C50*
Open 12–2.30 pm, 6.30–11.15 pm; closed Saturday
Moderate

- Access, Barclaycard
- Booking required
- Seats 46

- Parties catered for
- Taped music

In this neighbourhood of swank restaurants or pubs and wine bars, The Tent is a welcome oasis that offers plain and simple food in plain and simple surroundings. At lunchtime, mainly non-expense account people come in twos and fours to talk about their aspirations and ideas for self-improvement, and for the ample portions of *Steak and Kidney Pie*, *Chicken Breast with Mushroom and Cream Sauce*, *Rack of Lamb with Celery and Apricots*, *Fillet of Sole with Lemon and Herb Butter*.

In the evenings, candlelight and flickering shadows make the tearoom-style decor appear more intimate and interesting.

Pre-theatre; late dinner; Sunday lunch

ITALIAN
Topo Gigio

46 Brewer Street, W1   01–437 8516
⊖ **Piccadilly Circus**   *Map B65*
Open 12 noon–11.30 pm, 7 days
Moderate

- Access, American Express, Barclaycard, Diners
- Booking suggested

- Seats 160
- Small parties catered for
- Taped music

Topo Gigio (Little Mouse) is very popular at lunchtime with local business people who are, for the most part, eating non-expense account lunches. In the early evening, hungry theatre-goers tuck into big portions of *Ravioli*, *Veal Escalope alla Siciliana* or *Petto di Pollo alla Pavilion* (breast of chicken with ham and butter).

Service is briskly efficient, and the decor is vintage Soho *ristorante*: the colour scheme – wine red, parsley green and white – is the same as it was in the old Topo Gigio round the corner in Great Windmill Street, but there are fewer chianti bottles here.

Late lunch; pre-theatre; late dinner; Sunday lunch

CHINESE/CANTONESE

Wat's House

128 Allitsen Road, NW8 01–586 2391
⊖ St John's Wood   *Map E7*
Open 12–2.15 pm, 5.30–11.15 pm, 7 days
Moderate

- Access, American Express, Barclaycard, Diners
- Bookings accepted

- Seats 55
- Parties catered for
- Taped music

When you cannot explore the mythic kitchens of Shanghai or roam the legendary restaurants of Hong Kong, then trek on down to Wat's House in St John's Wood. It is an unpretentious restaurant that produces some serious Cantonese cuisine: *Crab Meat 'Po Yee Mein' Soup*, *Peking Duck with Pancake and Sliced Cucumber*, *Spring Onion and Plum Sauce*. In their book *Chinese Gastronomy*, Hsiang Ju Lin and Tsuifeng Lin compare Peking duck to an American bacon, lettuce and tomato sandwich in its distinction between textures and contrasting flavours. Other offerings to consider are *Grilled Prawn with Green Pepper in Black Bean Sauce*, *Dried Scallops with Fresh Asparagus* (when available) and *Beef and Bamboo Shoots*.

Pre-theatre; late dinner; Sunday lunch; take-away

Let's Lunch in London

INDIAN/VEGETARIAN

Woodlands Restaurant

77 Marylebone Lane, W1 01–437 4009
θ Bond Street *Map A12*
Open 12–3 pm, 6–11 pm Monday to Friday, 12 noon–11 pm
Saturday and Sunday
Moderate

- Access, American Express,
  Barclaycard, Diners
- Booking suggested
- Seats 70

- Parties catered for
- Taped music
- ঙ Access to restaurant

Western Musak is played in surroundings that look more like up-market Bognor Regis than Madrasi India. This is a Hindu vegetarian restaurant, a fairly rare type in London. Here you may eat *Pav Bhaji*, a fried vegetable curry; *Mixed Uthappam*, which is shaped like a pizza and filled with onion, tomatoes, cream of wheat and coconut; and *Vegetable Pilao Rice and Kurma*, which is also a curry.

Madras curries are wet in texture and strong in flavour. They are served with rice and usually eaten with a spoon and fork. In India and Pakistan, however, the custom is to scoop up the food with nan or a folded chapatti (bread pancake), and a little of the chapatti is eaten with each mouthful.

Pre-theatre; late dinner; Sunday lunch; take-away

More Informal

PAKISTANI/INDIAN

Agra

135–137 Whitfield Street, W1 01–387 4828
θ Warren Street *Map B1*
Open 12–3 pm, 6–12 midnight, 7 days
Inexpensive

- Access, American Express,
  Barclaycard, Diners
- Bookings accepted
- Seats 80

- Parties catered for
- Taped music
- ঙ Access to restaurant

The Agra is in the shadow of the Post Office Tower in a very unprepossessing little street in a neighbourhood of many exotic herb and spice shops. The long-established restaurant, in two separate shops with a connecting kitchen, has a fine reputation for authentic Indo-Pakistan food: specialities include *Tandooris* (more than curries), *Mutton Tikka*, *Chicken Tikka* and *Sheek Kabab*.

Pre-theatre; late dinner; Sunday lunch; take-away

AFRICAN

Calabash

African Centre, 38 King Street, WC2 01–836 1976
⊖ Covent Garden *Map B55*
Open 12.30–3 pm, 6.30–11 pm; closed Saturday lunch, Sunday
Inexpensive/Moderate

- American Express, Barclaycard, Diners
- Bookings accepted

- Seats 50
- Parties catered for
- Taped music

The informal dining room is in the basement of the Africa Centre, a non-profit-making meeting house and weekend disco where exhibitions, talks, plays and dances are regularly held.

A Senegalese chef prepares dishes from many African countries: Nigerian *Egusi* (beef stew with melon seeds), *Nyama Yo Phika*, a dish from Malawi, *Chicken Groundnut Stew*, from West Africa, *Beef Stew with Green Banana*, *Fish Fried in Palm Oil* and African vegetables such as *Yam*, *Blackeyed Beans* and *Ground Rice*.

The food tends to be spicy and very substantial. The portions are large, and the service is helpful and friendly.

Pre-theatre; late dinner

GREEK

Costa's Grill

14 Hillgate Street, W8 01–229 3794
⊖ Notting Hill Gate *Map D13*
Open 12 noon–10.30 pm; closed Sunday
Inexpensive

- Credit cards not accepted
- Booking suggested for lunch, required for dinner

- Seats 75
- Parties catered for

113

Let's Lunch in London

The atmosphere is always very lively in this simple, friendly and efficient paper-napkin kebab house where charcoal fires grill fresh *Sea Bream*, *Trout* and *Mackerel* as well as *Chicken* and *Lamb*. The chef is also proud of his *Moussaka*, *Kleftiko* (lamb cooked in the oven), *Dolmades* (stuffed vine leaves) and *Souvlakia* (kebabs).

Late lunch; pre-theatre; late dinner

POLISH

Daquise

20 Thurloe Place, SW7   01–589 6117
⊖ South Kensington   *Map C44*
Open 10 am–11.30 pm, 7 days
Inexpensive

- Credit cards not accepted
- Bookings accepted
- Seats 50
- Parties catered for

Daquise has been here since Second World War days when Polish émigrés made South Kensington their outpost. It is atmospheric, with a highly civilised, strictly regulated protocol between staff and venerable habitues. Everyone else receives brisk but efficient service. The place is usually busy, particularly at the weekend.

The menu varies little. Ample portions of *Polish Zrazy* and *Brackwith*, *Stuffed Cabbage*, *Bigos*, *Russian Zrazy*, *Pierozki* and *Kolduny*. Polish Tatra Zywiec is the only beer served, and is worth trying.

Late lunch; pre-theatre; late dinner; Sunday lunch; take-away

ENGLISH/FISH

Geale's Fish Restaurant

2 Farmer Street, W8   01–727 7969
⊖ Notting Hill Gate   *Map D14*
Open 12–3 pm, 6–11 pm; closed Sunday and Monday
Inexpensive

- Access
- Bookings not accepted
- Seats 100
- Parties catered for
- ♿ Access to restaurant

The Geale family opened this Notting Hill Gate landmark in 1919 when a substantial portion of fish and chips cost a penny-ha' penny. The fish and chips are still cooked in beef dripping but they cost about £1.50 now and, regretfully, they do not do take-aways any more.

There are two floors to this time-mellowed restaurant with a friendly, seaside tearoom atmosphere. The nicest place to sit is downstairs at a table in the window, watching the passers-by in these busy backstreets.

Pre-theatre; late dinner

INDIAN

Goan

16 York Way, N1 01–837 7517
⊖ King's Cross *Map F23*
Open 12 noon–12 midnight, 7 days
Inexpensive

- Access, American Express, Barclaycard, Diners
- Bookings accepted
- Seats 30
- Parties catered for

The Goan could easily set the style for the definitive tacky Indian restaurant. Not only is the interior cramped and unprepossessing, but the exterior, on the curve of a busy road, is not at all inviting. However, the smell of pungent spices used in authentic Goan dishes (from the west of India) will entice adventurous eaters. Specialities include *Sweetbreads with Prawn Curry*, *Vegetable Bhajee*, *Mackerel Fish Curry*, *Mutton Shakuti* and *Pork Vindaloo*.

Late lunch; pre-theatre; late dinner; Sunday lunch; take-away

AMERICAN

Le Grand Café

25 Battersea Rise, SW11 01–228 7984
⊖ None nearby; take 19, 49, 77 or 249 bus *Map C79*
Open 12 noon–3 pm, 6 pm–12 midnight; closed Sunday
Inexpensive/Moderate

- Credit cards not accepted
- Bookings not accepted
- Seats 56 (+20 in garden)
- Parties catered for
- Live and taped music

The name Grand Café evokes nostalgia for rococo decorations in the style of the Belle Epoch, not at all what the Battersea Grand Café is all about. This is a contemporary place, with blinking light bulbs and stripped walls painted black with fuschia trimmings

115

(fuschia is a Grand Café colour throughout). It has an open fire, a pretty tiled garden, and a young and friendly staff who keep the record player turning and the charcoal fire stoked, as well as serving *Deep Fried Clam Strips*, *Hamburgers*, *Chili Con Carne* and *Spaghetti*. There is American Schlitz Beer in the can, American cocktails, and live music in the evenings.

Pre-theatre; late dinner; outdoor eating

JEWISH

Harry Morgan's

31 St John's Wood High Street, NW8 01–722 1869
⊖ St John's Wood   *Map E8*
Open 12–3 pm, 6–10 pm; closed Friday dinner, Monday
Inexpensive

- Credit cards not accepted
- Bookings not accepted
- Seats 36

In this exceedingly busy and small restaurant it takes a long time for the staff to get to know a new customer, but once your face becomes familiar you will be treated like one of the family. The Morgan family have run this place for eighteen years. It is of the functional paper-napkin, formica-table genre, immaculately clean. *Salt Beef* is the *pièce-de-résistance*, and there is also *Calf's Foot Jelly*, *Chopped Liver*, *Gefilte Fish* (boiled and fried) and *Potato Pancakes*. You can also get steaks, veal, etc. but the best bets are the traditional Eastern European dishes. Incidentally, they do not serve chopped herring because they do not like the smell.

Pre-theatre; late dinner; Sunday lunch; take-away

GREEK/CYPRIOT

Koritsas

10 Kentish Town Road, NW1 01–485 5743
⊖ Camden Town   *Map E3*
Open 12 noon–12 midnight; closed Sunday
Inexpensive

- Access, American Express, Barclaycard, Diners
- Booking suggested for dinner
- Seats 80
- Parties catered for
- Taped music

116

There are two separate entrances and two different personalities to this fourteen-year-old kebab house that is run by the Paresheva family, who for many years had restaurants in Cyprus.

One side has an open kitchen, a colour telly sits on top of the fridge and grandma is usually here seeing to the preparation of vegetables while a few people wait for take-aways or to be served in this totally un-dressed little eating place.

Next door is quite another scene. Here is flocked wallpaper, coloured lights, bouzooki music, linened tables and strings of enormous worry beads hanging from the mouldings. The food for both places comes from the same kitchen: *Avgolemonon Soup*, *Kleftikon*, *Stifado*, *Arni Fasolaki*.

Late lunch; pre-theatre; late dinner; take-away

INDIAN/VEGETARIAN

Mandeer

21 Hanway Place, W1 01–323 0660
⊖ Tottenham Court Road   *Map B15*
Open 11 am–3 pm, 6–10.30 pm; closed Sunday
Inexpensive

- Access, American Express, Barclaycard, Diners
- Bookings accepted

- Seats 300
- Parties catered for
- Taped music

This friendly little Indian cultural centre and big vegetarian restaurant is at the Tottenham Court Road end of a winding alley that could have been the inspiration for the set designer of the musical *Cats*. Before you fully descend the stairs you are greeted by the taped sounds of sitar and tabla, and the pungent aromas of Indian spices.

Self-service lunches are available in the simply furnished Ravi Shankar Hall. (He actually opened it some years ago.) There is also a dining room with full service that has lots of authentic atmosphere. Specialities include *Crisp Dosai*, *Aubergine Bhajias* and *Kadhi Soup*. Or try the *Mandeer Thali*, a tray with samples of a number of dishes.

Pre-theatre; take-away

CHINESE

Poon's

4 Liecester Square, W1
⊖ Leicester Square   *Map B76*
Open 12 noon–1.30 pm, 7 days
Inexpensive

- Credit cards not accepted
- Booking suggested
- Seats 40
- Parties catered for

Poon's is not only tacky, it is downright uncomfortable. There are only three small tables downstairs, and four tables (for 6 each) on the first floor, up a precipitously steep staircase. Unless you go with your own party, be prepared to share a table.

However, the food served here takes you on a wondrous odyssey to Cantonese cuisine: *Wind-dried Duck, Mixed Barbecued Meats, Roasted Crispy Belly of Pork, Beef with Green Pepper and Black Beans.*

Since writing, the proprietors have moved to larger, and presumably more comfortable, premises at the above address.
Late lunch; pre-theatre; Sunday lunch; late dinner; take-away

MALAYSIAN

Satay House

13 Sale Place, W2 01–723 6763
⊖ Paddington, Edgware Road   *Map A8*
Open 12–3 pm, 6–11 pm, 7 days
Inexpensive/Moderate

- Access, American Express, Barclaycard, Diners
- Booking suggested
- Seats 200
- Parties catered for
- Taped music

A very busy, informal and cordial restaurant with a comprehensive selection of Malaysian dishes. The set menu is normally a good way to begin to taste a cuisine you are not familiar with, and if you do this here, start with the short menu. Extra dishes may not be necessary, as they serve large portions.

Malaysian food is a mixture of itself, Chinese and Indian. Trying too many different dishes in one meal tends to overwhelm the taste buds. Specialities include: *Soups, Satays, Kari* (curry), *Kambing, Ayam* (chicken), *Percik, Tahu* (bean curd), *Gado-Gada,* served with *Nasi* (rice).
Pre-theatre; late dinner; Sunday lunch; take-away

Eating Alone

The best thing about eating alone is having only your own mood to consider, so pamper yourself. Do you want to be in a quiet place where you can read or think, or is a busy restaurant with lots of action and interesting people to watch more to your liking? Or do you feel like treating yourself to a feast, beautifully served in elegant surroundings?

What one does not want when eating alone is to be marched off to the worst table in the house, between the toilets and the kitchen, and then have to wait and wait to be served. The following restaurants are thoughtful about the comfort and feeding of solitary eaters. As a rule, however, if you are eating alone you will get a more welcome reception before and after the midday rush, as many restaurateurs are reluctant to have half of a table for two remain empty at peak hours.

KOREAN
Arirang

31–32 Poland Street, W1 01–437 6633
⊖ Oxford Circus   *Map B22*
Open 12–3 pm, 6–11 pm; closed Sunday
Moderate

- All major credit cards
- Bookings accepted
- Seats 80

- Parties catered for
- Taped Korean music
- ♿ Access to restaurant

In Korean mythology, Arirang is like Olympus, a mountain top retreat of the gods and goddesses, and it is a common name for Korean restaurants. The cuisine is sweet and sour, partly Chinese, partly Indonesian in flavours. There is an 8-page menu at this Arirang, with hints on how to order and what to combine. Sip a salubrious Ginseng cocktail while deliberating over such specialities as *Tuejo Pokum* (fried chillied pork), *Bulgogi* (thinly sliced beef, marinated in sauces), or *Kal Bee Tang* (beef spare rib soup).

Graceful, short-stepping waitresses in native dress serve a clientele of Western devotees and Korean businessmen in banking, construction and the rag trade. Owner Eric Wee and his family preside over the two dining rooms: the ground floor one is more formal and comfortable than the room in the basement which conforms more to early Soho-Asian decor.

Pre-theatre; late dinner

THAI

Bangkok

9 Bute Street, SW7 01–584 8529
⊖ South Kensington *Map C43*
Open 12.30–2.15 pm, 6.30–11 pm; closed Sunday
Inexpensive/Moderate

- Credit cards not accepted
- Booking suggested for dinner
- Seats 50
- ♿ Access to restaurant, WC

Sauce for the grilled satays is a blend of crushed peanuts and hot oil. Thai cooking uses a skilful seasoning of onions, coriander, crushed roasted peanuts and fiery chillies, with lots of garlic, cucumbers, aromatic lemon juices and exotic Kaffir limes. Basil, lemon grass and curry spices also add character and flavour. These ingredients are all prepared beforehand and the basic stir-fry, steaming and grilling techniques are performed in the open kitchen while you wait for your *Savoury Beef Omelette*, *Fried Trout with Spicy Sauce*, *Thai Noodles*, *Chicken with Garlic or Ginger* and *Satays*.

The wood-topped tables are so close together that they almost meet. The decor is pleasant and modern, without a touch of ornamentation. The clientele seem serious about the cuisine and serious in general.

Pre-theatre; late dinner

GREEK

Beotys

79 St Martin's Lane, WC2 01–836 8768
⊖ Leicester Square *Map B78*
Open 12–2.30 pm, 5.30–11.30 pm; closed Sunday
Moderate

- Access, American Express, Barclaycard, Diners
- Booking suggested

- Seats 100
- Parties catered for
- ♿ Access to restaurant, WC

Like most successful restaurateurs, Kikis Poliviou projects the feeling that his restaurant is home and his guests are family, even if you are not a regular. They like good eaters at Beotys and there is real contact between you and the waiting staff. They describe the daily specialities in as much detail as you require. You may order an entree for an appetiser and share it with a companion. If in the middle of the meal you see a dish that looks good going to another table, you can order a half-portion.

Greek specialities include *Moussaka Khirokitia, Arnaki Melitzanes* and *Mosharake Spanahe*. If you like *Zabaglione*, ask Kikis himself to make you this frothy egg dessert.

Pre-theatre; late dinner

FRENCH

La Brasserie

272 Brompton Road, SW3 01–584 1668
⊖ South Kensington, Knightsbridge   *Map C24*
Open 8 am–12 midnight Monday to Friday, 10 am–12 midnight Saturday, 11 am–12 midnight Sunday
Moderate

- American Express, Barclaycard, Diners
- Booking suggested
- Seats 130

- Parties catered for
- Taped music
- ♿ Access to restaurant, WC

A brasserie is truly a brasserie when snacks and meals are served all day long, as they are in this lively neighbourhood meeting place where mirrors gleam and waiters in long white aprons bring large servings of *Blanquette de Veau, Boudin Noir Grillé, Andouillette Grillé, Pot au Feu, Boeuf Bourguignon.*

The atmosphere is unpretentiously Left Bank, and it is a good place to go when you think you may want to be alone but aren't sure. You can either eavesdrop on your neighbours' conversation, or read the newspapers on wooden rods provided by the management.

Late lunch; pre-theatre; late dinner; Sunday lunch; outdoor eating

Let's Lunch in London

INTERNATIONAL

Causerie at Claridge's Hotel

Brook Street, W1 01–629 8660
θ Bond Street *Map A22*
Open 12–3 pm, 6–11 pm; closed dinner Saturday, Sunday
Moderate/Expensive

- Access, Eurocard, Mastercharge
- Booking suggested for lunch
- Seats 40
- Jackets and ties required
- ♿ Access to restaurant, WC

A fresh feeling of awakening spring prevails in this pretty, brightly coloured, flower-decked dining room where there is a clubby complacency among the diners seated on upholstered armchairs and small sofas. Despite such comfortable seating, nobody slouches here. Rather, they maintain a posture of cultivated aloofness while formerly attired waiters deferentially serve à la carte selections from the repertoire of *chef de cuisine* M. Soubrand.

The *Salads*, *Herrings*, *Frikadeller* (meatballs) and various other hot and cold dishes from the serve-yourself smorgasbord are prepared by 'a Danish lady'. One does not think of Claridge's in terms of 'bargain' but this set price smorgasbord lunch is value for money. At the time of writing, for either £5.75 or £6.25, depending on your choice of drink, you may have one glass and any amount of food.
Pre-theatre; late dinner; Sunday lunch

CHINESE/SZECHUAN/PEKING

Crystal Palace

10 Hogarth Place, Hogarth Road, SW5 01–373 0754
θ Earl's Court *Map D30*
Open 12–3 pm, 7–12 pm, 7 days
Moderate/Expensive

- Access, American Express, Barclaycard, Diners
- Bookings accepted
- Seats 70
- Parties catered for
- Taped music
- ♿ Access to restaurant

Chinese chefs tend to go from restaurant to restaurant faster even than food critics. Before the ink dries on a review, the laudable chef has departed. One hopes that Hin Wah Shum will stay on at the Crystal Palace, preparing those *hsien* (tasty) Szechuan dishes that are so good and hot and spicy. If you are not familiar with this cuisine, the 9-course *Szechuan Feast* is a good introduction: *'Bang-Bang' Sesame Chicken Salad*, *Ganshow Prawns in Piquant Sauce*, *Double Cooked Pork and Peppers* and more, then end it with *Toffee Apples* or *Lychees*.

This is a very pretty place, classically simple with glossy white walls framed in black, and comfortable modern furniture. The host/partner, Ricky Cheung, and his staff are unusually friendly and helpful, making guests feel like Ming Dynasty nobles instead of treating them with the mildly hostile indifference which they (we) have almost come to expect.

Late dinner; Sunday lunch; take-away

ENGLISH

Ebury Court Hotel

26 Ebury Street, SW1 01–730 8147
Ø **Victoria** *Map C46*
Open 12–2 pm, 7–9 pm, 7 days
Moderate

- Access, Barclaycard
- Booking suggested
- Seats 40
- Taped music
- Jackets and ties required

There are only about a dozen tables here and many of them are in alcoves. Pink shades on little lamps give a rosy glow to striped wallpaper and chintz seat covers. This is no design-winner but it is a very pleasant place for a simple meal of Home-cooked Soup with bread, or *Kipper Pâté*, and main courses such as *Scotch Rump Steak with Garlic Butter* or *Grilled River Trout*.

The restaurant is in a small hotel made from four connecting terraced houses by the Topham family over forty-five years ago, and has always had a reputation for good food and pleasant service.

Sunday lunch

ENGLISH

English Garden

10 Lincoln Street, SW3 01–584 7272
Ø **Sloane Square** *Map C38*
Open 12–3 pm, 7–12 midnight, 7 days
Moderate

Let's Lunch in London

- American Express, Barclaycard, Diners, Eurocard
- Booking suggested
- Seats 60
- Taped music

Spring seems eternal in the English Garden, where horticulture that is not actually growing in pots has been dried and arranged in urns, or illustrated in large paintings and floral fabrics for the curtains and the chair seats. Both style and cuisine were developed by Malcolm Livingstone and Michael Smith, who created Walton's and the English House.

The menu should appeal to diet-conscious rising executives who cannot afford to fight off sleep in the office after lunch. You are actually encouraged to construct your own meal from a fairly long selection of dishes that may be ordered either as a light main course or as a starter. *English Garden Seafood Salad*, *Potted Arbroath Smokies with Whisky*, *Chicken and Asparagus Pancakes*, *English Garden Home-made Sausages*. The chef, Willie MacPherson, is a Scot.

Late dinner; Sunday lunch

ITALIAN

Il Girasole

126 Fulham Road, SW3 01–370 6656
⊖ South Kensington *Map C58*
Open 12–3 pm, 7–11.30 pm; closed Monday
Moderate

- American Express, Diners
- Booking required for dinner
- Seats 50
- ⑤ Access to restaurant

If you did not know that *girasole* means sunflower you would soon realise that it does as you bask in the bright and cheerful sunflower motif of this lively and unpretentious trattoria where Armando Otello and his chef Alfonso have, for over ten years, been looking after the pasta and antipasto needs of large families with small children and fashionable interior decorators with their clients. This end of the Fulham Road has some of the finest antiques and home furnishings shops in London. And where there is good shopping, there is usually also good eating. So try Alfonso's *Green and White Tortelloni*, *Tranetteral Pesto*, *Rack of Lamb with Mushrooms, Herbs and White Wine*, and his dishes from the different regions of Italy.

Late dinner; Sunday lunch; outdoor eating

JAPANESE
Hokkai

61 Brewer Street, W1 01–734 5826
ө **Piccadilly Circus**   *Map B71*
Open 12–2.30 pm, 6–10.45 pm; closed Sunday lunch
Moderate

- Access, American Express, Barclaycard, Diners
- Bookings accepted

- Seats 75
- Parties catered for

For all its colour, refinement, texture and flavour, Japanese food is still, to many Westerners, just a lot of pretty bits and pieces dipped in soy sauce. A Japanese meal is designed to satisfy whereas a Western meal is meant to fill you up. At the Hokkai both needs can be met. There are the *Sashimi* (raw fish) and the *Sushi*, the exquisite seaweed-wrapped mosaics of sweet-vinegar rice, studded with insets of fish, meat, vegetables, ginger or salmon roe. But here the emphasis is on homely, provincial-style cooking and large portions. You won't feel hungry soon after eating the *Tonkatsu* (deep-fried pork prepared in the Hokkai style), the *Suhiyaki*, *Hokkai Nabe* or *Tetsupanyaki*.

This well-established restaurant is a quiet dignified retreat from the busy streets of Soho.
Pre-theatre

INTERNATIONAL
The Ivy

1–5 West Street, WC2 01–836 4751
ө **Covent Garden, Leicester Square**   *Map B41*
Open 12–2.15 pm, 6–11 pm; closed Saturday lunch, Sunday
Expensive

- Access, American Express, Barclaycard, Diners
- Booking suggested
- Seats 105

- Parties catered for
- Jackets required
- &. Access to restaurant

The Ivy is a very large restaurant with an almost cathedral-like solemnity, replete with history and tradition (of government and theatre associations) and still patronised by a longstanding and faithful clientele who enjoy the calm atmosphere and attentive service.

The extensive menu will not challenge adventurous eaters but offers a wide selection, including *Escalopes de Veau Holstein*, *Dover Sole Marguery*, *Grilled Entrecôte with Garlic Sauce* and a buffet of cold meats with salad.
Pre-theatre; late dinner

GREEK/CYPRIOT
Kebab and Houmous

95 Charlotte Street, W1 01–636 3144
⊖ Goodge Street   *Map B6*
Open 12–3 pm, 6–11.30 pm; closed Saturday Lunch, Sunday
Moderate

- Access, American Express, Barclaycard, Diners
- Booking suggested for lunch
- Seats 60
- Parties catered for (up to 30 people)
- Taped music

This taverna provides a working definition of 'bustling', 'convivial' and 'cluttered'. Pictures of the Parthenon, hanging bottles and mementoes of Greece fill every empty space. Seating is so close that if you are on your own, you will not feel that you are eating alone. At lunchtime there is a clubby atmosphere among the regulars who are in advertising, films, publishing, fashion and the fine arts. Each group thinks this is a haunt of their own industry.

The proprietors take pride in their service and cuisine: starters of *Avgolemono* and *Kebabs*, and main courses including *Charcoal Grilled Chicken* and *Lamb Pseton* (kleftiko).
Pre-theatre; late dinner

FRENCH
Le Perroquet at the Berkeley Hotel

Wilton Place, SW1 01–235 6000
⊖ Knightsbridge, Hyde Park Corner   *Map C7*
Open 12.30–3 pm, 6.30 pm–2 am; closed Sunday
Moderate/Expensive

- Access, Eurocard, Mastercharge
- Booking suggested
- Seats 100
- Small parties catered for
- Live and taped music
- Jackets and ties required

The decor of Le Perroquet is an exercise in restrained flamboyance, in shades of purple and emerald with lots of etched mirror. The lighting is adroit and makes everyone look terrific – a good thing, because there is hardly any way you can look without seeing your own or someone else's reflection.

Service is cheerful and stylish. So too is the clientele. The wine list is a good one, and coffee is served 'with the compliments' of the house. The menu is undemanding at lunchtime: there are always three *Soups*, and light dishes such as *Haddock Mousse*, *Apricot and Chicken Salad*, *Caesar Salad*. There is also a good cheese board and tempting puddings.

The evening menu is much more extensive, and a simple after-theatre carte is served from 11.30 pm.

Pre-theatre; late dinner

LEBANESE

The Phoenicia

11–13a Abingdon Road, W8 01–937 0120
⊖ Kensington High Street *Map D21*
Open 12 midday–12 midnight, 7 days
Moderate

- Access, American Express, Barclaycard, Diners
- Seats 70
- Parties catered for
- Taped music
- &. Access to restaurant

The atmosphere of this friendy, informal neighbourhood restaurant conjures images of souks and sultans and attarine (spice stalls), yet the overall decor strikes one as more Cheltenham tearoom than Middle Eastern. Company directors and diplomats from the Arab world, with their families, sit round the large tables and take a long time over multi-course meals, talking or drinking wine or Arak, the Lebanese version of ouzo or Pernod. Service is attentive as waiters bring many selections of hot and cold starters that comprise the *Mezze*. Among the traditional Lebanese entrees are *Mahanek* (spicy Lebanese sausages), *Basturma* (smoked beef flavoured with chilli and paprika), and *Daoud Pasha* (meat, stewed with tomato and onion sauce and rice).

Late lunch; pre-theatre; late dinner; Sunday lunch; take-away

FRENCH

Les Trois Canards

13 Knightsbridge Green, SW1 01–589 0509
⊖ Knightsbridge *Map C2*
Open 12–2.30 pm, 7–11 pm; closed Sunday
Moderate

- Access, American Express, Barclaycard, Carte Blanche, Mastercharge
- Booking suggested
- Seats 45
- Parties catered for
- Taped music (evenings)
- ♿ Access to restaurant

Conveniently near the bustle of Knightsbridge shopping is the calm, welcoming Trois Canards, presided over by host/owner M. Sauzier. It is a pretty place, with candy-striped wallpaper and pink napery on the widely spaced tables.

If you want a meal that is light on the budget and the waistline, try two or three starters and skip the main course. There is no minimum charge here, and M. Sauzier is sensitive to the needs of his clientele. Starters include *Farci de Concombre aux Champignons* and *Terrine de Canard aux Legumes*. Among the main courses are *Magret de Canard au Poivre Vert* and *Grenadins de Veau aux Crevettes*.

Late dinner

With Children

Even picky eaters love to eat out, for they enjoy the ceremonies and the excitement of restaurants. Children also know that in a restaurant they can order their own meal and that the pressure is off about finishing their soup (or having soup at all). And they can look forward to dessert even when they do not finish their vegetables.

However it isn't advisable to ask children where they want to eat. Their choice is usually distinguished only by its monotony. It is wiser to tell them, very positively, where you're all going.

This section highlights London's diversity of choices, from soups to satays, from ethnic eclectic to space-age, that will appeal to children.

ITALIAN
Bertorelli

17 Notting Hill Gate, W11 01–727 7604
⊖ Notting Hill Gate   *Map D15*
Open 12–3 pm, 6–11.45 pm, 7 days
Moderate

- Access, American Express, Barclaycard, Diners
- Bookings accepted
- Seats 45

- Parties catered for
- Taped music
- ☵ Access to restaurant

There is a lot of unabashedly quaint, rustic-Italian decor in this scrupulously clean, friendly little restaurant where the regulars know the waiters and one another by sight. You should not expect invention here but you can anticipate a safe and solid meal, with home-made pastas – *Spaghetti Bolognese*, *Gnocci* and *Tortelloni*– and a selection of simple steak, chicken and scampi dishes.
Pre-theatre; late dinner; Sunday lunch; take-away

Let's Lunch in London

Century City

27 Davies Street, W1 01–499 3911
⊖ Bond Street *Map A25*
Open 12 midday–12 midnight, 7 days
Moderate

- Access, American Express, Barclaycard, Diners
- Bookings accepted
- Seats 100
- Parties catered for
- Taped music

In a Mayfair street of art galleries and other generally sedate enterprises stands this black and silver, padded and contoured space-age setting for inter-galactic gourmandising. The menu reads like a compendium of treats-of-all-nations: *Sicilian Skins* (potatoes with pepperoni and melted cheese), *Samosas*, *Mexi Pocket* (chili in a pitta pocket), *New York Treat* (bagels and Lox) and *Lamb Satay*, as well as *Hamburgers*, *Salads* and suchlike.

The barman turns out cocktails with familiar names and ingredients, and some rich, non-alcoholic concoctions as well.
Late lunch; pre-theatre; late dinner; Sunday lunch

CHINESE/CANTONESE

Chuen Cheng Ku

17–23 Wardour Street, W1 01–734 3281
⊖ Leicester Square, Piccadilly Circus *Map B73*
Open 11 am–11.30 pm, 7 days
Inexpensive/Moderate

- Credit cards not accepted
- Booking suggested
- Seats 550
- Parties catered for
- ♿ Access to restaurant

Hardly anything matches in this vast catering complex on three floors – no two walls even have the same colour or surface texture. On Sundays it is so crowded that diners are practically stacked at the tables, but the atmosphere is very lively and though service is brisk, customers are not hurried.

With approximately 270 separate items to choose from on the menu, it does seem easier to order one of the special menus, at the time of writing £9 for two people, £13.50 for three, £18 for four, and with each extra person an extra course is provided. However, another approach is to assume that ordering a Chinese meal is like exploring a box of filled chocolates, and take a bite out of enough different things so you get to know what you like. Among the many offerings are *Crab with Ginger or Black Beans*, *Shark's Fin Soup*, *Steamed Chicken Cubes with Black Mushrooms* and *Dim Sum* (served only until 6 pm).

Late lunch; pre-theatre; late dinner; Sunday lunch; take-away

There is another branch of **Chuen Cheng Ku** at 22 Lisle Street, WC2 (01–437 6332)
Open 4 pm–5 am, 7 days

INTERNATIONAL
Coffee House Restaurant
at the Inter-Continental Hotel

1 Hamilton Place, W1 01–409 3131
⊖ Hyde Park Corner   *Map A37*
Open 7 am–12 midnight, 7 days
Moderate

- Access, American Express, Barclaycard, Diners
- Bookings not accepted
- Seats 126
- Taped music

The name Coffee House is a bit of an understatement. This is an attractive, spacious, full-service restaurant with big windows facing the Wellington Museum and Hyde Park, and it is frequented by *les gens du monde*, fashionable people who come for the light snacks or the buffet luncheon. These include *Soups*, the *Cold meats*, *Fish* and *Salads* from the buffet (as much as you want), or à la carte choices: *Fisherman's Pot* (salmon, turbot, scallop, scampi and lobster dumpling poached in white wine with herbs and tomato), *Super Caesar Salad*, *Lamb Cutlets in Aubergine Béarnaise*, *Beef and Chillies in Oyster Sauce*. Cakes are made in the hotel's kitchen by a justly deserving gold-medalist pastry chef. There is a take-away counter for the pastries at the front of the restaurant.

Late lunch; pre-theatre; late dinner; Sunday lunch; take-away

ENGLISH

Dickens Inn by the Tower

St Katharine's Way, E1 01–488 9932

⊖ Tower Hill   *Map F26*

Open: Dickens Restaurant, 12–3 pm, 5–10 pm, closed Sundays;
Pickwick Restaurant 12–2 pm, 7–10 pm, closed Saturday lunch,
Sunday

Inexpensive/Moderate

- Access, American Express, Barclaycard, Diners
- Booking suggested

- Seats: Dickens 80, Pickwick 100
- Parties catered for

London has very few riverside restaurants and this one has a prime location, near the Tower, with a view of Tower Bridge. It is in the heart of St Katharine's Dock, the redevelopment area that contains, among other attractions, a floating maritime museum and a flotilla of historic sailing ships and Thames barges.

The building was an old warehouse that has been entirely reconstructed as a balconied inn 'of the Dickens period'. On the ground floor there is a vast pub, with a long snack bar packed with locals and tourists. The Pickwick Restaurant is on the first floor, serving mainly English food: *Grilled Pork Chop Stuffed with Stilton*, *Roast Rack of Lamb in Breadcrumbs*, *Filet Steak Stuffed with Oysters*.

The Dickens Restaurant, on the second floor, is a beamed and nautical-looking fish restaurant, with long tables for sharing and cubicles with tables for four. The menu includes *Mixed Fish Kebab*, *John Dory Grilled with Lemon Butter* and *Baked River Trout Stuffed with Spinach*. It may be difficult whole-heartedly to urge the children to finish everything on their plates, but the Inn is spacious and attractive, with friendly and helpful service.

Pre-theatre

FRENCH/ENGLISH/FISH

Flounders

19–21 Tavistock Street, WC2 01–836 3925

⊖ Covent Garden   *Map B48*

Open 12.30–3 pm, 5.30–12 midnight; closed Sunday

Moderate/Expensive

- Access, American Express, Barclaycard, Diners
- Booking suggested
- Seats 80

- Parties catered for
- Taped music
- &. Access to restaurant

This Covent Garden fish restaurant, in a little street of many restaurants, is close to the offices of assiduous lunchers in advertising and publishing and close to many theatres, among them the Aldwych. *Dramatis personae* from Royal Shakespeare productions often go there for a meal before and after rehearsals or performances.

The atmosphere is lively. The staff are pleasant. The menu is simple, the portions are generous: *Flounders Pancake*, *Nelson Fish Pie*, *Cod Mornay*, *Scallops Thermidor*, and fresh *Fish* prepared in cream sauces, grilled or fried.

Pre-theatre; late dinner

AMERICAN

Hard Rock Café

150 Old Park Lane, W1 01–629 0382
⊖ Hyde Park Corner *Map A40*
Open 12 midday–12.30 am, 7 days
Inexpensive/Moderate

- No credit cards
- Bookings not accepted
- Seats 100

- Taped music
- &. Access to restaurant

An everlasting restaurant success story is the much copied but still one-and-only Hard Rock Café, *de rigueur* for every tourist and teenager in London since it opened eleven years ago. It set the standard for dozens of subsequent establishments with its loud music, simple menu of *Charcoal Flavoured Hamburgers on Sesame Bun*, *Hard Rock's Club Sandwich*, *Banana Splits*, thick milk shakes and American beer, served by waitresses who all seem to bear an uncanny resemblance to Joan Crawford as housewife-turned-hashslinger in *Mildred Pierce*.

Late lunch; pre-theatre; late dinner; Sunday lunch; take-away

MEXICAN/AMERICAN

Parsons

311 Fulham Road, SW10 01–352 0651
⊖ South Kensington, then bus   *Map C64*
Open 12.30 pm–1 am, 7 days
Inexpensive

- Credit cards not accepted
- Bookings not accepted
- Seats 110
- Parties catered for
- Licensed for wine and beer only
- Taped music
- ♿ Access to restaurant

Parsons was the local haberdasher's (of the same name) until about a decade ago when the stockroom became a kitchen and the handsome old store was turned into a stylishly decorated restaurant in the American tradition of permissive gluttony. Since its opening, it has been the local pit-stop for a diverse Chelsea–Fulham clientele: Mrs Miniver middle-class families, 'Lumpen polytechnics' on their way to and from the neighbourhood cinemas, and lively youngsters who hang out there.

Originally it opened as a spaghetti house, but every few years the cuisine is changed. Now the heartiest appetites are generously served with *Tacos*, *Chili*, *Spare Ribs* and *Steaks*. Tapes of country music are played loud.

Late lunch; pre-theatre; late dinner; Sunday lunch; take-away

AMERICAN

Peppermint Park

13 Upper St Martin's Lane, WC2 01–836 5234
⊖ Leicester Square   *Map B42*
Open 12 noon–2 am, Monday to Saturday, 12 noon–12 midnight Sunday
Inexpensive/Moderate

- Access, American Express, Barclaycard, Diners
- Booking suggested at weekends
- Seats 150
- Parties catered for
- Taped music

Pink and green Peppermint Park is a cleverly devised environment. Large murals of restaurant scenes cover many walls and are reflected in well-placed mirrors which also reflect the real people, so you always feel that you are in a very popular place even during the rare moments when it is not entirely full.

The menu is a culinary description of ethnic America. The melting pot includes *New York Bagel with Smoked Salmon and Cream Cheese*, *Tacos*, *Hamburgers*, *Hotdogs* (a foot long), *Chili* and a big selection of crunchy salads.

There is a large bar that attracts cocktail drinkers, and on Fridays and Saturdays the restaurant stays open from 2 am to 6 am, for breakfast.

Late lunch; pre-theatre; late dinner; Sunday lunch; outdoor eating

AMERICAN

Rock Garden

6–7 The Piazza, Covent Garden, WC2 01–240 3961
⊖ Covent Garden   *Map B45*
Open 12 midday–2 am Monday to Wednesday, 12 midday to 6 am Thursday to Saturday, 12 noon–12 midnight Sunday
Inexpensive

- Credit cards not accepted
- Booking suggested at weekends
- Seats 110
- Parties catered for
- Rock music
- ♿ Access to restaurant

This is the first restaurant-cum-live music venue in the new Covent Garden. Georgie Fame and the Blue Flames opened the place in 1976 and it has been filled to capacity every evening since then. In good weather, when there is open-air dining on the Piazza, as many as a thousand people eat and drink here in a day.

An amusing 8-page comic book menu lists the 'eats and drinks' served in this converted vegetable warehouse made to look like an American roadside inn. Zombies and Tequilla Sunrises are among many cocktail specialities. You can order breakfast food day and night, or *Toureen de Mer*, *Hamburgers*, *Spare Ribs*. Marine Ices provide the ice cream for the *Splits* and *Sundaes*. Simple Simon is the baker, and the *Devil's Food Cake* is paradisaical.

Late lunch; pre-theatre; late dinner; Sunday lunch; take-away; outdoor eating

FRENCH
Le Routier

Commercial Place, Chalk Farm Road, NW1 01–485 0360
⊖ Camden Town, Chalk Farm   *Map E1*
Open 12.30–3 pm, 7.30–10.45 pm, 7 days
Moderate

- Access, American Express
- Booking suggested, especially on Sunday
- Seats 50
- Parties catered for
- Licensed for wine only
- Live and taped music
- ♿ Access to restaurant, WC

This informal café is in a big shed with many windows overlooking Camden Lock. There is also a large open patio right on the canal. Although popular with shoppers and West End business people, this is a family restaurant, where older men with new young wives, too tired to cook and too smart to settle for hamburgers, bring their babies for a meal with a view. Starters include *Mushrooms Stuffed with Snails* and *Deep Fried Camembert with Gooseberry Preserve*. Main courses feature *Rack of Lamb aux Herbes*, *Breast of Duck with Apricot Sauce* and *Guinea Fowl in Cognac Sauce*. There are *Grilled Steaks* too, and simpler fare for the babies.

Camden Lock is an old timber wharf on the Regents Canal which in the 1970s was turned into craft workshops. There is a market, open at weekends only.

Late dinner; Sunday lunch; outdoor eating

AMERICAN
Rumours

33 Wellington Street, WC2 01–836 0039
⊖ Covent Garden   *Map B62*
Open 11.30 am–4.30 pm, 5.30–11 pm; closed Sunday; meals served at lunchtime only
Inexpensive/Moderate

- Access, American Express, Barclaycard, Diners
- Booking suggested for lunch
- Seats 60
- Parties catered for
- Live music
- Children allowed in dining areas
- ♿ Access to restaurant

Rumours is in an old vegetable and fruit warehouse that was converted over four years ago into a non-membership drinking club and disco. The music still reverberates in the daytime, when the ground floor dining room/bar becomes a fancy sandwich shop where there are some ordinary sandwiches such as *Tuna on Rye Bread* (called 'Lana Tuna') and some rather contrived combinations with equally contrived names: *Lox Ness Monster* which consists of smoked salmon, cream cheese, black olives, onion and tomato on a two-foot long French loaf, and *The Mouth That Roared*, another two-foot sandwich (also for two, or more) of salami, bacon, cheese, pâté, lettuce and tomatoes.
Late lunch; take-away

ITALIAN
San Frediano

62 Fulham Road, SW3 01–584 8375
θ South Kensington   *Map C45*
Open 12.30–2.30 pm. 7.15–11.30 pm; closed Sunday
Moderate

- American Express, Barclaycard, Diners, Eurocard
- Booking suggested
- Seats 85
- ප Access to restaurant

Franco Buonoguidi is the slim and elegant owner of this ever popular seventeen-year-old trattoria designed by Enzo Appicello and maintained with the best of the 1960s spirit of London. The two bright, well-proportioned dining rooms, with spotless napery, cream stucco walls, ceramic tiled floors and red Magestretti chairs, are identical, yet as always regular patrons have strong preferences for one over the other. On weekdays the lunchtime crowd includes doctors and nurses from the nearby hospitals, computer people from south of the river and shoppers who may frequent the many smart boutiques along this patch of the Fulham Road. On Saturdays large families and Chelsea season-ticket holders on their way to Stamford Bridge stop by for the *Fegato alla Salvia, Scaloppine de Barbi* or *Wild Duck with Olives, Mushrooms and Wine*.
Late dinner

ENGLISH/FISH

Sea Shell Fish Bar

33-35 Lisson Grove, NW1 01–723 8703
⊖ Edgware Road *Map A1*
Open 12–2 pm, 5.30–10.30 pm; closed Sunday, Monday
Inexpensive

- Credit cards not accepted
- Bookings not accepted
- Seats 80
- Small parties catered for
- Unlicensed
- Taped music

Traditionally, fish and chips were sold in simple shops in working-class neighbourhoods and seaside resorts. Some of London's best were in the East End, close to Billingsgate where there has been a fish market for over eleven hundred years. At the Sea Shell, things are still done in the old tradition. *Haddock, Cod, Plaice, Sole* and that eel-like creature with pink flesh called *Rock Salmon* are deep fried in beef dripping and served in gigantic portions.

There are two dining rooms, both with a splashy coastal motif. It is quieter upstairs in this spotlessly clean establishment where there are usually queues around the block and limousines parked outside. The owners as well as the drivers are devoted customers.

Pre-theatre; take-away

AMERICAN

Texas Lone Star Saloon

154 Gloucester Road, SW7 01–370 5627
⊖ Gloucester Road *Map C39*
Open 12 noon–12 midnight, 7 days
Inexpensive

- Credit cards not accepted
- Bookings required for parties over 8 only
- Seats 180
- Parties catered for
- Country and Western music
- ♿ Access to restaurant, WC

There's a yellow rose of Texas deep in the heart of South Ken. Just sashay through the swing doors – they are the real thing, imported from the Lone Star State along with the cow-hide and brass nail chairs, the State flag, the recipes and lots of the ingredients. There is even a small collection of some of the 2,000 types of barbed wire ranchers used to fence their land.

There are *Tacos* and *Nachos* and *T-Bone Steaks* here; *Chili* and *Burgers* and *B.B.Q. ribs*; American beer and *Apple* and *Pecan Pies.*

Tim Rice compiles the music tapes and in the evenings the country and western music is live. So come on down and swing yo' partner.

Late lunch; pre-theatre; late dinner; Sunday lunch; take-away

There is another **Texas Lone Star Saloon** at 117 Queensway, W2 (01–727 2980)
Open 12–3 pm, 6.30–1 am; closed Sunday

POLYNESIAN/INTERNATIONAL

Trader Vic's at the Hilton Hotel

Park Lane, W1 01–493 8000
ᐱ Hyde Park Corner *Map A34*
Open 12–3 pm, 6.30–11.45 pm; closed for lunch Saturday and Sunday
Moderate/Expensive

- Access, American Express, Barclaycard, Diners
- Booking required

- Seats 220
- Parties catered for
- Taped music

It is forty-nine years since the old Trader, Victor Bergeron, came back from his first trip to Tahiti loaded with souvenirs with which he decorated his saloon, Hinky Dink's, in Oakland, California. Since then he has draped fishing nets and tapa cloths in luxurious 'South Sea Huts' filled with warrior gee-gaws all over the world. The decor, the dim and shadowy lighting and the taped music are hard to resist, and at some time everyone has a yen to go to Trader Vic's, to celebrate, or just to sit with friends or a friend and slowly sip sinful punches, and eat: *Waikiki* (half a fresh pineapple filled with fresh fruits), *Dover Sole Dali Dali, Pork Chops Polynesian, Minute Steak Trader Vic Style* or *Calves' Sweetbreads Poulette.*
Late dinner

139

INTERNATIONAL

The Upstairs at the Basil Street Hotel

8 Basil Street, SW3 01–581 3311
⊖ Knightsbridge *Map C12*
Open 12–3 pm; closed Sunday
Inexpensive

- Access, American Express, Barclaycard, Diners
- Bookings accepted (until 1 pm)
- Seats 80
- Parties catered for
- Licensed for wine and beer only
- Taped music

There is a bustling, informal atmosphere in this friendly, self-service, pine and print, modern-rustique setting in a space that was once the ballroom of the Basil Street Hotel. Now secretaries from the many nearby estate offices, weary shoppers and retired gentlemen with military moustaches serve themselves from the Copper Counter, which offers a hot main course with vegetables, dessert or cheese. The Salad Bowl is a separate counter where you help yourself to as much as you want of a big selection of cold meats and salads, sweets or cheese.

Quick and Quicker

There is no reason not to sit back, relax, and chew each bite twenty times, but if you are in a hurry, you will be served *toute de suite* at the restaurants described here.

Quick

FRENCH/CREPERIE
Asterix

329 King's Road, SW3 01–352 3891
⊖ Sloane Square, then bus   *Map C67*
Open 12 noon–12 midnight, 7 days
Inexpensive

- Credit cards not accepted
- Bookings not accepted
- Seats 60
- Licensed for beer and wine only

- Taped music
- ♿ Access to restaurant

This restaurant is named after the little Gaul who lived in the last remaining Gallic village in the Breton part of Roman occupied France (in the comic book series by Goscinny and Uderzo). Recipes for the *Crêpes* and *Galettes* are from Brittany too. There is also *French Onion Soup, Garlic Bread* and *Salads*... in portions generous enough to satisfy Asterix and even his ever-hungry friend Obelix.

Late lunch; pre-theatre; late dinner; Sunday lunch

ENGLISH
Buster Brown Café

61 The Cut, SE1 01–928 2157
⊖ Waterloo   *Map F32*
Open 11 am–12 midnight; closed Sunday dinner
Inexpensive

Let's Lunch in London

- Credit cards not accepted
- Bookings accepted
- Seats 71
- Parties catered for
- Taped music
- ♧ Access to restaurant, WC

Just over the road from the Young Vic Coffee Bar (see p. 152), with the same crowd, same management and same executive chef, but fancier surroundings and a cocktail bar.
Late lunch; pre-theatre; late dinner

ENGLISH

Café Royale Bar

68 Regent Street, W1 01–437 9090
϶ **Piccadilly Circus**   *Map B70*
Open 11.30 am–3 pm, 5.30–8 pm; closed Sunday
Inexpensive

- Access, American Express, Barclaycard, Diners
- Bookings accepted
- Seats 40
- Parties catered for
- Jackets and ties required
- ♧ Access to restaurant, WC by lift

More than a thousand meals a day are served in the formal surroundings of the public restaurants and private banqueting rooms of Charles Forte's very grand Café Royale. There is also The Bar, on the ground floor, a friendly and informal pub-like place where you can serve yourself from a plentiful array of hot and cold dishes, including: *Chicken Pie, Shepherd's Pie, Salads with Pâté, with Quiche, with Turkey*, and *Sandwiches* costing from 95p to £1.90 at the time of writing.

And, if you like cocktails, ask the barman Alf Brown to mix your favourite. He has been there a long time, and some folks go there to watch him at work, and to taste.
Pre-theatre

AMERICAN

Chicago Pizza Pie Factory

17 Hanover Square, W1 01–629 2669
϶ **Oxford Circus**   *Map B18*
Open 11.45 am–11.30 pm; closed Sunday
Inexpensive

- Credit cards not accepted
- Bookings not accepted
- Seats 270
- Parties catered for
- Taped music
- No-smoking area

A Chicago pizza is rather like a quiche. It is cooked in a deep pan and there is more filling than dough. This is the house speciality and it is served with various fillers. Also on the limited menu are *Stuffed Mushrooms, Garlic Bread, Cheesecake* and soft and hard drinks. However, you may not have coffee before 2.15 pm, and in the evening only one cup per person is served. Speedy turnover is a priority, as there are always long queues at peak times.

This is a 'theme' restaurant and the walls are covered with ephemera of Chicago and posters of every film ever made about the 'windy city'. Many of these films are so obscure you will not find them in Kevin Brownlow's histories of the cinema. And tapes from a local Chicago radio station are flown in weekly and played loud during the day, l-o-u-d-e-r at night. Tables may be shared and the crowd is as mixed as a random sample for a national opinion poll.

Late lunch; pre-theatre; late dinner; take-away

INDIAN/VEGETARIAN
Diwana Bhel Poori House

121 Drummond Street, NW1 01–387 5556
⊖ Euston *Map E10*
Open 12 noon–1 am; closed Monday
Inexpensive

- Access, Barclaycard
- Bookings accepted
- Seats 40

- Unlicensed
- Taped music
- Ⴔ Access to restaurant

The twain meet in this neighbourly spot that offers an authentic and sustaining repertory of Gujerati (western Indian) vegetable dishes in scrupulously clean, modern and rather spartan surroundings. The restaurant is not licensed yet few of the Indian families or the serious-meined and soberly dressed occidentals bring wine or spirits to their tables. Instead, they drink lassi or orange juice or brightly coloured Falooda with their meals of *Deluxe Dosa* (a long, crispy pancake filled with vegetables and served with coconut chutney and savoury sauce). *Thali* is a set meal on a tray consisting of *Nan* (bread) and four or five selections.

Late lunch; pre-theatre; late dinner; Sunday lunch; take-away

There is another **Diwana Bhel Poori House** at 50 Westbourne Grove, W2 (01–221 0721) *Map D4*

HEALTH FOOD/VEGETARIAN

Food For Thought

31 Neal Street, WC2 01–836 0239
⊖ Covent Garden *Map B37*
Open 12 noon–8 pm; closed Saturday and Sunday
Inexpensive

- Credit cards not accepted
- Bookings not accepted
- Seats 46
- Unlicensed
- No-smoking area

You would think the doors to the Ark were about to close by the size of the queues waiting to get into this narrow, tight and spartan self-service restaurant on two floors where tables are shared. Pulse, sprouts and legume fanciers are happy to wait for the hearty *Soups, Salads, Quiches, Curries* and delectable desserts.
Late lunch; pre-theatre; take-away

WHOLEFOOD

The Granary

39 Albermarle Street, W1 01–493 2978
⊖ Green Park *Map B81*
Open 11 am–7 pm; closed Saturday dinner, Sunday
Inexpensive

- Credit cards not accepted
- Bookings not accepted
- Seats 120
- Licensed for wine and beer only
- Taped music
- ♿ Access to restaurant

The Granary is a Mayfair-rustic, self-service storehouse providing wholesome fare: colourful *Salads, Flans,* varied *Casseroles* and *Gratinées.* Their mad keen pastry chef has a repertory of 23 very nourishing desserts.
Late lunch; pre-theatre; take-away

AMERICAN

L. S. Grunt's

12 Maiden Lane, WC2
⊖ Charing Cross, Covent Garden *Map B60*
Open 12 noon–11.30 pm: closed Sunday
Inexpensive

- Access, Barclaycard
- Bookings not accepted
- Seats 100
- Parties catered for
- Taped music
- ♧ Access to restaurant, WC

This big American-style pizzeria is in an old power station. It has a long courtyard entrance, a fair-ground atmosphere, an American cocktail bar and a predictable menu.

Tasty, deep-dish *Pizzas* with lots of cheese, oregano, tomatoes and the extras – pepperoni, sausage, mushrooms, you name it – are served here. There are *Garlic Stuffed Mushrooms* to start, and *Garlic* and *Herb Breads*. Help yourself to salads which are in a big Victorian bath tub. For the still hungry, there is *Ice cream* and *Cheesecake*.

Late lunch; pre-theatre; late dinner; take-away

JEWISH

Hatchetts Salt Beef Bar

5 Clerkenwell Road, EC1 01–251 2587
϶ **Barbican** *Map F24*
Open 8 am–6 pm; closed Saturday
Inexpensive

- Credit cards not accepted
- Booking suggested
- Seats 45

This is a pit-stop for those in search of the lean-lean salt beef sandwich on rye bread with gherkins. It is a small, unpretentious, family-run café with something for everyone, from *Fish and Chips* to *Gefilte Fish with Chraine* (horse radish), *Cheese Blintzes*, *Lockshen Pudding* (noodles). On Sundays the activity comes from Petticoat Lane; the weekday lunch crowd includes city gents and taxi drivers.

Late lunch; Sunday lunch; take-away

VEGETARIAN

Healthy, Wealthy and Wise

9 Soho Street, W1 01–437 1835
϶ **Tottenham Court Road** *Map B23*
Open 9 am–9 pm; closed Sunday
Inexpensive

Let's Lunch in London

- Credit cards not accepted
- Bookings accepted
- Seats 110
- Parties catered for
- No alcohol or cigarettes permitted in restaurant
- Taped music

On the site of an old Soho pub is the London headquarters of the Hare Krsna Society and their restaurant, run co-operatively by members to support temple activities. The dining room is immaculately clean, bright and cheerful, with a self-service counter and long pine tables. Daily specials are listed on a blackboard menu: *Stuffed Vine Leaves*, *Vegetable Curry and Rice*, *Spring Rolls and Rice*, varied salads and wholemeal bread.

There are hardly any saffron robes here during the weekday lunch hours. The regulars wear casual-to-tailored clothes and are in fashion, film and music, and seem to relax while eating their pulses and beans, listening to meditative music.

Late lunch; pre-theatre; take-away

INTERNATIONAL/WHOLEFOOD

Justin de Blank Food and Drink

54 Duke Street, W1 01–629 3174
Θ **Marble Arch**   *Map A19*
Open 8.30 am–3.30 pm, 4.30–9 pm Monday to Friday, 9 am–3 pm Saturday; closed Sunday
Inexpensive/Moderate

- Credit cards not accepted
- Bookings not accepted
- Seats 60
- Parties catered for
- Licensed for wine and beer only

Slim celebrants of the body who believe that papayas improve the personality and wonder if broccoli will give them courage find much to munch on at the long self-service counter here: *Roast Scottish Beef*, *Blanquette of Lamb*, *Vegetarian Lasagne*, *Haddock Roulade* and various salads; for dessert there are *Seasonal Fruit Salads* and *Fruit Brûlé*.

Expect to queue at lunchtime. Shoppers and local business people share wide, zinc-topped tables for six. The restaurant is attractive and the staff is friendly and helpful, but seating on the high-backed cane benches is somewhat tight when every place is taken.

Pre-theatre; take-away

ENGLISH
The Muffin Man

12 Wright's Lane, W8 01–937 6652
⊖ High Street Kensington *Map D23*
Open 8.45 am–6.30 pm; closed Sunday
Inexpensive

- Credit cards not accepted
- Bookings accepted
- Seats 32
- Parties catered for
- Unlicensed
- ⚹ Access to restaurant

You will find real country tea-room atmosphere just off Kensington High Street, where serving staff instinctively know who is in a hurry and who wants to relax a bit. There are home-made *Soups, Flans, Salads,* and generously filled sandwiches.
Late lunch; pre-theatre

INDIAN
New Bengal

187-189 Queensway, W2 01–229 1640
⊖ Queensway, Bayswater *Map D6*
open 12–3 pm, 5.30–12 midnight, 7 days
Inexpensive

- Access, American Express, Barclaycard, Diners
- Bookings accepted
- Seats 50
- Parties catered for
- Taped music

This is an unassuming and authentic little place where a meal can be a single dish or many. Afficionados come for the *New Bengal Special Chicken with Rice,* which arrives crackling and sizzling hot from the oven. There is also *Tandoori Chicken, Tandoori Lamb, Chicken Tikka, Mutton Tikka* and various curries.
Pre-theatre; late dinner; Sunday lunch; take-away

FRENCH/CREPERIE
Obelix

294 Westbourne Grove, W11 01–229 1877
⊖ Notting Hill Gate *Map D3*
Open 12 noon–11 pm, 7 days
Inexpensive

Let's Lunch in London

- Credit cards not accepted
- Bookings accepted
- Seats 65
- Parties catered for
- Taped music
- ♿ Access to restaurant

Asterix comic book fans will want to sit near the big comic strip painting on the wall of this friendly eatery where Getafix the Druid would approve of the offerings, which are big enough to satisfy even Obelix's gargantuan appetite: *Galettes*, or Breton-style crêpes made with buckwheat flour and filled with fresh ingredients. Choose one of the many combinations: *Tuna and Ratatouille, Bacon and Spinach, Chicken and Asparagus*, or make up your own from the long list of fillings. If, like Obelix, you spent the morning hunting Romans (in the Portobello Road) and are really hungry, you can also have *Side Salads, Garlic Bread* and *French Onion Soup*. There are sweet crêpes too, with a variety of fillings, and cakes.

Late lunch; pre-theatre; late dinner; Sunday lunch; take-away; outdoor eating

ENGLISH
The Palm Court at the
Waldorf Hotel

Aldwych, WC2 01–836 2400
϶ Holborn, Temple *Map B49*
Open 11 am–11 pm, 7 days
Moderate

- Access, American Express, Barclaycard, Diners
- Booking suggested for lunch
- Seats 90
- Parties catered for
- Live music
- Jackets recommended

Elevenses, or a mid-morning refreshment, a light lunch and the classic English tea are served here in gracious surroundings. The Palm Court was built in 1908 and was recently restored to its original Louis XVI style. Lunch offerings include *Omelette 'Arnold Bennett', The Waterloo Burger* and *Club Sandwiches*. Tea drinkers may note that fresh brewed Balijen Indian and Lapsang Souchong China teas are served.

Late lunch; pre-theatre; late dinner; Sunday lunch; take-away

INTERNATIONAL

The Picnic Basket at the
Selfridge Hotel

Orchard Street W1 01–408 2080
ⓔ **Marble Arch**   *Map A15*
Open 7 am–12.30 am, 7 days
Moderate

- Access, American Express, Barclaycard, Diners
- Bookings not accepted
- Seats 94
- Parties catered for
- Taped music
- Jackets required
- ♿ Access to restaurant, WC

A light and airy dining room where one can eat quickly or linger in comfort at large, separate tables where there is space for parcels and to open a newspaper if you are eating alone. The lunch menu includes *Chicken Holstein, Chef's Picnic Salad* or *The Roast of the Day.*
Late lunch; pre-theatre; late dinner; Sunday lunch

MALAYSIAN

Rasa Singapore

232-234 Brompton Road, SW3 01–584 3493
ⓔ **South Kensington**   *Map C16*
Open 12.30–3 pm, 6–10.30 pm; closed Thursday
Inexpensive

- Access, American Express, Barclaycard, Diners
- Bookings accepted
- Seats 30
- Parties catered for
- Taped music

This pretty little restaurant served by genuinely helpful staff provides the kind of food associated with the legendary street stalls of Singapore. Portions are small, so you can try a variety: *Crispy Fried Wan Tan, Laksa* (rice noodles with shrimps, fish cakes and bean sprouts), *Sambal Ikan Bilis* (fish in spicy sauce) and *Ngo Hiang* (fried meat roll wrapped with bean curd).
Pre-theatre; Sunday lunch

VEGETARIAN/HEALTH FOOD

Riverside Studios

Crisp Road, W6 01–741 2251
⊖ **Hammersmith** *Map D31*
Open 11 am–10.30 pm
Inexpensive

- Credit cards not accepted
- Bookings not accepted
- Seats 72
- Parties catered for
- ♿ Access to restaurant, WC

Down by the riverside in Hammersmith's flourishing arts centre is this bustling, country-food cafeteria where creators and appreciators sit at rows of long refectory tables and discuss the arts and the foibles of our polymorphous society over generous portions of home-made *Soups, Casseroles* and *Salads*. Busy at lunchtime as well as in the evenings.
Late lunch; pre-theatre; late dinner; Sunday lunch

VEGETARIAN/WHOLEFOOD

Slenders

41 Cathedral Place, EC4 01–236 5974
⊖ **St Paul's** *Map F12*
Open 8 am–6.15 pm; closed Saturday and Sunday
Inexpensive

- Credit cards not accepted
- Bookings not accepted
- Seats 107
- Unlicensed
- Taped music
- No-smoking area
- ♿ Access to restaurant

A flourishing health food oasis in the covered modern square near St Paul's Cathedral is this large self-service restaurant where pine tables and hanging plants complement the colourfully arranged counter filled with steaming hot daily specials such as *Lentil, Pepper and Mushroom Cutlets, Cheese and Vegetable Flan, Vegetable Casseroles, Salads* and a wide selection of desserts.
Late lunch

HEALTH FOOD
Wholefood

110-112 Baker Street, W1 01–935 3924
⊖ Baker Street *Map A2*
Open 8 am–8 pm Monday to Friday, 8 am–3 pm Saturday; closed Sunday
Inexpensive

- Diners
- Booking suggested
- Seats 100

- Parties catered for
- No smoking

Wholefood is a haven for non-smoking, fitness dilettantes – a simply furnished self-service restaurant where, they say, even the wine is organically produced. Generous portions of daily specials include *Pork Casserole, Shepherd's Pie, Braised Onions, Mixed Root Vegetable Casserole*; there are always hearty soups and lots of big, sticky desserts.

Just next door is the country-smelling Wholefood Shop, and round the corner, in Paddington Street, is the Wholefood meat shop, one of the few butchers in London that sells organically grown meats.
Late lunch; take-away

ENGLISH
Windsor Lounge at the Atheneum Hotel

116 Piccadilly, W1 01–499 3464
⊖ Green Park *Map A38*
Open 24 hours a day, 7 days
Inexpensive/Moderate

- Access, American Express, Barclaycard, Diners
- Bookings not accepted

- Seats 30
- ♿ Access to restaurant

Hotels can be havens for hungry, thirsty and foot-sore non-residents as well as for paying guests. At the Windsor Lounge for instance, light lunches, tea and snacks are available throughout the day in very comfortable surroundings. The menu includes *Soups, Club Sandwich, Steak Sandwich, Smoked Salmon Platter* and fruit. Service is deft and swift. Wine is served by the glass, but spirit drinkers may want to stop in the bar which has an impressive array of bottles, a capable barman and an unusually comprehensive selection of pure malt whiskies.

Late lunch; pre-theatre; late dinner; Sunday lunch

ENGLISH

Young Vic Coffee Bar

66 The Cut, SE1 01–633 0133
⊖ Waterloo *Map F30*
Open 12.30–2.30 pm; closed Saturday and Sunday
Inexpensive

- Credit cards not accepted
- Bookings not accepted
- Seats 60
- Licensed for wine and beer only

As fast as it is redecorated, the paint wears off this ever-crowded and friendly snack bar where students, aspiring actors and theatre-goers can get anything from a cup of coffee and a sticky bun to thick soups, fresh salads, quiches, casseroles and quite a good glass of wine.

Big notice boards keep up-to-date listings of what is on and where in London.

Quicker

INTERNATIONAL/CREPERIE

Ambrosiana

194 Fulham Road, SW10 01–937 0762
⊖ South Kensington, then bus *Map D37*
Open 12 noon–12 midnight, 7 days
Inexpensive

- Credit cards not accepted
- Bookings accepted
- Seats 60
- Parties catered for
- Taped music
- ♿ Access to restaurant

For over five years a very regular clientele has been going to Alfonso Cretella's cosy restaurant for the *Crêpes* (made with white self-raising flour) and filled with sturdy meats and savoury combinations. *Salads, Omelettes* and *Sweet Crêpes* are also available, and Mr Cretella is proud of his Italian house wine (*vino da tavalo*) which he pours into very large glasses.

Late lunch; pre-theatre; late dinner; Sunday lunch

ENGLISH
R. Cooke's Eel and Pie Shop

The Cut, SE1 01–928 5931
⊖ **Waterloo** *Map F29*
Open 10.30 am–2.30 pm; closed Sunday
Inexpensive

- Credit cards not accepted
- Bookings not accepted
- Seats 60
- Unlicensed

Refinements are cut to a minimum in this Victorian, family-run eel and pie shop, one of the few remaining in London. Local students and working people sit three a side on the wooden benches at formica-topped tables eating big portions of *Jellied Eels, Stewed Eels and Mash, Meat Pies and Mash*, served with *Parsley Sauce*. For added flavour, souse with vinegar. There is only orange juice or coke to drink.
Take-away

INTERNATIONAL/CREPERIE
Crêperie

56A South Moulton Street, W1 01–629 4794
⊖ **Bond Street** *Map A20*
Open 10 am–12 pm; closed Sunday
Inexpensive

- Credit cards not accepted
- Bookings accepted
- Seats 120
- Taped music

In a quiet corner of this short and smartly-boutiqued walking street is the ever-busy Crêperie, with lots of tables on three floors of a narrow building, and more tables outside, weather permitting. *Galettes*, thin buckwheat pancakes folded over a varied choice of meats, savouries and vegetables, are a sustaining lunch, with a glass of wine or cider and a *Crêpe au Marnier* to follow. There are also *Soups, Salads* and *Ice Creams*.
Late lunch; pre-theatre; late dinner; take-away; outdoor eating

There are two other branches, at 21 Covent Garden, WC2 (01–836 2137) and 26 James Street, W1 (01–493 1030), both open 7 days a week

HEALTH FOOD

Jack Sprat

17 George Street, W1 01–486 5909
⊖ Bond Street, Baker Street *Map A11*
Open 11.30 am–3.30 pm, 5.30–8 pm Monday to Friday,
11.30 am–2.30 pm Saturday; closed Saturday dinner, Sunday
Inexpensive

- Credit cards not accepted
- Bookings not accepted
- Seats 40
- Licensed for wine only
- ⅏ Access to restaurant

Jack Sprat substitutes low-calory yoghurt for cream in the appropriate dishes, and the chalk menu behind the busy self-service counter lists not only the price but also the calory count of each daily special: *Carrot Soup*, 70p – 40 calories; *Leek and Watercress Soup*, 70p – 85 calories; *Chicken, Aubergine and Pepper Casserole with Brown Rice*, 254 calories; *Tuna and Egg Salad*, 142 calories.

This is a cheerful place with only a few tables. Most seating is at a quite comfortable counter.
Pre-theatre; take-away

FRENCH

Maison Bouquillon

45 Moscow Road, W2 01–229 8684
⊖ Bayswater, Queensway *Map D9*
Open 9 am–8 pm, 7 days
Inexpensive

- Credit cards not accepted
- Bookings not accepted
- Seats 40
- Unlicensed

Near the grand Russian Orthodox church is this small, orthodox French patisserie with petite tables and chairs where any time of the day *Cheese filled Croissants, Pâtisseries* of many sorts, *Charcuterie, Salads* and light main courses are served.
Late lunch; pre-theatre; late dinner; Sunday lunch; take-away; outdoor eating

INTERNATIONAL/CREPERIE

My Old Dutch

131-132 High Holborn, WC1 01-404 5008
⊖ Holborn, Chancery Lane   *Map B16*
Open 12 midday–12 midnight Sunday to Wednesday, 12 noon–1 am Thursday to Saturday
Inexpensive

- Access, American Express, Barclaycard, Diners
- Bookings accepted for parties only
- Seats 160
- Taped music
- ♿ Access to restaurant

In a big, brightly decorated, two-storey restaurant near the Holborn Tube Station is My Old Dutch, where *Pannekoecken* (pancakes) made from a traditional Dutch recipe are cooked in deep pans and served flat on 15-inch plates, beneath mini-meal servings of meats, savouries and vegetables. *Cold meats* and *Salads* are also available.

There is also a cocktail bar.

Late lunch; pre-theatre; late dinner; Sunday lunch

HEALTH FOOD/VEGETARIAN

Neal's Yard Bakery and Tea Room

6 Neal's Yard, WC2 01-836 5199
⊖ Covent Garden   *Map B36*
Open 10.30 am–5 pm (3.15 Wednesday, 4.15 Saturday); closed Sunday
Inexpensive

- Credit cards not accepted
- Bookings not accepted
- Seats 24
- Unlicensed
- No smoking

Neal's Yard is a country-like little courtyard with genuine old cobble stones and ivy-covered buildings in the heart of Covent Garden, where clever entrepreneur Nicholas Saunders created a healthfood complex for seekers of the elixir of life. The Bakery is downstairs, for take-aways. Upstairs is the Tea Room, with counter service: *Quiches, Pizzas, Pasties, Soups*, interesting wholemeal sandwiches and lots of sweet treats.

Late lunch; take-away

ENGLISH
Olive's Pantry

27 Neal Street, WC2 01–836 2840
✆ Covent Garden   *Map B38*
Open 8.30 am–4.30 pm; closed Saturday and Sunday
Inexpensive

● Credit cards not accepted

Olive's Pantry does yeoman's service for those too hungry and impatient to wait in the long queues outside its neighbouring healthfood restaurants in Neal Street. It is a clean and friendly snack bar with a few tables in two rooms where you can get soup, sandwiches and *Quiches*.
Late lunch; take-away

FRENCH
Pâtisserie Valerie

44 Old Compton Street, W1 01–437 3466
✆ Leicester Square, Tottenham Court Road   *Map B30*
Open 8.30 am–7 pm; closed Sunday
Inexpensive

● Credit cards not accepted   ● Unlicensed
● Bookings not accepted   ♿ Access to restaurant, WC
● Seats 50

Pastries are baked on the premises and displayed in the window of this pâtisserie. Few pudding fanciers pass by without stopping to look. The little formica-topped tables are filled most of the day. Each table has a plate of *Pastries* waiting to be eaten. There are also sandwiches made to order and *Quiches*. The coffee is fresh and strong, the tea is brewed in individual pots. Regulars include theatre people and *Private Eye* stringers.
Late lunch; pre-theatre; take-away

ITALIAN
Pucci Pizza Vino

205 King's Road, SW3 01–352 2134
✆ Sloane Square   *Map C69*
Open 11.30 am–12 midnight; closed Sunday
Inexpensive

- Credit cards not accepted
- Bookings accepted
- Seats 50

- Parties catered for
- Taped music

The name says it all, except that the *Pizza* served here has a very good proportion of bread (as they call the crust) to cheese and fillers which include mushroom, pepperoni, olives and suchlike. The little kitchen also produces *Escalope Milanese*, *Pasta*, *Mozzarella Salad* and *Roast Chicken*. This is a busy place, so be prepared to wait at peak times.

Late lunch; pre-theatre; late dinner; take-away

FRENCH
Le Relais Basque

28 Westbourne Grove, W2 01–229 2107
⊖ Bayswater, Queensway   *Map D5*
Open 9 am–11.15 pm Tuesday to Friday, 8.30 am–11.15 pm Saturday and Sunday; closed Monday

- Credit cards not accepted

Same menu, same management as Maison Bouquillon, p. 154, but different procedure. Queue at the counter downstairs, give your order and go upstairs to wait (rather a long time when it is busy) and your food is brought to you. Both places tend to be very busy at conventional snack times.

Late lunch; pre-theatre; late dinner; Sunday lunch; take-away

Pubs

With few exceptions, nearly all pubs in London open at 11 in the morning, close at 3 o'clock in the afternoon (Sundays 12 until 2), open again at 5.30 and close at 11 pm (Sundays 7 pm to 10.30 pm). These licensing hours are learned like the arithmetic tables, and are as exasperating to the English as they are puzzling to foreigners, who wonder why conditions so clearly disliked have been tolerated for so long.

Most London pubs are divided into at least two bars: the Saloon Bar and the Public Bar, where the beer is a bit cheaper and the fittings plainer. Between these two ends of the house you may also find the Lounge Bar, superior to the Saloon, with lounge chairs and occasionally waiter service. Sometimes there are doors marked Private Bar; this area is not at all private, but is the place for the ladies and for quiet talks. These differences between the pub divisions, however, are becoming less pronounced nowadays.

Pubs are highly individual places. There are arty pubs, classy pubs, bawdy pubs. There are rococo Victorian pubs, mews ale shops with sawdust on the floor, and modern pubs with electronic game machines. Some pubs specialise, offering big selections of whiskies, many types of beer and ale, dozens of different wines to serve by the glass. The pubs listed here were chosen primarily for the quality of food served and also for their warm atmosphere and attractive surroundings.

ENGLISH/INTERNATIONAL
The Admiral Codrington

17 Mossop Street, SW8 01–589 4603
⊖ South Kensington *Map C31*
Open 11 am–3 pm, 7–11 pm; closed Sunday
Moderate

- Credit cards not accepted
- Bookings accepted
- Seats 30
- Parties catered for
- Taped music
- ♿ Access to restaurant
- Beer: Stones, Charrington IPA
- Children allowed in dining area

Hand pumps pull real ale at the big bar frequented by rich and playful young bucks and does. The interior is rich too, in mahogany, glass, brass and traditional pub accoutrements. There is a champagne-and-shell-fish bar in the pretty covered garden at the rear.

Some pubs specialise. The Admiral Codrington once kept more than 100 different whiskies and still has a pretty good selection of them. But since Susan and Melvyn Barnett took it over, this popular Chelsea 'local' has evolved from gaslit, Victorian pub to gastronomic pub/wine bar.

The lunch menu includes *Home Made Steak and Mushroom Pie with Two Vegetables, Fried Cod and Chips, Charcoal Grilled Steaks* and *Whole Baby Lobster and Salad*. The dinner menu is more extensive.

Outdoor eating

INTERNATIONAL

The Britannia

1 Allen Street, W1 01–937 1864
ϴ Kensington High Street   *Map D22*
Open 12–2.30 pm; snacks served 5.30–9 pm
Inexpensive

- Credit cards not accepted
- Booking suggested
- Seats 30
- Small parties catered for
- ♿ Access to restaurant
- Beer: Young's
- Children not allowed in dining areas

The Britannia is a comfortable and spacious wood-panelled pub of no particular architectural distinction. It has a pretty rear garden, a gas fire, and more windows than most pubs so it is light and airy. At weekends it is filled with locals who are much like the weekday crowd – people in property, insurance, the arts, a judge or two and the odd Lord.

There is Young's Real Ale and good food in a casual setting without pretension or fuss: *Coq au Vin, Venison, Veal.*

Outdoor eating

Let's Lunch in London

ENGLISH/INTERNATIONAL

The Bunch of Grapes

16 Shepherd Market, W1 01–629 4989
⊖ Green Park *Map A35*
Open 11–3 pm, 5.30–11 pm; Pub open 7 days, Restaurant closed
Sunday
Inexpensive/Moderate

- Credit cards not accepted
- Bookings not accepted
- Seats 30 (Restaurant)
- Parties catered for
- Taped music

- Beer: Fremlins Tusker, Wells Eagle, Wethered
- Children allowed in dining areas

Shepherd Market is a tourist area, broadly speaking, offering a variety of activities such as browsing in its several antique shops or sipping and eating in the cheerful atmosphere of this hundred-year-old Gin Palace. The Gin Palace style is a great Victorian contribution to pub architecture: lots of carved, tongued and grooved mahogany, lots of cut, etched and polished glass, and a coal fire that is a focal point of the room.

Customers drink Wethered's Real Ale, Charles Wells Ale or Fremlins Tusker. They eat *Chicken Curry Mayonnaise*, *Pork in Cider*, *Skate in Garlic Butter* or *Sherried Kidneys* in the Saloon, or they go to Ted's Pantry, a little carvery in the back, for *Meat Platters* or *Cold Salmon*. There is a small wine bar upstairs.

ENGLISH

The Cross Keys

2 Lawrence Street, SW3 352 1893
⊖ South Kensington, Sloane Square, then bus *Map C71*
Open 11 am–3 pm, 5.30–10 pm, 7 days
Inexpensive

- Access, American Express, Barclaycard, Diners
- Bookings not accepted
- Seats 20
- ♿ Access to pub, WC

- Beer: Courage
- Children allowed in dining areas

The Cross Keys, in Chelsea just behind the Albert Bridge, looks like an old coaching terminus. It has a courtyard with long tables and benches, hanging plants and a handsome façade. The interior is small and intimate. The neighbourhood is quaint: narrow streets lined with unselfconscious cottages that have been decoratively drawn up the social scale. Enthusiastic tourists and local residents, civilised and authoritarian in bearing, slake their thirst on the hand-pumped real ale.

Mrs Goodall, the tenant, welcomes children in the dining room and in the garden, and provides half-size portions at half prices of home-cooked Pub Grub: *Lamb's Liver and Bacon, Homemade Steak and Kidney Pie, Chili and Rice, Corned Beef Hash* and *Shepherd's Pie*.

Pre-theatre; Sunday lunch; take-away; outdoor eating

ENGLISH
Devonshire Arms

21A Devonshire Street, W1 01–935 6121
⊖ Regent's Park *Map A5*
Open 11–3 pm, 5–30–11 pm, 7 days; snacks served in the evening, no food at the weekend
Inexpensive

- Credit cards not accepted
- Bookings not accepted
- Seats 80
- Beer: Ind Coope, Allied Beers (Real Ales)

- Children not allowed in dining areas

Each customer may not be greeted with a 'Now what can we do for you, love?' but this is a friendly, enduring and unpretentious Victorian pub, with tiled walls, etched glass and wood panelling. It is always tightly packed from wall to wall with people who manage to make room for one more body to get to the bar for the *Salads, Steak and Kidney Pie, Chicken and Mushroom Pie, Shepherd's Pie* and *Pastas.*

Eaters as well as drinkers are catered for here. The grub is made on the premises.

Pre-theatre; take-away

ENGLISH
Fox and Anchor

115 Charterhouse Street, EC1 01–253 4838
⊖ Farringdon, Barbican *Map F2*
Open 6 am–3 pm; closed Saturday and Sunday
Inexpensive/Moderate

Let's Lunch in London

- Credit cards not accepted
- Bookings accepted
- Seats 80
- Parties catered for
- Beer: Burton Ale
- Children allowed in dining areas

Before you enter, stop to look at the lovely Royal Doulton façade of moulded stone, and once inside, try to avoid eye contact with the Fox in the Box at the rear of this authentic Victorian pub where Mrs Evelyn Zied has been providing hearty breakfasts and lunches to a contented following (many buyers and butchers from the Smithfield Market) who appreciate simple English cooking based upon plenty and quality, at good and simple prices.

On Wednesday mornings only there is smoked haddock, but every day there are *Home-made Soups*, *Cold Buffet*, *Salads* and *Grills*. The *Mixed Grill* is served on a platter-sized plate, about 3 inches deep with steak and liver, kidney and bacon, hamburger, deep fried chicken leg, mushrooms, chips and grilled tomato halves. And if you get to the bottom of the plate, you will find a pork sausage.

ENGLISH

The George Inn

77 Borough High Street, SE1 01–407 2056
⊖ London Bridge   *Map F33*
Open 12–2 pm, 6.30–9 pm, 7 days
Inexpensive/Moderate

- Access, American Express, Barclaycard, Diners
- Booking suggested
- Seats 50
- Parties catered for
- Jackets and ties preferred in restaurant
- Beer: Wethered, Fremlins Tusker
- Children allowed in dining rooms

Shakespeare and Dickens both knew the hospitality of the George Inn, and so do hosts of tourists who come to see the low eaves, sloping wood floors, oak settles and heavy balustrades of London's last remaining galleried tavern, rebuilt in 1667, shortly after the Great Fire. As in days of yore, plays are still given in the courtyard on summer evenings, and Morris Dancers perform indoors all year round, in the evening.

There are two dining rooms on the first floor. One has an à la carte menu, the other a three-course table d'hôte menu. Selections from both include traditional English fare: *Roast Beef, Barnsley Chop, Gammon Steak, Grilled Sardines.*

Hot snacks only are served at the bar on the ground floor which looks most authentically old. Notice the Parliament Clock, purchased in 1797, and have a pint of Thomas Wethered's Bitter, brewed in Marlow, Berkshire.

Pre-theatre; Sunday lunch

ENGLISH/SCOTTISH
Grafton Arms

72 Grafton Way, W1 01–387 7923
⊖ Warren Street *Map B2*
Open 11 am–3 pm, 5.30–11 pm, 7 days
Inexpensive

- Credit cards not accepted
- Bookings accepted
- Seats 36
- Parties catered for
- Taped music

- Beer: Whitbread, Wethered
- Children under 14 not allowed in dining areas

Much of the best Scottish food never leaves home but you can get a taste of honest Highland fare in Bloomsbury where Jen Robertson and her Scottish helpers prepare *Highland Stew, Haggis and Neeps* (the latter are swedes mashed with pepper, butter and herbs), *Mince and Potatoes with Vegetables* and *Hot Scotch Broth* in a mug. In winter Graham Robertson mixes hot Scotch toddies with whisky, cloves, sugar and water. Some of the daily specials are available in the pub. The wine bar has a full menu.

The Grafton Arms is a lively, attractively re-made pub with a 'Victorian' interior, and a rather earnest young clientele of men and women from offices and schools round Gower Street.

Pre-theatre; late dinner; outdoor eating

ENGLISH
The Grenadier

18 Wilton Row, SW1 01–235 3074
⊖ Knightsbridge, Hyde Park Corner *Map C8*
Open 11 am–3 pm, 5.30–11 pm Monday to Saturday, 12–2 pm, 7–10.30 pm Sunday
Moderate

- Access, American Express, Barclaycard, Diners
- Booking suggested
- Seats 21
- Parties catered for
- Beer: Watney's
- Children allowed in dining areas

Pubs grew like mushrooms in the last century, but their social status was questionable in Victorian England, so a speculative builder such as Thomas Cubitt hid them in mews when he developed aristocratic Belgravia. However the Grenadier was not purpose-built: it was the mess for the Duke of Wellington's officers, and the Duke himself is alleged to have played cards there. It is very attractive, with a beautiful old pewter bar, lots of shiny military memorabilia, a red sentry box outside and the Duke's mounting block nearby.

Predictably, the Grenadier is very popular with tourists and with aristocratic Belgravians for whom it is a local which happens to have quite a good restaurant. Specialities are *Soup of the Day*, *Beef Bourguignon*, *Chicken Maryland*, *Roast Joint*, *Waterloo Dinner*, *Duckling in Orange Sauce* or *Beefsteak, Kidney and Mushroom Pie*.

Sunday lunch; outdoor eating

ENGLISH
The Guinea

30 Bruton Place, W1 01–629 5613
⊖ **Green Park, Bond Street**   *Map A26*
Open 11.30–3 pm, 5.30–11 pm; closed Saturday lunch, Sunday; food served at lunchtime only
Moderate

- Access, American Express, Barclaycard, Diners
- Booking suggested
- Seats 30
- Beer: Young's
- Children allowed in dining areas

The licence for this Mayfair tavern dates from 1423, the first year of the reign of Henry IV. The pub though is Edwardian, and may be one of the busiest in London, with its own regular custom plus many people passing through to the restaurant in the back, whose speciality is charcoal-grilled Scottish beef. The pub serves off-cuts from the restaurant's prime beef in its *Shepherd's Pie* and *Roast Beef Sandwiches*. Go early because these are usually all gone long before the afternoon closing time.

The big and lively crowd go there for the food and bitter.

ENGLISH
The King's Head

115 Upper Street, N1 01-226 8561
⊖ Highbury and Islington, Angel   *Map F20*
Open 11 am-3 pm, 5.30-11 pm; food served until 8 pm (no food on Sunday)
Inexpensive

- Credit cards not accepted
- Bookings accepted for dinner in theatre
- Seats 80 (Theatre)
- Parties catered for
- Live music (evenings)

- & Access to restaurant
- Beer: Taylor Walker, Burton Ale
- Children allowed in dining areas

Britain has more than 400 pubs named King's Head. This well-worn King's Head became a theatre-pub when Dan Crawford, an American with a keen interest in theatre, took over as landlord and made it one of London's leading fringe venues. John Fowles' *The Collector* was its first success, back in the early 1970s, Robert Patrick's *Kennedy's Children* and *Da* by Hugh Leonard are among numerous past triumphs.

The theatre is in a back room. Seats are available for those who wish to see the play only. The set dinner is optional.

Predictably, many young, aspiring theatre people frequent this pub, and on Wednesdays and Saturdays shoppers and stall-holders from the nearby Camden Passage market also drop in for a pint of Taylor Walker or Burton Ale, and *Chicken Pie*, *Lasagne* or *Curry*. This pub still trades in pounds, shillings and pence.
Pre-theatre

ENGLISH
The Lamb

94 Lamb's Conduit Street, WC1 01-405 5962
⊖ Holborn, Russell Square   *Map B3*
Open 11 am-3 pm, 5.30-11 pm, 7 days; food served at lunchtime only
Inexpensive

- Credit cards not accepted
- Bookings not accepted
- Seats 30
- & Access to restaurant, WC

- Beer: Young's
- Children not allowed in dining areas

Let's Lunch in London

The Lamb was Charles Dickens' local and has always been a haunt of Bloomsbury poets and painters, and somewhat more recently of racing-car buffs. The interior was redone in 1960, leaving intact such features as the long, curved bar with etched glass snob screens. These small revolving partitions were meant to shield a customer from the eyes and ears of bar-mates. The walls are lined with rows of Edwardian music hall photographs. Only purists of ale-house architecture would say that restoration made it more Victoriana than Victorian.

It is a friendly local, serving a vast selection of beers and such victuals as *Steak and Kidney Pie*, *Cottage Pie* and *Chili Con Carne*.

Outdoor eating

ENGLISH

The Lamb and Flag

33 Rose Street, WC2 01–836 4108
⊖ Leicester Square *Map B53*
Open 11 am–3 pm, 5.30–11 pm; snacks only served evenings and weekends.
Inexpensive

- Credit cards not accepted
- Bookings not accepted
- Seats 30

- Parties catered for
- ♿ Access to restaurant
- Beer: Courage

In olden days, when the seventeenth-century poet John Dryden was a regular, this was called a 'spit and sawdust' pub. These days it is described, architecturally, as an Alehouse: handsome, functional, solid carpentry, oak-grained and rugged. In keeping with old traditions, there is often music and poetry reading in the upstairs room.

This must be one of the most crowded pubs in the West End. More people seem to be going in than coming out of the alley entrance in a little winding passage near Garrick Street. There are lots of old school ties here, drinking the Courage Directors and Best Bitter, and eating the *Quiches*, *Pâté and Bread*, *Sausages* and *Hot Pies*.

Pre-theatre

ENGLISH
Ye Olde Cheshire Cheese

Wine Office Court, 145 Fleet Street, EC4 01–353 6170
⊖ Chancery Lane, Blackfriars   *Map F7*
Open 12–2.30 pm, 6–8.30 pm; closed Saturday and Sunday
Moderate

- Credit cards not accepted
- Bookings accepted
- Seats 97
- Parties catered for
- ♿ Access to restaurant
- Beer: Marston's
- Children allowed in dining areas

Atmosphere rather more than gastronomy is the drawing card to this famous old tavern rebuilt in 1667: sashed windows, saw-dusted floors, oaken tables, rows of clay pipes in pots. Once eminent visitors were given a pipe and tobacco free, but times have changed. They do not let you forget that this was a literary haunt, of Johnson, Thackery, Dickens, to name a few. (Dr Johnson's house, where he laboured over the dictionary, is close by in Gough Square).

'The Cheese' is a low-ceilinged, rambling tied-house with three small bars and three small restaurants. There are snacks at the bars, and Marston's dry-hopped bitter from the brewing town of Burton-on-Trent. 'Ye Fare' in the restaurants is solid English cooking: *Steak, Kidney, Mushroom and Game Pie* or *Pudding , Roast Beef* with traditional trimmings, *Grills, Bread and Butter Pudding, Pancakes* and English cheeses.

ENGLISH
Princess Louise

208 High Holborn, WC1 01–405 8816
⊖ Holborn   *Map B17*
Open 11–3 pm, 5.30–11 pm; lunch Monday to Saturday, snacks in the evening (no food on Sunday)
Inexpensive/Moderate

- Credit cards not accepted
- Bookings not accepted
- Seats 40
- Live and taped music
- Beer: 11 Real Ales

There are walls of etched glass and floral-patterned ceramic tiles, curtained booths, fringed lamp shades, and the original plaster work in this rococo Victorian pub with a good range of beers and ales. Mr Caley, the tenant, lists the specials on a slate above the bar. Among the eleven Real Ales are 'Albert Ale', a dark bitter, Bourne Valley Brew, Ruddle's County and Sam Smith Strong Brown.

Students and soberly dressed articled clerks, chartered accountants and solicitors talk about sports, the weather and their social lives as they sip and nibble. Food is available in the main bar and upstairs in the wine bar. Hot and cold dishes of the good Pub Grub variety change each day and include: *Lasagne, Cotswold Cottage Pie, Sweet and Sour Chicken, Quiches, Chicken and Ham Pie, Vegetarian Pie.*

ENGLISH

Rossetti

23 Queen's Grove, NW8 01–722 7141
⊖ St John's Wood   *Map E4*
Open 11–3 pm, 5.30–11 pm, 7 days (no food on Sunday)
Moderate

- Credit cards not accepted
- Bookings not accepted
- Seats 100
- Beer: Fuller's London Pride and ESB
- Children not allowed in dining areas

None of the dark Victorian cosiness of an English pub here, and no dart boards or space invaders either. This place is modern, bright and leafy, spacious enough to allow potted plants to grow as big as trees.

There is lots of space too to stand around the big art-deco style bar, and nicely spaced tables and chairs in front of big windows. The daily offerings are *Quiches, Pizzas, Sausages* and freshly made *Salads.*
Pre-theatre

ENGLISH

Scarsdale Arms

23A Edwardes Square, W8 01–937 4513
⊖ Kensington High Street, then bus   *Map D25*
Open 11 am–3 pm, 5.30–11 pm; closed Sunday
Inexpensive

- Credit cards not accepted
- Bookings accepted
- Seats 80
- Parties catered for

  ♿ Access to restaurant, WC
- Beer: Watney's
- Children allowed in patio area

G. K. Chesterton is said to have taken his pint at the Scarsdale Arms, a local where strangers stand out. The pub is midway between very much sought-after property in Edwardes Square and Pembroke Square, a sequestered enclave of domestic, late Georgian terraced houses situated just off Kensington High Street.

The Scarsdale is the prototype of a Victorian pub, with a spacious arrangement of dark, comfortable rooms inside and a forecourt stacked with rustic tables and chairs where fresh-air-loving patrons meet at the merest glimpse of the sun.

Outdoor eating

Wine Bars

English tastes are altering dramatically. Beer consumption is going down, wine consumption is increasing, and the demand for more foods from different parts of the world is also on the rise. Wine bars provide a lively atmosphere in which to enjoy the new eating and drinking habits.

ENGLISH

Angela and Peter

300 Battersea Park Road, SW11 01–228 6133
⊖ None near; take 19, 39, 45 or 49 bus   *Map C77*
Open 12–3 pm, 7–11 pm, 7 days
Inexpensive/Moderate

- Credit cards not accepted
- Booking suggested
- Seats 30
- Parties catered for
- Licensed for wine only
- Taped music
- ♿ Access to restaurant, WC

In this wine bistro you can eat at the bar or at tables, or in the garden when the weather allows. Peter Evans is usually behind the bar, creating a casual, friendly atmosphere, as though he were in his own home and his best buddies had called in to chat. It's a nice place for lunch after exploring Battersea Park and children are welcomed.

The food is by two young, English, cordon-bleu trained cooks, Julia Hawk and Georgina Sparrow. The menu changes daily and includes *Leek and Potato Soup* and *Smoked Trout* for starters, and entrees such as *Stilton and Mushroom Quiche, Tagliatelle with Chicken, Mushroom and Garlic Sauce, Trout with Buttered Almonds and Parsley, Ham and Leeks in a Cheese Sauce* and *Duck Cooked in Port.*
Late dinner; Sunday lunch; outdoor eating

INTERNATIONAL
The Archduke

Concert Hall Approach, South Bank, SE1 01–928 9370
⊖ Waterloo   *Map F27*
Open 11–3 pm, 5.30–12 midnight; closed Saturday lunch, Sunday
Moderate

- Access, American Express, Barclaycard, Diners
- Booking required for lunch and pre-theatre
- Seats 70
- Parties catered for
- Licensed for wine only
- Taped music (lunchtime) live jazz (evenings)
- & Access to Wine Bar only

There are three levels to The Archduke, where music is the *leitmotif.* Hoffner cartoons decorate the wine list and the regulars are savvy concert-goers who do not fall for the trap near the end of Schubert's Trout Quintet and applaud too soon at the false ending.

Hunt Thompson designed this vaulted and bright wine bar underneath the railway arches near the South Bank arts complex in hi-tech style: brightly painted beams and pipes, Italian industrial lighting, stripped brick walls.

The menu varies according to the season. Sometimes there is *Red Mullet en Papillote*, *Harvest Pie* or chicken dishes in various sauces. Always there are *Pork Sausages* from France, *British Bangers* from Mr D. J. MacDonald of Marylebone High Street, and *Venison Sausages* and *Greek Peasant Sausages*, served with potatoes and salad.
Pre-theatre; late dinner

ENGLISH
Bill Bentley's

31 Beauchamp Place, SW3 01–589 5080
⊖ Knightsbridge   *Map C21*
Open 11.30–3 pm, 5.30–11 pm; closed Sunday
Expensive

- Access, American Express, Barclaycard, Diners
- Booking suggested
- Seats 30
- Licensed for wine only

Beauchamp Place may have more restaurants per store front than any other boutique-lined street in London. Near the Pont Street end, in a little Georgian house, is Bill Bentley's, a small, crowded and convivial Oyster and Wine Bar where you can try a variety of wines (by the glass) without having to cope with a wine list. You can also sample an assortment of simple foods: *Native Oysters, Wiltshire Pink Trout Meunière, Whole Lobster Salad, Grilled Dover Sole, Fillets of Lemon Sole Meunière.* Hot entrees such as *Entrecôte au Poivre Vert* and *Grilled Lamb Cutlets* are also available.

Pre-theatre; outdoor eating

There are other branches of **Bill Bentley's** at 239 Baker Street, NW1 (01–935 3130) and Swedeland Court, 202 Bishopsgate, EC2 (01–283 1763). They share the wine lists, menus, style and traditional character of the Knightsbridge restaurant.

Open 11.30–3 pm; closed Saturday and Sunday

INTERNATIONAL
Blakes

34 Wellington Street, WC2 01–836 5298
⊖ Covent Garden   *Map B47*
Open 11 am–3 pm, 5–10.30 pm, 7 days
Inexpensive/Moderate

- Access, Barclaycard
- Booking suggested
- Seats 125

- Parties catered for
- Licensed for wine only
- Taped music

I wonder what the sensualist poet, Omar Khayam, would say about all the jugs of wine and loaves of bread that are consumed at Blakes, which must have stretch walls to accommodate the crowds. Lots of businessmen in open-necked shirts and businesswomen in three-piece suits frequent the place at lunchtime when there is a large buffet with a very tempting array of *Olde English Meat Pies, Smoked Fish,* cheese, salads and sweets at the ground floor food and wine bar. Downstairs there is a bistro with hot dishes which change with the seasons.

Pre-theatre; Sunday lunch

ENGLISH
Bow Wine Vaults

10 Bow Church Yard, EC4 01–248 1121
⊖ St Paul's, Mansion House   *Map F15*
Open 12–3 pm; closed Saturday and Sunday
Moderate

- Credit cards not accepted
- Booking suggested
- Seats 48
- Fully licensed (but beer not sold)

- Children allowed in dining areas

Well within the sound of Bow bells is this high-ceilinged, fifteen-year-old wine bar frequented by men exuding the manly odour of Brut and the knowledge of gilt-edged securities. There are two counters upstairs, with a choice of a dozen wines by the glass and about a hundred different bottles, which include many lesser known French wines. Sandwiches may be had, and cheeses from Paxton and Whitfield.

Cases of wine line the staircase to the basement restaurant under a skylight, with a linen-covered counter and tables served by cheerful staff. The varied menu changes daily, from starters to puddings. *Plats du jour* may be *Roast Veal Stuffed with Spinach and Bacon*, *Noisettes of Lamb with a Madeira Sauce*, *Cold Duck Pie with Cumberland Sauce*.

INTERNATIONAL
Brahms and Liszt

19 Russell Street, WC2 01–240 3661
⊖ **Covent Garden** *Map B46*
Open 11.30–3 pm, 5.30–11 pm; closed Sunday
Inexpensive/Moderate

- American Express, Barclaycard, Diners
- Booking suggested
- Seats 80

- Parties catered for
- Licensed for wine and beer only
- Taped music

This old warehouse looks as though it had an easy conversion to a popular wine bar. The vaulting gives character to the snug basement room, and on the ground floor the weathered wooden floors and general proportions create a cosy, sedate and faintly shabby charm that inspires devotion among habitués – a young, friendly but serious-looking crowd, dressed mainly in dark clothes and bulky sweaters, who seem not to mind the constant very loud music that is by neither Brahms nor Liszt.

The kitchen produces *Steak and Kidney Pie*, *Chicken Pilaff*, and *Venison Ragout*.
Pre-theatre; late dinner

FRENCH

Café des Amis du Vin

11–14 Hanover Place, WC2 01–379 3444
⊖ Covent Garden   *Map B43*
Open 12 noon–12 midnight; closed Sunday
Moderate

- Access, American Express, Barclaycard, Diners
- Booking required
- Seats 135
- Parties catered for
- Taped music
- ♿ Access to restaurant

This big and busy, smartly done-up wine bar on two floors of an old Covent Garden warehouse has a very festive spirit, where all *des amis* seem to be having a happy time. Something about the decor or the placing of tables or the lighting makes everyone look unusually animated. Of course it could be the wine, of which there is quite a good selection.

Every day there are three *plats du jour*, and there are always: *Saucisses de Toulouse*, *Sélection de Charcuterie Fine*, *Les Trois Filets Sauce Béarnaise*. Snacks – *Omelettes*, *Quiches* and *Charcuterie* – are served between normal mealtimes.

Late lunch; pre-theatre; late dinner

ENGLISH

City Vaults

2 St Martins-le-Grand, EC1 01–606 8721
⊖ St Paul's   *Map F5*
Open 11.30 am–3 pm, 5–7 pm; closed Saturday and Sunday
Moderate

- Access, American Express, Barclaycard, Diners
- Booking suggested for lunch
- Seats 60
- Parties catered for
- Licensed for beer and wine only
- Jackets and ties required

It is hard to believe that only a few years before this was a fast food restaurant, but these days 'Victorian' wine bars are created with the ease of a card player dealing a hand, and many are owned by wine merchants. The City Vaults, a Davy's Wine Bar, is down a steep flight of stairs next to St Paul's tube station. Besides little tables round a long bar and buffet, there are dim alcoves behind glass partitions for quiet, romantic meetings. One must book ahead for these tables.

The cold buffet offers *Smoked Salmon*, *Pâtés*, *Game Pie*, *Ham* and *Roast Beef, Mixed Salads*, all temptingly fresh and nicely displayed. The house wines are good and there is a range of more expensive bottles.

Pre-theatre

INTERNATIONAL

Daly's

210 The Strand, WC2 01–583 4476
θ Temple *Map F16*
Open 8.30 am–11 pm; closed Saturday and Sunday
Moderate

- Access, American Express, Barclaycard, Diners
- Booking suggested for lunch in restaurant
- Seats 60
- Parties catered for
- Taped music

Although it looks like an old and well-established favourite hangout, Daly's is a recently created wine bar but a definitive example of the genre: painted walls with mirrors and some pictures of character, rotating ceiling fans, lots of greenery, daily newspapers supplied gratis and the prototypical hard little chairs that are not meant for comfortable sitting of any duration.

It is a jolly place with a generally jolly staff. The food and wine bar is on the ground floor and has an extensive selection of meat pies, salads, cheese and sweets, and wines by the glass. The wine list needs some re-thinking to become more interesting.

There is a lunch-only restaurant downstairs, open for private parties in the evening, and facing on to Essex Street is a little shop called Mace and Potts with a very big selection of cheeses.

Late lunch; pre-theatre

FRENCH

Ebury Wine Bar

139 Ebury Street, SW1 01–730 5447
θ Victoria *Map C49*
Open 11–3 pm, 5.30–11 pm Monday to Saturday, 12–2 pm, 7–10.30 pm Sunday
Moderate

- Access, American Express, Barclaycard, Diners
- Booking required
- Seats 60
- Parties catered for
- Live music

Let's Lunch in London

Champers corks and labels from the great vineyards decorate the walls of this snug and crowded 1960s wine bar in a bow-fronted house in the heart of Belgravia. There is no loud music here to drown the sound of popping corks and the quiet conversation of habitués who give the impression of being securely rich and seriously sophisticated.

Young cookery school cooks, who tend to work in pairs, prepare the simple and imaginative dishes of *Goose*, *Pigeon*, *Chicken*, *Turkey*, *Fish Pie*.

There is a good choice of wines.

Pre-theatre; Sunday lunch

GERMAN

Jörgen's Weinstube

22 Harcourt Street, W1 01–402 5925
⊖ Edgware Road   *Map A6*
Open 12–3 pm, 5.30–11 pm; closed Sunday
Inexpensive

- Access, American Express, Barclaycard
- Booking suggested
- Seats 45
- Parties catered for
- Licensed for wine only
- Live music

No leather pants or beer in this small *weinstube*, but owner/manager Jörgen Kunath plans to import that rather unusual apple (*apfel*) wine from Germany. The food is basically German, with Nouvelle Cuisine influences. There are of course *Frankfurters* and *Bratwurst* with *Red Cabbage*, *Sauerkraut* or *Potato Salad*. But the *Herrings* are not the very vinegary rollmops; they are done in a sweet and sour marinade, the way the Danes do them. And Anton's *Cheese and Pork Strudel* is a mix of minced pork, cheese and spices wrapped in light pastry.

There is no bar at which to stand and drink. In both dining rooms, customers sit at tables in amiable, simple and tastefully furnished surroundings.

Pre-theatre; late dinner

ENGLISH/INTERNATIONAL

Julie's Wine Bar

137 Portland Road, W11 01–727 7985
⊖ Holland Park   *Map D2*
Open 11 am–11 pm Monday to Saturday, 11 am–10.30 pm Sunday;
tea served 3–5.30 pm
Moderate/Expensive

- Credit cards not accepted
- Bookings not accepted
- Seats 80
- Parties catered for
- Taped music

Julie's is a friendly wine bar with a very wide reach. People come
from all over London to these black-painted, rambling rooms,
filled with stained glass panels and vast amounts of Victorian
furniture, potted palms and carpet cushions. It looks much nicer
than it sounds, and is attended by alert and proficient staff.

If you do not go early (before 12.45 pm) you will have to wait
for a table, and if you wait too long, you will not have a full choice
from the short menu that changes daily: thick and creamy *Soups*,
Grilled Fresh Sardines, *Smoked Trout*, *Sausages*, *Quiches* and
Salads. Between 3 and 5.30 pm teas are served with assorted
cakes, flans, fresh scones and cream.

In summer a little back garden is set with tables for lunch only;
in the evening it is used by **Julie's Restaurant** which is next door
at no. 135 (01–229 8331) and open for dinner only.
**Late lunch; pre-theatre; late dinner; Sunday lunch; outdoor
eating**

INTERNATIONAL

Loose Box

136 Brompton Road, SW3 01–584 3344
⊖ South Kensington, Knightsbridge   *Map C15*
Open 11 am–3 pm, 5.30–11 pm (dinner served until 9.30 pm);
closed Sunday
Moderate

- Credit cards not accepted
- Bookings accepted
- Seats 80
- Parties catered for
- Licensed for wine only
- Taped music

You enter through Searcy's, the caterers which is an English
institution rather like Crufts or the Royal Family. There are three
levels, including a small roof garden; all are comfortable, cheer-

fully decorated and populated by a decorative and convivial crowd. At lunchtime, men tend to congregate at the bar and tables on the ground floor, while young women, many with large Knightsbridge carrier bags tucked under their tables, have their heads together deep in conversation at tables on the first floor.

The offerings are listed on blackboard menus, but it is easier to choose from the display on the heavily laden buffets: *Hungarian Goulash*, *Seafood Salad*, *Chicken and Ham Pie*, *Pâté*.
Pre-theatre

INTERNATIONAL
Mildred's

135 Kensington Church Street, W8 01–727 5452
⊖ Notting Hill Gate *Map D16*
Open 12–3 pm, 5.30–11 pm; closed Saturday lunch, Sunday
Moderate

- Credit cards not accepted
- Booking suggested
- Seats 30
- Parties catered for
- Licensed for wine only
- Taped music

The chef of this snug 30-seater is an English trained Iranian whose daily specials, the *Soups* and *Casseroles*, have more zest and flavour than do the regular menu items such as *Steak and Kidney Pie* or *Pork Chop with Apple Sauce*.

The decor is standard wine bar: brick walls, dim lights, much foliage.

The lunchtime clientele is mostly people who work in the nearby shops, design studios and estate agencies. In the evenings the place is filled with locals from this high-priced residential area in which narrow winding streets take remarkable shortcuts through wider, tree-lined streets.
Pre-theatre

ENGLISH
Mother Bunch's Wine House

Arches F&G, Old Seacoal Lane, EC4 01–236 5317
⊖ St Paul's *Map F9*
Open 11.30–3 pm, 5.30–8.30 pm; closed Saturday and Sunday
Inexpensive

- Access, American Express, Barclaycard, Diners
- Booking suggested for lunch
- Seats 90
- Parties catered for
- Licensed for wine only

Fleet Street and City people go to Mother Bunch's, situated in a slightly hidden location under the railway arches in a twisting Dickensian lane close to Ludgate Circus and St Bride's Church, 'the parish church of the press'. This cellar wine bar is done in exuberant nineteenth-century style, with a wealth of dust-catching objects.

A consistently good and attractively displayed cold table offers: *Soups of the Day*, *Smoked Salmon*, *Plates of Ham*, *Roast Beef*, *Game Pie*, *Salads* – everything one would want for a jolly good picnic lunch. The house wines are reliable and served in 9 oz glasses.

Pre-theatre

ENGLISH

Russkies

6 Wellington Terrace, W2 01–229 9128
⊖ Notting Hill Gate   *Map D10*
Open 11 am–3 pm, 5–11 pm Monday to Saturday, 7–10.30 pm Sunday; closed Sunday lunch
Inexpensive

- Credit cards not accepted
- Bookings accepted
- Seats 50
- Taped music

Russkies is a popular local that is stylish and intimate, owned by a wine shipper, and facing the Russian Embassy, hence the name. It is not, however, frequented by Embassy staff.

It offers snug but comfortable surroundings, pleasant service, and a wine list that includes reasonably priced bottles from vineyards round the world. Vintage jazz records are played very softly when the place is busy but other times you can ask the bartender to turn up the sound.

The food is simple and reliable: *Shepherd's Pie*, *Smoked Chicken and Salad*, *Chili con Carne* and the seemingly obligatory *Quiche with Salad*.

Pre-theatre

Let's Lunch in London

INTERNATIONAL

Tuttons

⊖ Covent Garden   *Map B57*
Open 9 am–1.30 am, 7 days
Inexpensive/Moderate

- Access, American Express, Barclaycard, Diners
- Bookings accepted (downstairs restaurant only)

- Seats 200
- Parties catered for
- Live and taped music

A sturdy vegetable warehouse was converted into this big, lively and competent restaurant with many windows and splendid views of the Covent Garden Piazza. In warm weather tables are set up outside under a big awning. Furnishings are simple, attractive and informal. The real decoration is the crowd, mostly people in their twenties and thirties dressed in jeans, T-shirts, one-offs made at home, three-piece suits, cotton drill, with beards, shaved heads, coiffed heads, ponytails.

The big money was spent on the super-functional kitchen which produces breakfasts, snacks or 3-course meals all day long: *Steak and Kidney Pie*, *Spicy Chicken Kebabs*, *Salmon Trout Mayonnaise*, *Vegetarian Coulibiac*. There are two dining rooms. Prices are lower in the one on the ground floor.

Late lunch; pre-theatre; late dinner; Sunday lunch; outdoor eating

ENGLISH

Vats

51 Lamb's Conduit Street, WC1 01–242 8963
⊖ Russell Square, Holborn   *Map B8*
Open 12–3 pm, 5.30–8.30 pm; closed Saturday and Sunday
Moderate

- Access, American Express, Barclaycard, Diners
- Booking suggested
- Seats 75–80

- Parties catered for
- Licensed for wine only
- ♿ Access to restaurant

Vats is a long, dim and woody wine bar. The seats are a tight fit. The atmosphere is paper-napkin-informal, and customers usually sit where their favourite waiter or waitress is serving. This is a lunch hour local where fairly equal numbers of ambitious middle management men and women in law, advertising, fashion

and newspapers meet to talk about business, to make out and to relax while eating the chef's home-made *Soups, Casserole of Liver and Bacon Cooked in Red Wine and Herbs, Steak, Kidney and Mushroom Pie Cooked in Wine and Port* and *Apple Pie.*
Pre-theatre

INTERNATIONAL
Whittington's

21 College Hill, EC4 01–248 5855
⊖ Cannon Street, Mansion House *Map F18*
Open 11.30–3 pm; closed Saturday and Sunday
Inexpensive

- Access, American Express, Barclaycard
- Bookings not accepted for the bar

- Seats 100

Whittington's is a historic place, verifiably associated with its namesake, Dick. He may even have lived above the very busy, brightly lit, rambling, vaulted wine cellar where the regular clientele meet to eat and talk in amiable but necessarily loud voices about career opportunities and plans for success.

You know the cold buffet is fresh daily when before the end of the lunch hour there is very little left of the *Pâtés, Salads, Cold Meats* and *Pies.* There is also an à la carte restaurant. This is one of the few wine bars with a full licence, providing the choice of both spirits or a good selection of wines from France, Germany and Italy.

ENGLISH
Wine Press at the Whitehouse Hotel

Albany Street, NW1 01–387 1200
⊖ Great Portland Street *Map D9*
Open 11 am–3 pm, 5.30–11 pm (food served until 9.30 pm)
Inexpensive

- American Express, Barclaycard, Diners
- Bookings accepted for over 10 people

- Seats 65

Let's Lunch in London

Down a steep flight of stairs in the hotel lobby is the Wine Press, wood beamed, tiled and pub-like with lots of hanging brass cooking utensils. On weekdays, at about 12.45 pm, a very large crowd from a rather small radius of neighbouring offices in ad agencies, Thames TV and Capital Radio begins to arrive. By 1 o'clock, the place defies the old law of physics that no two things (or people?) can occupy the same space at the same time.

The menu is geared to pub/wine bar food, with a daily selection of *Pâtés*, *Shepherd's Pie*, *Game Pies*, *Salads* and sweets. The hot food comes from the hotel kitchens of the chef, Ian Douglas Brown, and whatever is bought in is highly selective Pub Grub.

Pre-theatre

Shops and Museums

Department stores have always provided food in settings designed to be functional and comfortable. Now many of these eating places have pizzazz, bright lights, decorative themes, and often include wine bars and healthfood bars and varied cuisine. Many offer breakfast, morning coffee, and afternoon tea as well as lunch.

Most of these oases are open for refreshment from about half an hour after the stores open until about half an hour before closing time.

Shops

ENGLISH

Fortnum and Mason

181 Piccadilly, W1 01-734 4938
⊖ Piccadilly Circus, Green Park   *Map B84*
Open 9.30 am–11.30 pm; closed Sunday
Inexpensive/Moderate

- Access, American Express, Barclaycard, Carte Blanche, Diners
- Bookings accepted for dinner

- Seats 95
- Small parties catered for
- ♿ Access to restaurant

The Fountain Restaurant

The Fortnum's Fountain has long been an oasis for ice cream (and ice cream soda) lovers, and was one of the few places providing both full meals and light snacks from early morning to after theatre time when almost no one else in London did this. The ten-page menu includes everything from Ovaltine to American cocktails, including *Game Pie*, *Scotch Roast Beef*, *Tivoli Platter*, *Fruits with Salads*, *Ice Cream Sodas*, *Frappés* and *Shake Floats*.

The big, columned, muraled, chandeliered Fountain is decorated in fruit-flavoured, ice cream colours, has linened tables, and a big counter for quick eating. The restaurant has a separate entrance in Jermyn Street. There is also a soda fountain and dining room on a half-landing up from the august food halls.

Late lunch; pre-theatre; late dinner

ENGLISH

The General Trading Company

144 Sloane Street, SW1 01–730 0411
⊖ Sloane Square   *Map C33*
Open 9.30–5 pm Monday to Friday, 9.30–1.30 pm Saturday; closed Sunday
Inexpensive

- Credit cards not accepted
- Bookings not accepted
- Seats 60
- Licensed for wine and beer only

- Taped music
- ♿ Access to restaurant, WC

This store is comfortably designed for browsing and creatively stocked. It also provides breakfast, lunch and tea in the Café, where Charles Part prepares *Boeuf Carbonnade*, *Endives Milanaise*, *Moussaka*, *Quiche*, *Veal and Pork Terrine*, *Cauliflower Cheese* and *Bubble and Squeak*.

The Café overlooks the plants department and a pretty enclosed garden where you can sit in fine weather.

Late lunch; outdoor eating

INTERNATIONAL

Habitat

206 King's Road, SW3 01–352 1211
⊖ Sloane Square   *Map C61*
Open 10 am–4.30 pm; closed Sunday
Inexpensive

- Access, American Express, Barclaycard, Diners
- Bookings accepted
- Seats 90

- Licensed for wine and beer only
- Taped music

This spacious, leafy, country-style dining room is, naturally, fitted with Habitat pine furniture and kitchen accessories and is a very popular buffet lunch stop. The kitchen area is grandly utilitarian and the offerings are good and simple: *Pâté and Gherkin*, *Chicken and Ham Pie*, *Jacket Potatoes*, and *Pastries*.
Late lunch

INTERNATIONAL
Hamleys

188–196 Regent Street, W1 01–734 3161
☉ **Oxford Circus, Piccadilly Circus** *Map B26*
Open 9.30 am–5.30 pm, 9.30 am–7.30 pm Thursday; closed Sunday

- Credit cards not accepted   • Unlicensed
- Bookings accepted

Hamleys may be the biggest toy shop in the universe, as well as in London. The restaurant is a jolly place for extrovert children, but at weekends and holiday times it may be overwhelming for introvert parents. There is a self-service section for light meals, and table service for hot food. *Hamburgers* and *Hotdogs* are standard fare, and there are daily specials such as *Goulash*, *Fried Plaice* and *Steak*. It is done up like an open-air café. The staff are brightly costumed and wear straw boaters.

INTERNATIONAL
Harrods

Knightsbridge, SW1 01–730 1234
☉ **Knightsbridge** *Map C10*
Open 9 am–5 pm Monday, Tuesday, Thursday, Friday, 9–6 pm Wednesday, 9–7 pm Saturday; closed Sunday

- Access, American Express, Barclaycard, Diners

OMNIA, OMNIBUS, UBIQUE (Everyone, Everything, Everywhere) is the aptly chosen motto of this six-storey, red brick, turreted store of stores where the appetites of hungry shoppers are well looked after.

The Georgian Room and Knightsbridge Restaurant (4th Floor)

Together these adjoining dining rooms, where morning coffee, lunch and afternoon tea are served, are large enough to land several small aircraft. Both have linened tables and waitress service. There is a cold buffet and a hot carvery table in the Georgian Room. The Knightsbridge Restaurant is somewhat more formal and has a more extensive menu.

Harrods Circles

Upper Circle and Way In (4th Floor)
Dress Circle (2nd Floor)
Leisure Circle (Ground floor, with own entrance in Hans Road)
These four attractive and busy self-service restaurants provide snacks and light meals throughout the day: *Quiches*, *Salads*, *Cheese*, *Pâtés*, *Pork Pies*, *Pastries*, *Gâteaux*. Wine is served by the glass or carafe.

Health Juice Bar (Ground Floor)

This is a little mecca for the health conscious, where all day food processors whirr and churn out designer-coloured, thick shakes made of fresh vegetables, fruit, eggs and yoghurt. There are also salads of brown rice, carrots and nuts, or cheese and fruit.

The Green Man (Ground Floor, Men's Store)

Open 9.30–11.30 pm for coffee, 11.30–3 pm for lunch, 3–4.30 pm for tea; also open 5.30–6.45 pm Wednesday
Children not allowed during pub hours
Some real bits but mostly reproduction decorations create a pub atmosphere in this dimly lit, low-ceilinged room where Tennent's Export Lager and Worthington E is on tap. There is Pub Grub, with some of the *Salads*, *Cold Meats* and *Pâtés* coming from the Food Hall. You can also have desserts and coffee.

ENGLISH

Harvey Nichols

Knightsbridge, SW1 01–235 5000
⊖ Knightsbridge *Map C4*
Open 9.30 am–5.30 pm (6.30 pm Wednesday); closed Sunday

- Access, American Express, Barclaycard, Diners

At Harvey Nichols, flagship of the Debenham group of stores, you can get a comprehensive look at the top names in British design and the best American and European fashions, and eat well too.

Harveys at the Top (5th Floor)

Moderate

- Booking suggested
- Seats 96
- Parties catered for
- ♿ Access to restaurant

This is a spacious, attractive, air-conditioned restaurant with full service, and a patio that is used in the summer, weather permitting.

Early morning shoppers can have a full English breakfast before starting on their rounds. Cream teas are served in the afternoon, and every day there are different lunch specials: *Avocado Vinaigrette with Salad, Beef Curry with Rice, Chili with Crackers, Omelettes* and large *Sandwiches* with various fillers.
Outdoor eating

Harveys One-O-Nine (Basement)

Inexpensive

- Bookings not accepted
- Seats 100

Meals and snacks are served all day here: *Assorted Quiches, Open Sandwiches, Salads, Pastries.* This restaurant has its own entrance in Seville Street. At the exit at the bottom of the stairs is a discreet sign which reads, 'If the alarm sounds, please contact a member of staff to have your Inventory Control Tag removed'.

VEGETARIAN/WHOLEFOOD

Heal's

196 Tottenham Court Road, W1 01–636 1666
⊖ Goodge Street *Map B7*
Open 10 am–5 pm; closed Sunday

Heal's, originally trading in feather dressing back in 1810, now has a royal warrant for bedding and specialises in fabrics, china and kitchenware. There are interesting gift and toy departments.

Cranks in Heal's (4th Floor)

- Credit cards not accepted
- Licensed to sell wine and
  beer only
- No-smoking area

This is a neatly designed, bright and leafy self-service restaurant that serves wholesome vegetarian food: *Soups, Pizzas, Pies and Flans, Salads* and desserts of *Muesli* and *Fresh Fruit Trifle*.

ENGLISH
Liberty

Regent Street, W1 01–734 1234
⊖ Oxford Circus, Piccadilly Circus   *Map B19*
Open 9.30–11.30 am for coffee, 12–2.30 pm for lunch, 3.30–4.45 pm for tea; closed Sunday
Moderate

- Access, American Express,
  Barclaycard, Diners
- Bookings accepted
- Seats 52
- Small parties catered for
- ⅗ Access to restaurant, WC

Liberty's is a polite and very comfortable store full of dark wood panelling, and an extensive selection of carpets, modern furniture and fabrics.

The restaurant (on the fourth floor) is quiet, done up in shades of beige and subtle good taste. The tables are predictably covered in Liberty print clothes. The clientele has shopped in the store for generations and frequently there is granny, mother and daughter enjoying the *Three-Course Carvery Luncheon, Selection of Salads* or *Various Omelettes*.

ENGLISH
Peter Jones

Sloane Square, SW3 01–730 3434
⊖ Sloane Square   *Map C34*
Open 9.30 am–5 pm Monday to Friday, 9.30–12.30 pm Saturday; closed Sunday

- Access, American Express,
  Barclaycard, Diners

Peter Jones, the sensible store that is 'never knowingly under-sold' (their motto), is also sensible because it does not continually rearrange itself. After an absence of several years one can still unerringly find the china and glass departments, or the carpets or restaurants.

The Crock Pot (4th Floor)

Open 9.30–11.45 am for snacks, 11.45 am–3 pm for lunch, 3–5 pm for snacks
Inexpensive

The lunch menu offers: *A Meal of Soup* (served with roll and butter), *Omelette Supreme, Choice of Two Traditional Cold Meat Pies*, and for dessert *King's Road* (chocolate ripple and mint ice creams with walnuts, marshmallows and chocolate sauce).

The Restaurant (4th Floor)

Open 11.45 am–2.30 pm Monday to Friday for lunch; morning and afternoon tea also served
Moderate

The Restaurant is almost the same as The Crock Pot, but here the tables are covered in linen. A Children's Menu is tempting for tots and served all day: *Fish Cakes or Sausages* and *Baked Beans* with *Chips or Mashed Potatoes, Spaghetti Bolognaise*. Breakfast and traditional high tea are also served.

The Coffee Shop (5th Floor)

● Licensed to sell wine and
  beer only

This is a bright, cheerful, modern cafeteria where snacks and light meals are available all day.

VEGETARIAN/WHOLEFOOD

Peter Robinson

214 Oxford Street, W1 01–636 7700
⊖ Oxford Circus *Map B14*
Open 10 am–5.30 pm; 10 am–7.30 pm Thursday; closed Sunday

Peter Robinson is a big open-plan store divided into boutique-like sections, with a wide variety of women's (only) fashions and accessories.

Cranks in Peter Robinson (1st Floor)

- Credit cards not accepted
- No-smoking area
- Licensed to sell wine and
  beer only

This is a gazebo-like restaurant with lots of trailing foliage and a buffet counter offering the famous Cranks fare: *Salads, Filled Wholemeal Rolls, Nut Cutlets, Flans, Biscuits* and *Cakes*.

ENGLISH
Simpson's

203 Piccadilly, W1 01–734 2002
⊖ Piccadilly Circus, Green Park *Map B85*
Open 9 am–5.30 pm, 9 am–6.30 pm Thursday; closed Sunday

- Access, American Express,
  Barclaycard, Diners

Simpson's is noted for its selection of European menswear, active sportswear for both sexes, and a classic range of women's fashions.

The Restaurant (Lower Ground Floor)

Expensive

A large, quiet, comfortable full-service restaurant where you may help yourself to the cold buffet, or order à la carte: *Roast Beef with Yorkshire Pudding, Fried Plaice, Bread and Butter Pudding, Savouries*.

Jermyn Street Wine Shop

Open 9 am–5.30 pm

- Licensed to sell wine
  during pub hours only

This attractive wine shop, with its own entrance in Jermyn Street, is a convenient place to meet friends for a glass of wine and a light lunch.

Museums

British Museum

Great Russell Street, WC1 01–636 1555
⊖ Russell Square, Tottenham Court Road   *Map B12*

Self-Service Restaurant (Ground Floor)

Open 10.30 am–4.15 pm Monday to Saturday, 3–5.15 pm Sunday

- Credit cards not accepted
- Bookings not accepted
- Licensed for wine and beer at lunchtime only

Commonwealth Institute

Kensington High Street, W8 01–602 3246
⊖ Kensington High Street, then bus   *Map D18*

Flags Restaurant (Ground Floor)

Open 12–2.30 pm, 6.30–10 pm; closed Monday dinner, Sunday

- Access, Barclaycard
- Booking suggested
- Fully licensed

Coffee Shop (Ground Floor)

Open 10 am–5 pm, 7 days

- Credit cards not accepted
- Bookings not accepted
- Unlicensed

Bar

Open 11 am–3 pm

- Credit cards not accepted
- Bookings not accepted
- Fully licensed

Institute of Contemporary Arts

Nash House, The Mall, SW1 01–930 0493
⊖ Charing Cross   *Map B95*

Restaurant (Main Floor)

Open 12 noon–8 pm; closed Monday

- Credit cards not accepted
- Bookings not accepted
- Licensed for wine and beer

Museum of London

London Wall, EC2 01–600 3699
⊖ Barbican   *Map F4*

Cafeteria/Sandwich Bar (Lower Ground Floor)

Open 10 am–5.45 pm Tuesday to Saturday, 2–5.45 pm Sunday; closed Monday

- Credit cards not accepted
- Bookings not accepted
- Unlicensed

National Gallery

Trafalgar Square, WC2 01–839 3321
⊖ Charing Cross, Leicester Square   *Map B89*

Restaurant (Main Floor)

Open 10 am–5 pm Monday to Saturday, 2–5 pm Sunday

- Credit cards not accepted
- Bookings not accepted
- Licensed for wine and beer at lunchtime only

Natural History Museum

Cromwell Road, SW7 01–589 6323
⊖ South Kensington   *Map C41*

Cafeteria (1st Floor)

Open 10 am–5.30 pm Monday to Saturday; closed Sunday

Snack Kiosk (Ground Floor)

Open 2.30–5.30 pm Sunday only

- Credit cards not accepted
- Bookings not accepted
- Unlicensed

Royal Academy

Burlington House, Piccadilly, W1 01–734 9052
⊖ Piccadilly Circus, Green Park *Map B82*

Restaurant (Ground Floor)

Open 10.30 am–5 pm, 7 days

- Credit cards not accepted
- Bookings not accepted
- Fully licensed

ENGLISH/FRENCH

Royal Institute of British Architects

66 Portland Place, W1 01–580 5533
⊖ Oxford Circus, Regent's Park *Map B4*
Open 9.30 am–5 pm (last orders for lunch 2.15 pm, tea served
3–5 pm); closed Saturday and Sunday
Inexpensive

- Credit cards not accepted
- Bookings accepted
- Seats 42
- Parties catered for
- ♿ Access to restaurant, WC

Coffee Shop (6th Floor)

Naturally this is a frequent haunt of architects, town planners and designers, but it is also open to the public even though a sign says 'For Members Only'. The simple, sixth-floor dining room has nice views, a terrace, a little bar with the usual choice of drinks including *Scrumpy*, and a buffet table where you serve yourself from *Salads, Home-made Pâté, Wholemeal Quiche, Roast Chicken à l'Orange, Fillet of Cod Provençal.*

Science Museum

Exhibition Road, SW7 01–589 3456
⊖ South Kensington   *Map C40*

Cafeteria (3rd Floor)

Open 10 am–5.30 pm Monday to Saturday, 2.30–5.30 pm Sunday

- Credit cards not accepted
- Bookings not accepted
- Unlicensed

ENGLISH

Tate Gallery

Millbank, SW1 01–834 6754
⊖ Pimlico   *Map C57*
Open 12–3 pm: closed Sunday
Moderate

- Credit cards not accepted
- Booking suggested
- Seats 140
- No-smoking area
- ♿ Access to restaurant, WC

London museums, as a rule, have restaurants of no particular distinction. An exception is the Tate Gallery, where Michael Driver's cuisine and an outstanding and reasonably priced wine list are taken seriously by a loyal clientele who do not necessarily visit the traditional and contemporary collections before going to their white-linened tables in the low-ceilinged dining room whose walls are lined with a complete series of fanciful murals by Rex Whistler.

There is always *Roast Beef with Yorkshire Pudding* and *Poached Turbot*, but the initiated go, and go back, to sample Driver's olde English revivals: *Crab, Hindle Wakes* (a medieval chicken recipe from the spinners of Lancashire) and *Elizabeth Veal Kidneys Florentine*.

There is also a **Coffee Shop**, open 10.30 am–5.30 pm, 7 days a week.

Victoria and Albert Museum

Cromwell Road, SW7 01–589 6371
⊖ South Kensington   *Map C42*

Cafeteria (Ground Floor)

Open 10.15 am–5 pm Monday to Thursday and Saturday, 2–5 pm Sunday; closed Friday

- Credit cards not accepted
- Bookings not accepted
- Fully licensed

Index of Food Types

African
Calabash

American
Chicago Pizza Pie Factory
Le Grand Café
Hard Rock Café
Joe Allen
L. S. Grunt's
Peppermint Park
Rock Garden
Rumours
Surprise
Texas Lone Star Saloon

Austrian
Kerzenstüberl

Brazilian
Paulo's (A Taste of Brazil)

Ceylonese
Sri Lanka

Chinese
Chuen Cheng Ku
City Friends
Crystal Palace
Gallery Boat Chinese Restaurant
Gallery Rendezvous
I Ching
Joy King Lau
Ken Lo's Memories of China
Luxuriance
Man Fu King
Mr Chow's
Poon's
Poon's Covent Garden
Tai Pan
Wat's House

Creole
Le Dodo Gourmand

English
Admiral Codrington (Pub)
Angela and Peter (Wine Bar)
Baron of Beef
Bentley's
Bill Bentley's (Wine Bar)
Bow Wine Vaults (Wine Bar)
Bunch of Grapes (Pub)
Buster Brown Café
Café Royale Bar
Chanterelle
City Vaults (Wine Bar)
R. Cooke's Pie and Eel Shop
Cowcross Restaurant
Cross Keys (Pub)
Dan's
Devonshire Arms (Pub)
Dickens Inn by the Tower
Drone's
Dorchester Hotel, Grill Room
Drakes
Ebury Court Hotel
English Garden
English House
Flounders/Also French
Fortnum and Mason Fountain
The Fox and Anchor (Pub)
Geale's
General Trading Co. Café
George Inn (Pub)
The Grafton Arms (Pub)
The Grange
The Greenhouse
The Grenadier (Pub)
The Guinea Grill
The Guinea (Pub)
Harvey Nichols
King's Head (Pub)
The Lamb (Pub)
The Lamb and Flag (Pub)
Liberty
Lockets
Lunch Room, RIBA

Fish and Seafood

French

Index of Food Types

Au Quai St Pierre
Le Relais Basque
Restaurant and Brasserie SW1
Le Routier
Savoy Hotel Grill Room
Le Suquet
La Tante Claire
Thierry's
La Toque Blanche
Flounders
Les Trois Canards
Wheeler's
White House Restaurant

German
Jörgens Weinstube

Greek/Cypriot
Beoty's
Costa's Grill
Kebab and Houmous
Koritsas
Nontas
White Tower

Health Food
Crank's in Heal's (Vegetarian)
Crank's in Peter Robinson
   (Vegetarian)
Food for Thought (Vegetarian)
The Granary
Healthy, Wealthy and Wise
   (Vegetarian)
Jack Sprat
Neal's Yard Bakery and Tea
   Room (Vegetarian)
Riverside Studios
Slenders
Wholefood

Hamburgers – see American

Hungarian
Gay Hussar

Indian/Pakistani
Agra
Diwana Bhel Poori (Vegetarian)

Goan
Khan's
Kundan
Last Days of the Raj
Mandeer (Vegetarian)
New Bengal
Salloos
Shezan
Veeraswamy's
Woodlands (Vegetarian)

International
The Archduke (Wine Bar)
The Upstairs, Basil Street Hotel
Bewick's
Blakes Hotel Restaurant
Blakes Wine Bar
Brahms and Liszt (Wine Bar)
Britannia (Pub)
Café Royale, Grill Room
Le Caprice
Carrier's
Century City
Claridge's Causerie
Coconut Grove
Coffee House Restaurant, Inter-
   Continental Hotel
Daly's (Wine Bar)
L'Escargot
Foxtrot Oscar
Foxtrot Qango
Frederick's
Golden Carp
Grahame's Sea Fare
Habitat Café
Hamley's
Harrods
The Ivy
Julie's Wine Bar
Justin de Blank
Lane's at Inn on the Park
Langan's Bistro
The Loose Box (Wine Bar)
Mildred's (Wine Bar)
Monkeys
Neal Street Restaurant
Newports
Le Perroquet, Berkeley Hotel

Pomegranates
Ritz Hotel Restaurant
Rossetti (Pub)
RSJ
Savoy Hotel, River Room
South of the Border
Summit Restaurant, St George's
  Hotel
Tapas
The Tent
Thomas de Quincey
Tutton's (Wine Bar)
Whittington's Wine Bar

Italian
Apicella
La Barca SE1
La Barca SW7
Bertorelli
Bertorelli Brothers Restaurant
Bianchi's
Cecconi's
La Famiglia
Al Gallo D'Oro
Il Girosole
Manzi's
Meridiano
Montpeliano
La Nassa
Pontevecchio
Pucci Pizza Vino
Rugantino W1
Rugantino East EC4
Sambuca
San Frediano
San Lorenzo
Santa Croce
Tiberio
Topo Gigio

Japanese
Ajimura
Defune
Ginnan
Hiroko, Kensington Hilton
Hokkai
Mima
Sakura
Suntory

Jewish
Harry Morgan's
Hatchett's Salt Beef Bar

Korean
Arirang

Malay/Thai
Bangkok (Thai)
Bunga Raya (Malay)
Busabong (Thai)
Chaopraya (Thai)
Rasa Singapore (Malay)
Satay House (Malay)

Middle Eastern
Al Amir (Lebanese)
Al Bustan (Lebanese)
Caravan Serai (Afganistan)
Efe's Kebab House (Turkish)
Fakhreldine (Lebanese)
Phoenicia (Lebanese)

Pizzas – see American

Polynesian
Trader's Vic's, Hilton Hotel

Portuguese
Os Arcos

Russian
Luba's Bistro

Polish
Daquise

Spanish
Dulcinea

Swiss
Swiss Centre

Restaurant Spotter

Page No.	Restaurant Name (Food type)	Map ref.	Late Lunch	Pre-theatre	Late dinner	Sun lunch	Outdoors	Take-away
158	The Admiral Codrington *English/International*	C31					●	
112	Agra *Pakistani/India*	B1		●	●	●		●
92	Ajimura *Japanese*	B40		●	●			●
58	Alonso's *Spanish/International*	C78			●			
152	Ambrosiana *International/Creperie*	D37	●	●	●	●		
15	Al-Amir *Lebanese*	A10	●	●		●	●	
170	Angela and Peter *English*	C77			●	●	●	
28	Apicella 81 *Italian*	B25			●		✓	
171	The Archduke *International*	F27		●	●			
119	Arirang *Korean*	B22		●	●			
141	Asterix *French/Creperie*	C67	●	●	●	●		
151	Atheneum Hotel, Windsor Lounge *English*	A38	●	●	●	●		
120	Bangkok *Thai*	C43		●	●			
73	La Barca (SE1) *Italian*	F34			●			
93	La Barca (SW7) *Italian*	D39			●			
45	Baron of Beef *English*	F6	●				●	
140	Basil St Hotel, The Upstairs	C12						
74	Bentley's *Fish*	B83	●				●	
120	Beoty's *Greek*	B78		●	●			
126	Berkeley Hotel, Le Perroquet *French*	C7		●	●			
1	The Berkeley Hotel Restaurant *French*	C7			●	●		
129	Bertorelli *Italian*	D15		●	●	●		●
75	Bertorelli Bros Restaurant *Italian/International*	B10	●					
29	Bewick's *French/International*	C27	●					
75	Bianchi's *Italian/International*	B31		●	●	●		
171	Bill Bentley's *English*	C21	●				●	
59	Blakes, Blakes Hotel (SW7) *International*	D34			●			
172	Blakes (WC2) *International*	B47		●		●		
59	Boulestin *French*	B58			●			
172	Bow Wine Vaults *English*	F15						
173	Brahms and Liszt *International*	B46		●	●			
121	La Brasserie (SW3) *French*	C24	●	●	●		●	
76	La Brasserie (W1) *French*	A21	●	●	●			
17	La Brasserie Du Détour *French*	D19	●	●	●	●		
16	Brasserie and Restaurant des Amis *French*	C13		●	●	●	●	
30	Brasserie St Quentin *French*	C18		●	●	●		

Page No.	Restaurant Name (Food type)	Map ref.	Late Lunch	Pre-theatre	Late dinner	Sun lunch	Outdoors	Take-away
159	The Britania *International*	D22					●	
191	British Museum	B12						
93	Bubb's *French*	F3						
160	The Bunch of Grapes *English/International*	A35						
94	Bunga Raya *Malaysian*	D7	●	●	●			●
95	Busabong *Thai*	C63	●	●	●			●
60	Al Bustan *Lebanese*	C17	●	●		●		●
141	Buster Brown Café *English*	F32	●	●	●			
174	Café des Amis du Vin *French*	B43	●	●		●		
61	Café Jardin *French*	A23			●		●	
142	Café Royale Bar *English*	B70	●					
2	Café Royale Grill Room *French*	B70	●	●	●			
113	Calabash *African*	B55	●	●				
3	The Capital Hotel Restaurant *French*	C11	●		●			
30	Le Caprice *International*	B91	●	●				
61	Caravan Serai *Afghan*	A7	●	●	●			●
46	The Carlton Tower Hotel Rib Room *English*	C5	●		●			
17	Carrier's *French/International*	F22			●			
122	Causerie Claridge's Hotel *International*	A22	●	●	●			
76	Cecconi's *Italian*	B68			●			
130	Century City *International*	A25	●	●	●	●		
31	Chanterelle *French*	D33			●	●		
62	Chaopraya *Thai*	A16			●			●
95	Le Chef *French*	A14			●			
3	The Chelsea Room, Carlton Tower Hotel *French*	C5			●	●		
142	Chicago Pizza Pie Factory *American*	B18	●	●	●			●
130	Chuen Cheng Ku *Chinese/Cantonese*	B73	●	●	●	●		●
46	City Friends *Chinese/Cantonese*	F11			●			●
174	City Vaults *English*	F5	●					
47	Claridge's Hotel, The Restaurant *French*	A22			●	●		
122	Claridge's Hotel, Causerie *International*	A22	●	●	●			
63	Coconut Grove *International*	A17	●	●	●	●	●	
131	Coffee House Restaurant, Inter-Continental Hotel *International*	A37	●	●	●	●		●
191	Commonwealth Inst., Flags Restaurant	D18						
48	Connaught Hotel, Restaurant and Grill *French*	A28				●		
153	R Cooke's Eel and Pie Shop *English*	F29						●
96	La Corse *French*	C66			●			●
113	Costa's Grill *Greek*	D13	●	●	●			
18	Cowcross Restaurant *English*	F1				●		

Page No.	Restaurant Name (Food type)	Map ref.	Late Lunch	Pre-theatre	Late dinner	Sun lunch	Outdoors	Take-away
187	Cranks in Heal's *Vegetarian/Wholefood*	B7						
189	Cranks in Peter Robinson *Vegetarian/Wholefood*	B14						
153	Crêperie *International/Crêperie*	A20	●	●	●		●	●
63	La Croisette *French/Fish*	D35			●	●		
160	The Cross Keys *English*	C71		●		●	●	●
122	Crystal Palace *Chinese/Szechuan/Peking*	D30			●	●		●
175	Daly's *International*	F16	●	●				
96	Dan's *English/Novelle Cuisine*	C60			●	●	●	
114	Daquise *Polish*	C44	●	●	●	●		●
48	Defune *Japanese*	A9			●	●		●
161	Devonshire Arms *English*	A5			●			●
132	Dickens Inn by the Tower *English*	F26			●			
77	Didier's *French/Nouvelle Cuisine*	D1						
143	Diwana Bhel Poori House *Indian/Vegetarian*	D4 E10	●	●	●			●
97	Le Dodo Gourmand *Creole*	A13						
4	Dorchester Hotel, Grill Room *English/International*	A31		●	●	●		
98	Drakes *English*	C36			●	●		
31	Drones *English/International*	C23	●		●			
32	Du Rollo *French*	B33			●	●		
19	Dulcinea *Spanish*	C47			●	●		
19	Eatons *French/International*	C51			●			
123	Ebury Court Hotel *English*	C46				●		
175	Ebury Wine Bar *French*	C49		●		●		
5	A L'Ecu de France *French*	B86			●	●		
98	Efe's Kebab House *Turkish*	B5	●	●	●			●
123	English Garden *English*	C38			●	●		
64	The English House *English*	C29			●			
32	L'Escargot *French/International*	B32	●		●			
20	Fakhreldine *Lebanese*	A36	●	●	●	●		●
33	La Famiglia *Italian*	D38			●	●		
132	Flounders *French/English/Fish*	B48		●	●			
144	Food for Thought *Health Food/Vegetarian*	B37	●	●				●
183	Fortnum and Mason, The Fountain *English*	B84			●			
183	The Fountain, Fortnum and Mason *English*	B84			●			
21	Four Seasons *French/Nouvelle Cuisine*	F19			●		●	
161	Fox and Anchor *English*	F2						
34	Foxtrot Oscar *International*	C73			●	●		●
34	Foxtrot Qango *International*	D36			●	●		

Restaurant Name (Food type)	Map ref.	Late lunch	Pre-theatre	Late dinner	Sun lunch	Outdoors	Take-away
49 Le Français *French*	C59	●					●
64 Frederick's *French/International*	F21			●		●	
35 Fuji *Japanese*	B66	●					●
65 The Gallery Boat Chinese Restaurant *Chinese/Peking*	E5	●	●	●			●
36 Gallery Rendezvous *Chinese/Peking*	B29	●	●	●			●
21 Al Gallo D'Oro *Italian*	D24			●	●		
99 Le Gamin *French*	F10						
5 Le Gavroche *French*	A24						
78 Gay Hussar *Hungarian*	B27	●	●				
114 Geale's Fish Restaurant *English/Fish*	D14	●	●				
184 The General Trading Company *English*	C33						
162 The George Inn *English*	F33	●			●		
78 Ginnan *Japanese*	F13	●					
124 Il Girasole *Italian*	C58		●	●	●		
115 Goan *Indian*	F23						
79 The Golden Carp *International/Fish*	A29	●	●				
163 Grafton Arms *English/Scottish*	B2	●				●	
80 Grahame's Sea Fare *International/Fish*	B21	●					●
144 The Granary *Wholefood*	B81	●	●				●
115 Le Grand Café *American*	C79	●	●		●		
80 The Grange *English/International*	B56		●				
81 The Greenhouse *English/International*	A30		●				
163 The Grenadier *English*	C8			●	●		
52 The Grill Room, Savoy Hotel *French*	B63	●	●				
144 L. S. Grunt's *American*	B60	●	●	●			●
50 The Guinea *English*	A26						
164 The Guinea Grill *English*	A26		●				
184 Habitat *International*	C61	●					
99 Les Halles *French*	B13						
185 Hamleys *International*	B26						
133 Hard Rock Café *American*	A40	●	●	●	●		●
185 Harrods *International*	C10						
116 Harry Morgan's *Jewish*	E8	●	●		●		●
186 Harvey Nichols *English*	C4					●	
145 Hatchetts Salt Beef Bar *Jewish*	F24	●			●		●
187 Heal's, Cranks *Vegetarian/Wholefood*	B7						
145 Healthy, Wealthy and Wise *Vegetarian*	B23	●	●				●
139 Hilton Hotel, Trader Vic's *Polynesian/International*	A34			●			
100 Hiroko, Kensington Hilton *Japanese*	D11	●			●		

Page No.	Restaurant Name (Food type)	Map ref.	Late Lunch	Pre-theatre	Late dinner	Sun lunch	Outdoors	Take-away
125	Hokkai Japanese	B71	●					
22	I Ching Chinese	D26	●	●	●	●		●
7	Inigo Jones French	B52		●	●			
131	Inter-Continental Hotel, Coffee House Restaurant International	A37	●	●	●	●		●
7	Interlude de Tabaillau French	B44			●			
192	Institute of Contemporary Arts	B95						
125	The Ivy International	B41		●	●			
154	Jack Sprat Health Food	A11	●					●
101	Jacaranda French	C28			●	●		
81	Joe Allen American	B61	●	●	●	●		
176	Jörgen's Weinstube German	A6	●	●				
101	Joy King Lau Chinese	B75	●	●	●			●
177	Julie's Wine Bar English/International	D2	●	●	●	●		●
146	Justin de Blank Food and Drink International/Wholefood	A19	●					●
126	Kebab and Houmous Greek/Cypriot	B6	●	●				
23	Ken Lo's Memories of China Chinese	C48			●			
100	Kensington Hilton, Hiroko Japanese	D11	●			●		
102	Kerzenstüberl Austrian	A18						
102	Khan's Indian	D8			●	●		●
165	The King's Head English	F20	●					
116	Koritsas Greek/Cypriot	E3	●	●	●			●
23	Kundan Indian/Pakistani	C56			●			●
165	The Lamb English	B3				●		
166	The Lamb and Flag English	B53	●					
24	Lane's, The Inn on the Park International	A39	●	●	●			
36	Langan's Bistro International/French/English	A4			●			
37	Langan's Brasserie French	B80			●			
38	Last Days of the Raj Indian	B28	●	●				●
82	Legends French	B67			●	●	●	
188	Liberty English	B19						
8	Lockets English	C55	●	●				
177	Loose Box International	C15	●					
103	Luba's Bistro Russian	C20	●	●			●	
104	Luxuriance Chinese/Peking/Shanghai	B72	●	●	●			●
25	Ma Cuisine French	C26			●			
104	Maggie Jones English	D17			●	●		
154	Maison Bouquillon French	D9	●	●	●	●	●	●
105	Man Fu King Chinese/Cantonese	B88	●	●	●	●	●	●
117	Mandeer Indian/Vegetarian	B15	●					●

Page No.	Restaurant Name (Food type)	Map ref.	Late lunch	Pre-theatre	Late dinner	Sun lunch	Outdoors	Take-away
105	Manzi's *Fish*	B74		•	•	•		
66	Meridiano *Italian*	C35			•	•	•	
50	Mijanou *French*	C52						
178	Mildred's *International*	D16	•					
51	Mima *Japanese*	D20		•	•	•		
8	Mirabelle *French*	A33			•			
38	Monkeys *French/International*	C62			•			
106	Mon Plaisir *French*	B35		•	•			
66	Montpeliano *Italian*	C9			•		•	
178	Mother Bunch's Wine House *English*	F9		•				
39	Mr Chow's *Chinese/Peking*	C1			•	•		•
147	The Muffin Man *English*	D23	•	•				
192	Museum of London	F4						
155	My Old Dutch *International/Crêperie*	B16	•	•		•		
39	La Nassa *Italian*	C65	•		•	•		
192	National Gallery	B89						
192	Natural History Museum	C41						
83	Neal Street Restaurant *International*	B39			•			
155	Neal's Yard Bakery and Tea Room *Health Food/Vegetarian*	B36	•					•
147	New Bengal *Indian*	D6		•	•	•		•
40	Newport's *English*	C3			•			
107	Nontas *Cypriot*	E6		•	•			•
147	Obelix *French/Crêperie*	D3	•	•	•	•	•	•
67	Odette's Restaurant *French*	E2				•	•	
83	Odins *French*	A3			•			
156	Olive's Pantry *English*	B38	•					•
25	Os Arcos *Portuguese*	C54			•			
68	The Palm Court, Ritz Hotel *English*	B90						
148	Palm Court, Waldorf Hotel *English*	B49	•	•	•	•		•
107	Paulo's (A Taste of Brazil) *Brazilian*	B50	•	•				
134	Parsons *Mexican/American*	C64	•	•	•	•		•
156	Pâtisserie Valerie *French*	B30	•	•				•
134	Peppermint Park *American*	B42	•	•	•	•	•	
126	Le Perroquet, Berkeley Hotel *French*	C7		•	•			
188	Peter Jones *English*	C34						
189	Peter Robinson, Cranks *Vegetarian/Wholefood*	B14						
127	The Phoenicia *Lebanese*	D21	•	•	•	•		•
149	The Picnic Basket, Selfridge Hotel *English*	A15	•	•	•	•		
84	Poissonnerie de l'Avenue *French/Fish*	C37			•			•

Page No.	Restaurant Name (Food type)	Map ref.	Late lunch	Pre-theatre	Late dinner	Sun lunch	Outdoors	Take-away
68	Pomegranates *International*	C76			●			
69	La Pomme d'Amour *French*	D12						
108	Pontevecchio *Italian*	D32			●	●	●	
118	Poon's *Chinese*	B76	●	●	●	●		●
40	Poon's of Covent Garden *Chinese/Cantonese*	B54	●	●	●			●
9	Le Poulbot *French*	F14						
69	La Poule au Pot *French*	C53			●			
167	Princess Louise *English*	B17						
156	Pucci Pizza Vino *Italian*	C69	●	●	●			●
70	Au Quai St Pierre *French/Fish*	D28			●	●		●
149	Rasa Singapore *Malaysian*	C16		●		●		
157	Le Relais Basque *French*	D5	●	●	●	●		●
41	Restaurant and Brasserie *French*	C75	●	●	●	●		
10	Restaurant, Ritz Hotel *International*	B90		●	●	●		
84	The River Restaurant, Savoy *French*	B63			●	●		
150	Riverside Studios *Vegetarian/Health food*	D31	●	●	●	●		
135	Rock Garden *American*	B45	●	●	●	●	●	●
168	Rossetti *English*	E4		●				
136	Le Routier *French*	E1			●	●	●	
85	Rowley's *English/Steak*	B87	●	●	●			
193	Royal Academy	B82						
193	Royal Institute of British Architects	B4						
86	RSJ *French*	F28			●			
86	Rugantino (W1) *Italian*	B34		●	●			
87	Rugantino East (EC4) *Italian*	F8						
51	Rules *English*	B59		●	●			
136	Rumours *American*	B62	●					●
179	Russkies *English*	D10		●				
89	St George's Hotel, Summit Restaurant *International*	B9		●		●		
42	Sakura *Japanese*	B24		●		●		
71	Salloos *Pakistani*	C6			●			●
42	Sambuca *Italian*	C32			●			
137	San Frediano *Italian*	C45			●			
71	San Lorenzo *Italian*	C22			●			
88	Santa Croce *Italian*	C70			●		●	
102	Satay House *Malaysian*	A8		●	●	●		●
52	Savoy Hotel, The Grill Room *French*	B63		●	●			
84	Savoy Hotel, The River Restaurant *French*	B63			●	●		
168	Scarsdale Arms *English*	D25					●	
194	Science Museum	C40						

Page No.	Restaurant Name (Food type)	Map ref.	Late Lunch	Pre-theatre	Late dinner	Sun lunch	Outdoors	Take-away
10	Scotts *English/Fish*	A27	●	●				
138	Sea Shell Fish Bar *Fish*	A1	●					●
53	Sheekey's *Fish*	B79	●	●				
149	Selfridge Hotel, The Picnic Basket *English*	A15	●	●	●	●		
11	Shezan *Pakistani*	C14			●			●
190	Simpson's (W1) *English*	B85						
53	Simpson's-in-the-Strand *English*	B64	●					
54	Simpson's of Cornhill *English*	F25						
150	Slenders *Vegetarian/Wholefood*	F12	●					
88	South of the Border *English/International*	F31		●	●	●	●	
108	Sri Lanka *Ceylonese*	D29		●	●	●		●
89	Summit Restaurant, St George's Hotel *International*	B9		●		●		
12	Suntory *Japanese*	B94						●
43	Le Suquet *French*	C30		●	●			
89	Surprise *American*	B20		●	●	●		
55	Sweetings *English/Fish*	F17						●
109	Swiss Centre *Swiss*	B77	●	●	●	●		●
43	Tai Pan *Chinese/Hunan/Peking/Szechuan*	C19			●	●		●
12	La Tante Claire *French*	C72			●			
44	Tapas *International*	C74			●			
194	Tate Gallery Restaurant *English*	C57						
110	The Tent *International*	C50		●	●	●		
138	Texas Lone Star Saloon *American*	C39	●	●	●	●		●
72	Thierry's *French*	C68			●			
90	Thomas de Quincey *French*	B51		●	●			
26	Tiberio *Italian*	A32			●			
110	Topo Gigio *Italian*	B65	●	●		●		
27	La Toque Blanche *French*	D27			●			
139	Trader Vic's, Hilton Hotel *Polynesian/International*	A34			●			
128	Les Trois Canards *French*	C2			●			
180	Tuttons *International*	B57	●	●	●	●	●	
140	The Upstairs, Basil Street Hotel	C12						
180	Vats *English*	B8	●					
55	Veeraswamy's *Indian*	B69		●	●	●		●
195	Victoria and Albert Museum	C42						
148	Waldorf Hotel, Palm Court *English*	B49	●	●	●	●		●
13	Walton's *English/International*	C25			●	●		
111	Wat's House *Chinese/Cantonese*	E7		●	●	●		●
56	Wheeler's *French/Fish*	B93						

Page No.	Restaurant Name (Food type)	Map ref.	Late Lunch	Pre-theatre	Late dinner	Sun lunch	Outdoors	Take-away
14	The White House Restaurant *French*	E9		●	●			
181	White House Hotel, Wine Press *English*	E9		●				
56	The White Tower *Greek/Mediterranean*	B11						
181	Whittington's *International*	F18						
151	Wholefood *Health food*	A2	●					●
57	Wilton's *English/Fish/Game*	B92						
151	Windsor Lounge, Atheneum Hotel *English*	A38	●	●	●	●		
181	Wine Press, White House Hotel *English*	E9		●				
112	Woodlands Restaurant *Indian/Vegetarian*	A12		●	●	●		●
167	Ye Olde Cheshire Cheese *English*	F7						
152	Young Vic Coffee Bar *English*	F30	●					

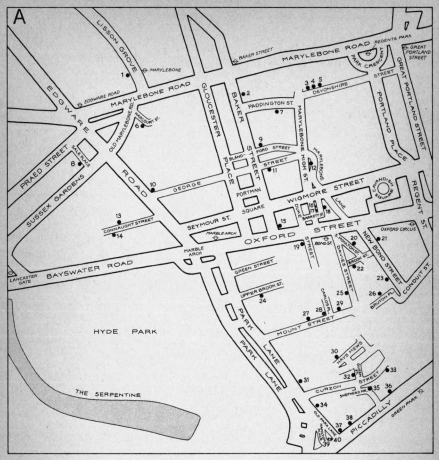

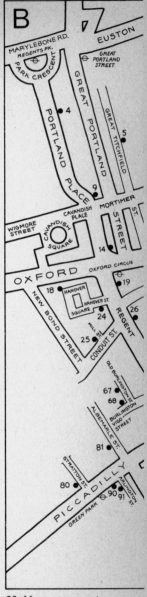

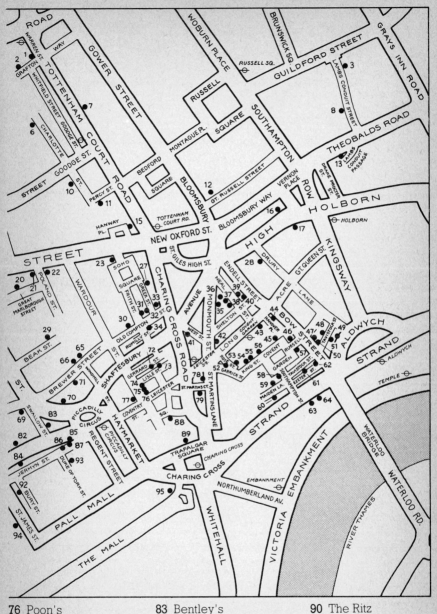

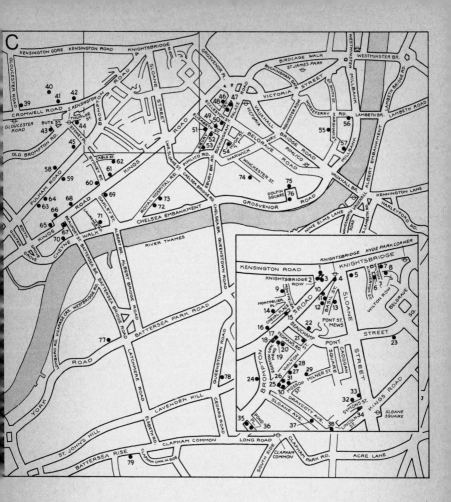

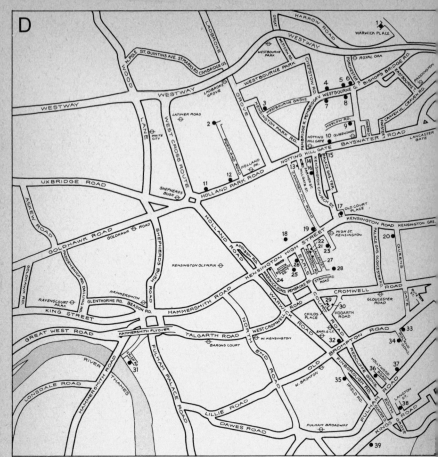

D

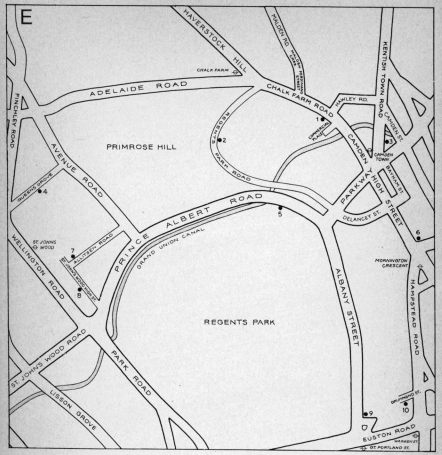

1 Le Routier
2 Odette's Restaurant
3 Koritsas
4 Rossetti
5 Gallery Boat Chinese Restaurant
6 Nontas
7 Wat's House
8 Harry Morgan's
9 White House Hotel
10 Diwana Bhel Pouri House

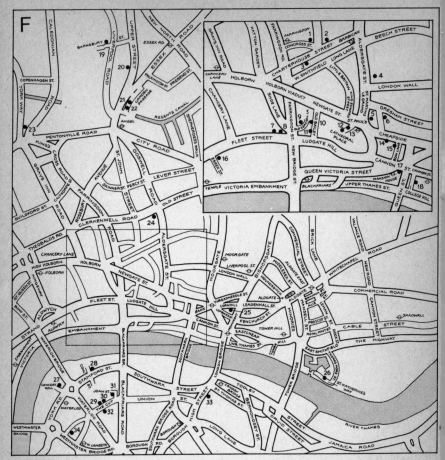

F

1 Cowcross Restaurant	18 Whittington's Wine Bar
2 Fox and Anchor	19 Four Seasons
3 Bubb's	20 King's Head
4 Museum of London	21 Frederick's
5 City Vaults	22 Carrier's
6 Baron of Beef	23 Goan
7 Ye Olde Cheshire Cheese	24 Hatchett's Salt Beef
8 Rugantino East	25 Simpson's of Cornhill
9 Mother Bunch's Wine House	26 Dickens Inn by the Tower
10 Le Gamin	27 The Archduke
11 City Friends	28 RSJ
12 Slenders	29 R. Cooke's Eel and Pie Shop
13 Ginnan	30 The Young Vic
14 La Poulbot	31 South of the Border
15 Bow Wine Vaults	32 Buster Brown Café
16 Daly's	33 The George Inn
17 Sweetings	34 La Barca